Reviewing
Basic
Grammar

Reviewing Basic Grammar

A Guide to Writing Sentences and Paragraphs

Fifth Edition

Mary Laine Yarber
Robert E. Yarber
Emeritus, San Diego Mesa College

Longman

New York • San Francisco • Boston
London • Toronto • Sydney • Tokyo • Singapore • Madrid
Mexico City • Munich • Paris • Cape Town • Hong Kong • Montreal

Senior Acquisitions Editor: Steven Rigolosi
Development Editor: Jennifer Krasula
Marketing Manager: Melanie Goulet
Supplements Editor: Donna Campion
Production Manager: Joseph Vella
Project Coordination, Text Design, and Electronic Page Makeup: Thompson Steele, Inc.
Cover Designer/Manager: Wendy Ann Fredericks
Cover Illustration/Photo: Michael Goldman/FPG International
Senior Manufacturing Buyer: Dennis Para
Printer and Binder: R.R. Donnelly & Sons, Inc.—Harrisonburg
Cover Printer: Coral Graphic Services, Inc.

For permission to use copyedited material, grateful acknowledgement is made to the copyright holders on pp. 363–65, which are hereby made part of this copyright page.

Library of Congress Cataloging-in-Publication Data

Yarber, Mary Laine.
    Reviewing basic grammar: a guide to writing sentences and paragraphs / Mary Laine Yarber, Robert E. Yarber.—5th ed.
        p. cm.
    Includes index.
    ISBN 0-321-04579-3
        1. English language—Grammar. 2. English language—Sentences. 3. English language — Paragraphs. I. Yarber, Robert E. II. Title.

PE1112 .Y37 2001
428.2—dc21   00-028200

Copyright © 2001 by Addison Wesley Educational Publishers, Inc.

All rights reserved. No part of this publication may be reproduced, stored in a retrieval system, or transmitted, in any form or by any means, electronic, mechanical, photocopying, recording, or otherwise, without the prior written permission of the publisher. Printed in the United States.

Please visit our website at http://www.awl.com

ISBN 0-321-04579-3

12345678910—DOH—03020100

Brief Contents

Detailed Contents

© 2001 Addison-Wesley Educational Publishers Inc.

© 2001 Addison-Wesley Educational Publishers Inc.

© 2001 Addison-Wesley Educational Publishers Inc.

Preface

Like its predecessors, this edition of *Reviewing Basic Grammar* has been written for those college and university students who need to refresh their grammar and basic writing skills before taking Freshman English. Designed to be used in developmental writing courses, writing laboratories, and self-tutorial formats, it features the essentials of grammar and usage, as well as a structured approach to writing that will help students become confident, competent, and effective writers.

Previous users of this book will recognize (in addition to a new title) several new features, many in response to their suggestions and requests. Among the most significant are the additional emphasis on writing and an expanded recognition of the needs of the student for whom English is a second language.

These changes have not been introduced at the expense of previous editions. Like them, this revision of *Reviewing Basic Grammar* has been guided by the following principles:

- It must emphasize the essentials of sentence structure, grammar, punctuation, and spelling, while avoiding technical terminology.

- It must include writing because grammar and usage cannot be taught in a vacuum. The writing assignments must be meaningful, and they should reflect students' interests and concerns.

- It must be concise, clear, and interesting to both the student and the instructor, with abundant exercises and opportunities for evaluation.

- It must recognize the ethnic and cultural diversity of today's student body.

Features and Organization

Chapter 1, new to this edition, emphasizes the **importance and relationship of acceptable usage and grammar with effective writing.** This chapter also contains an introduction to paragraph writing, in addition to a section on writing with the computer.

Each succeeding chapter presents a complete and concise examination of the common problems in basic usage, followed by a sequential study of **paragraph writing.** The result is a thorough and seamless coverage of the fundamentals of usage and writing that will prepare the student for the challenges of Freshman English.

The grammar and usage sections provide **clear explanations and examples,** as well as **exercises in a variety of formats,** including sentence completion, multiple choice, sentence generation, and editing. Among the topics are the following:

- Sentence fragments, comma-splices, and fused sentences
- Subject-verb agreement
- Pronoun-antecedent
- Confusion of the subject and object forms of pronouns
- Use of adjectives for adverbs and vice versa
- Use of indefinite pronouns such as *anyone, anybody, someone, neither,* and *none*
- Use of verbs
- Punctuation, possessives, numbers, and capitals
- Sexism in the use of pronouns

Answers to odd-numbered exercises in odd-numbered chapters and to even-numbered exercises in even-numbered chapters are included at the end of the textbook so that students may evaluate themselves as they move through the chapters. Two review tests, identical in format and difficulty, conclude the grammar and usage section of each chapter.

After the overview of the paragraph in Chapter 1, subsequent chapters present the topic sentence, methods to assure coherence by various organizational patterns, the use of transitions within the paragraph, and strategies for paragraph development. **Student paragraphs** and **memorable prose by professional writers** are included to illustrate the various rhetorical patterns introduced in each chapter.

Boxed, readily identifiable **Writing Tips** are included on such practical matters as the proper format for submitted papers, selecting the best dictionary, and building one's vocabulary. A **Computer Activity** is similarly included in each chapter for those classrooms equipped with computers. Each computer activity may be easily adapted to any word-processing program used in the class.

Many students in our classes are from homes in which English is not spoken or from families whose use of English can best be described as nonstandard. In this book we stress that we are not expecting them to change abruptly the way they speak to their family and friends. Rather, they are adding another dialect to their linguistic repertoire—the form of the language usually recognized and accepted as the norm for educated users of the language in this country. In other words, Standard English will supplement—not supplant— the dialect they have brought to the classroom. As we point out, the failure to acquire this tool can exact vocational, financial, and social penalties. For these reasons, and in response to suggestions from many instructors, we have introduced **A Checklist for the ESL Writer** in

© 2001 Addison-Wesley Educational Publishers Inc.

the Appendix. Cross-referenced with the chapters in this book, it addresses the most troublesome and confusing problems encountered by the student whose first language is not English. To supplement this appendix, qualified adopters of this book may obtain ESL Worksheets (ISBN 0-321-01955-5) by contacting their Addison-Wesley Longman representative. Written by Jocelyn Steer, a recognized authority on the teaching of English to ESL students, they provide extra practice in the areas that require additional attention.

The Teaching and Learning Package

Each component of the teaching and learning package for *Reviewing Basic Grammar*, 5/E has been crafted to ensure that the course is a rewarding experience for both instructors and students.

Instructor's Manual/Test Bank

The instructor's manual/test bank (0–321–04581–5), provided free to adopters of *Reviewing Basic Grammar*, provides the following teaching aids:

- Answers to the chapter review exercises
- Three tests on grammar and usage (Forms A, B, and C), identical in difficulty and format, for chapters 2–13, with an answer key
- Four cumulative final examinations on grammar and usage (Forms A, B, C, and D), identical in difficulty and format, with an answer key
- A list of twenty-five spelling words to supplement each of the first ten chapters for instructors who wish to introduce spelling throughout the semester rather than devote an entire chapter to spelling. The words are based on the list on pages 302–305 of the chapter on spelling.

In addition, an **Electronic Test Bank for Writing** is also available. Available in December 2000, this electronic test bank features more than 5,000 questions in all areas of writing, from grammar to paragraphing, through essay writing, research, and documentation. With this easy-to-use CD-ROM, instructors simply choose questions from the electronic test bank, then print out the completed test for distribution. 0–321–08117–X

The Reviewing Basic Grammar Website

For additional exercises, summaries, and interactive activities, be sure to visit our **book-specific website at http://awl.com/yarber**. *Reviewing Basic Grammar Online* provides a wealth of resources, including gradable quizzes, e-mail capabilities, and interactive chat. Stop by for a visit!

Electronic Supplements

The Writer's ToolKit Plus.   This CD-ROM offers a wealth of tutorial, exercise, and reference material for writers. It is compatible with either a PC or Macintosh platform, and is flexible enough to be used either occasionally for practice or regularly in class lab sessions. The Writer's ToolKit is available free with this text. To order a free Writer's Toolkit CD-ROM with your student's text, please contact your AWL sales representative.

Daedalus Online.   Addison Wesley Longman and The Daedalus Group are proud to offer the next generation of the award-winning Daedalus Integrated Writing Environment. Daedalus Online is an Internet-based collaborative writing environment for students. The program offers prewriting strategies and prompts, computer-mediated conferencing, peer collaboration and review, comprehensive writing support, and secure, twenty-four hour availability.

For educators, Daedalus Online offers a comprehensive suite of online course management tools for managing an online class, dynamically linking assignments, and facilitating a heuristic approach to writing instruction. For more information, visit **http://www.awlonline.com/daedalus,** or contact your Addison Wesley Longman sales representative.

The Longman English Pages Web Site. Both students and instructors can visit our free content-rich Web site for additional reading selections and writing exercises. From the Longman English pages, visitors can conduct a simulated Web Search, learn how to write a résumé and cover letter, or try their hand at poetry writing. Stop by and visit us at **http://www.awlonline.com.**

The Longman Electronic Newsletter.   Twice a month during the spring and fall, instructors who have subscribed receive a free copy of the Longman Developmental English Newsletter in their e-mailbox. Written by experienced classroom instructors, the newsletter offers teaching tips, classroom activities, book reviews, and more. To subscribe, send an e-mail to **Basic Skills@awl.com.**

Teaching Online: Internet Research, Conversation, and Composition, Second Edition. Ideal for instructors who have never surfed the Net, this easy-to-follow guide offers basic definitions, numerous examples, and step-by-step information about finding and using Internet sources. Free to adopters. 0-321-01957-1

Researching Online, Third Edition.   A perfect companion for a new age, this indispensable new supplement helps students navigate the Internet. Adapted from *Teaching Online,* the instructor's Internet guide *Researching Online* speaks directly to students, giving them detailed, step-by-step instructions for performing electronic searches. Available free when shrinkwrapped with any Longman Developmental English text. Contact your AWL sales representative for more information.

© 2001 Addison-Wesley Educational Publishers Inc.

For Additional Reading and Reference

The Dictionary Deal.   Two dictionaries can be shrinkwrapped with any Longman title at a nominal fee. *The New American Webster Handy College Dictionary* is a paperback reference text with more than 100,000 entries. *Merriam Webster's Collegiate Dictionary*, tenth edition, is a hardback reference with a citation file of more than 14.5 million examples of English words drawn from actual use. Contact your AWL sales representative for more information.

100 Things to Write About.   This one hundred-page book contains one hundred individual assignments for writing on a variety of topics and in a wide range of formats, from expressive to analytical. Ask your AWL sales representative for a sample copy. 0-673-98239-4

The Longman Textbook Reader.   This supplement, for use in developmental reading courses, offers five complete chapters from AWL textbooks: computer science, biology, psychology, communications, and business. Each chapter includes additional comprehension quizzes, critical thinking questions, and group activities. Available free with the adoption of any Longman text. Contact your AWL sales representative for more information.

Teaching Writing to the Non-Native Speaker.   This booklet examines the issues that arise when non-native speakers enter the developmental classroom. Free to instructors, it includes profiles of international and permanent ESL students, factors influencing second-language acquisition, and tips on managing a multicultural classroom. 0-673-97452-9

The Pocket Reader, First Edition.   This inexpensive volume contains 80 brief readings (1–3 pages each) on a variety of themes: writers on writing, nature, women and men, customs and habits, politics, rights and obligations, and coming of age. Also included is an alternate rhetorical table of contents. 0–321–07668–0

Testing and Exercising Packages

Competency Profile Test Bank, Second Edition.   This series of sixty objective tests covers ten general areas of English competency, including fragments; comma splices and run-ons; pronouns; commas; and capitalization. Each test is available in remedial, standard, and advanced versions. Available as reproducible sheets or in computerized versions. Free to instructors. Paper version: 0-321-02224-6. Computerized IBM: 0-321-02633-0. Computerized Mac: 0-321-02632-2.

Diagnostic and Editing Tests, Second Edition.   This collection of diagnostic tests helps the instructors assess students' competence in Standard Written English for the purpose of placement or to gauge progress. Available as reproducible sheets or in computerized versions, and free to instructors. Paper: 0-321-02222-X. Computerized IBM: 0-321-02629-2. Computerized Mac: 0-321-02628-4.

ESL Worksheets, Second Edition.   These reproducible worksheets provide ESL students with extra practice in areas they find the more troublesome. A diagnostic test and post-test are provided, along with answer keys and suggested topics for writing. Free to adopters. 0-321-01955-5

80 Practices.   A collection of reproducible, ten-item exercises that provide additional practice for specific grammatical usage problems, such as comma splices, capitalization, and pronouns. Includes an answer key; free to adopters. 0-673-53422-7

CLAST Test Package, Fourth Edition.   These two forty-item objective tests evaluate students' readiness for the CLAST exams. Strategies for teaching CLAST preparedness are included. Free with any Longman English title. Reproducible sheets: 0-321-01950-4. Computerized IBM version: 0-321-01982-2. Computerized Mac version: 0-321-01983-0.

TASP Package, Third Edition.   These twelve practice pre-tests and post-tests assess the same reading and writing skills covered in the TASP examination. Free with any Longman English title Reproducible sheets: 0-321-01959-8. Computerized IBM: 0-321-02623-3. Computerized Mac: 0-321-02622-5.

Acknowledgments

We are grateful to the many instructors in colleges and universities throughout the country who continue to express their pleasure with previous editions of this book.

Mary Laine Yarber acknowledges that there is a team of treasured people behind every writer's name, and therefore wishes to thank her colleagues Clara Beard, Mark Berger, Mark Black, Eileen Corliss, Diana Garcia, David Herrera, Lorri Horn, Carol Jago, Liam Joyce, Linda Kovaric, Mary Lelewer, Meredith Louria, Ron Mills-Coyne, Cynthia Milwe, Sylvia Rousseau, Bryan Sanders, Debbie Skaggs, and Rob and Linda Thais for their invaluable encouragement and entertainment; her neighbors in West Hollywood, Michael and Elizabeth Bates, Vick Brown, Jeff Crans, Karen Wood Elliott, Josh Finkelstein and Diana Wong, Cindy Matta, Thomas and Solace Pineo-Meurer, Ira and Rita Schwartz, and Tony Wood for turning a nurturing home into a fruitful workspace; and her friends Terry Dool, Lisa Fimiani, Ronna Hersh, Beth Lebowsky-Rosch, April Quaker, Sherry Talsky, Cathy Tangum, and Theresa Wallace for suggesting needed diversions from work at all the right times.

Mary Yarber also thanks her family, Robert E. Yarber, Mary Winzerling Yarber, Donald and Sylvia Yarber, and Charles Yarborough for decades of encouragement.

As always, Susan Strom and Terry Wolverton served as role models in the mission of making words and ideas clear and accessible to all who seek their power.

© 2001 Addison-Wesley Educational Publishers Inc.

Robert E. Yarber again gratefully acknowledges the contributions of his daughter and co-author, Mary Laine Yarber. Her knowledge, energy, wit and concern for her students are obvious throughout this book as well as in the classroom. He also is pleased to acknowledge the contributions of his wife, Mary Winzerling Yarber, a writer and master teacher who also served as a referee when needed during the revisions of this book.

Finally, we would like to thank the following reviewers for sharing their insights and suggestions:

Jonathan Alexander, University of Cincinnati

Robin Cosgrove, University of Minnesota, Duluth

Andrew Hoffman, San Diego Mesa College

Carolyn Kershaw, Allegany Community College

John Kopec, Boston University

Martha Knight, Bossier Parish Community College

Tom LaJeunesse, University of Minnesota, Duluth

Jane Maher, Nassau Community College

Karen Mason, Bossier Parish Community College

Sam Rogal, Illinois Valley Community College

Alice Sink, High Point University

William Wilson, Palm Beach Community College

Holly Young, Arkansas State University at Beebe

Mary Laine Yarber
Robert E. Yarber

Reviewing
Basic
Grammar

ur instructors in classrooms. In informal conversations, of course, you can
he principles of standard written English. Most **slang,** for example, is per-
to many speakers of American English. But if such expressions appear in
get in the way of the writer's ideas and distract the reader.

u wear while working on your car or painting your room would not be ap-
interview. Nor would the expressions you use with your friends be appro-
peak to a traffic judge whom you are trying to impress. To be a good writer,
ll be expected to follow the principles of standard written English—in
e language that is right for the job. If your writing does not follow those
filled with errors in grammar, spelling, and punctuation—it will confuse
reader. It could even convince him or her that you and your ideas should
usly.

ns, the following chapters will give you a quick review of the parts of
eal with the most serious kinds of errors that writers encounter. You will
ost important rules of punctuation and spelling. But do not get the idea
e of errors equals good writing. You will also need practice in writing sen-
phs that are interesting, coherent, and correct.

WRITE: A COLLABORATIVE CHECKLIST

uestions with other students in your class.

e a job, explain the situations in which writing is important.
al do you follow before you write? Do you like to have music on? Drink
you sharpen your pencils, clean your room, or play a computer game?
he routine you follow in order to get started.
ers read. What do you read regularly? Which magazines, books, or news-
ho are your favorite authors, or what are your favorite types of books?
ass an example of writing by a professional reporter or author whom you
do you like about it? Read the example to the class and see if others
ey do not, examine their reasons.
our strengths as a writer? Try to be specific: mention ideas, vocabulary,
n, or any other aspect of your writing that does not present problems

our weaknesses as a writer? Again, try to be specific: getting started,
ulary, poor spelling, shortage of ideas, and so on.
ass some of your own writing that you like. Read it to the class (or have
se read it) to get their reaction.

© 2001 Addison-Wesley Educational Publishers Inc.

CHAPTER **1**

Getting Stal
Computers,
and Paragra

or radio and by y
ignore many of t
fectly acceptable
writing, they can

The clothes yo
propriate for a jol
priate when you s
therefore, you wi
other words, to u
principles—if it i
and mislead your
not be taken serio

For these reaso
speech and then d
also review the m
that the avoidanc
tences and paragra

| STANDARD ENGLISH: WHO NEEDS |

The English language is spoken an
around the world. In Europe, which is
guages, English is increasingly the lang
English is spoken and written in both
business and cultural influence.

In the United States, the ability to
in most occupations. Reports, proposal
day's work world. These must be not on
in grammar, spelling, and punctuation

The ability to use the English langu
job. Almost every class that you will t
be expected to write exams, reports, e
and convincing, and to follow the pri

Fortunately, you already know and
dard written English. The chapters t
and structure. Standard written Eng
books, newspapers, and articles, and t

PREPARING TO

Discuss these

1. If you hav
2. What ritu
   coffee? D
   Describe t
3. Good writ
   papers? W
4. Bring to c
   like. Wha
   like it. If t
5. What are
   organizatic
   for you.
6. What are
   weak voca
7. Bring to cl
   someone e

Getting Started: Computers, Grammar, and Paragraphs

STANDARD ENGLISH: WHO NEEDS IT?

The English language is spoken and written by almost five hundred million people around the world. In Europe, which is uniting rapidly and which has at least fifteen languages, English is increasingly the language that Europeans use to communicate. In Asia, English is spoken and written in both business and social settings as a result of American business and cultural influence.

In the United States, the ability to use the English language effectively is a requirement in most occupations. Reports, proposals, summaries, and letters are typically required in today's work world. These must be not only factually accurate, but also free of serious mistakes in grammar, spelling, and punctuation.

The ability to use the English language effectively is not a skill that is helpful only on the job. Almost every class that you will take in college requires writing of some kind. You will be expected to write exams, reports, essays, and term papers that are well organized, logical, and convincing, and to follow the principles of **standard written English.**

Fortunately, you already know and unconsciously follow most of the principles of standard written English. The chapters that follow in this book will build on that knowledge and structure. Standard written English is the kind of English that you find in reports, books, newspapers, and articles, and that you hear spoken by news announcers on television or radio and by your instructors in classrooms. In informal conversations, of course, you can ignore many of the principles of standard written English. Most **slang,** for example, is perfectly acceptable to many speakers of American English. But if such expressions appear in writing, they can get in the way of the writer's ideas and distract the reader.

The clothes you wear while working on your car or painting your room would not be appropriate for a job interview. Nor would the expressions you use with your friends be appropriate when you speak to a traffic judge whom you are trying to impress. To be a good writer, therefore, you will be expected to follow the principles of standard written English—in other words, to use language that is right for the job. If your writing does not follow those principles—if it is filled with errors in grammar, spelling, and punctuation—it will confuse and mislead your reader. It could even convince him or her that you and your ideas should not be taken seriously.

For these reasons, the following chapters will give you a quick review of the parts of speech and then deal with the most serious kinds of errors that writers encounter. You will also review the most important rules of punctuation and spelling. But do not get the idea that the avoidance of errors equals good writing. You will also need practice in writing sentences and paragraphs that are interesting, coherent, and correct.

Preparing to Write: A Collaborative Checklist

Discuss these questions with other students in your class.

1. If you have a job, explain the situations in which writing is important.
2. What ritual do you follow before you write? Do you like to have music on? Drink coffee? Do you sharpen your pencils, clean your room, or play a computer game? Describe the routine you follow in order to get started.
3. Good writers read. What do you read regularly? Which magazines, books, or newspapers? Who are your favorite authors, or what are your favorite types of books?
4. Bring to class an example of writing by a professional reporter or author whom you like. What do you like about it? Read the example to the class and see if others like it. If they do not, examine their reasons.
5. What are your strengths as a writer? Try to be specific: mention ideas, vocabulary, organization, or any other aspect of your writing that does not present problems for you.
6. What are your weaknesses as a writer? Again, try to be specific: getting started, weak vocabulary, poor spelling, shortage of ideas, and so on.
7. Bring to class some of your own writing that you like. Read it to the class (or have someone else read it) to get their reaction.

© 2001 Addison-Wesley Educational Publishers Inc.

THE PARAGRAPH: AN OVERVIEW

Most of the writing that you will be asked to do in college will be in the form of paragraphs. A *paragraph* consists of several related sentences that deal with a single topic, or an aspect of a topic. Paragraphs frequently stand alone, as in the case of responses to questions on examinations. Usually, however, paragraphs are parts of longer pieces of writing, such as essays, reports, and term papers. In such cases paragraphs help your reader by breaking down complicated ideas into manageable parts and relating each part to the main idea or thesis of your composition.

Regardless of whether it is freestanding or part of a larger unit, a well-organized paragraph has three characteristics:

- ◆ A good paragraph is *unified:* all of its sentences are related to one main idea.

- ◆ A good paragraph is *coherent:* the thought proceeds logically from sentence to sentence.

- ◆ A good paragraph is *developed:* it contains enough information to convey the idea of the paragraph in a reasonably thorough way.

In the following chapters you will practice writing paragraphs that are unified, coherent, and developed. As mentioned above, a *unified* paragraph is about a single idea or topic. The sentence that states the paragraph's topic is the *topic sentence*, and it is developed and supported by the specifics in the sentence that follow or precede it. In Chapter 2 you will learn to recognize topic sentences and to write your own paragraphs with topic sentences.

Good paragraphs are *coherent*. This means that the sentences are in the right order with the right connecting words so that the reader is not confused. Chapters 3–6 will introduce you to the ways to make your paragraphs coherent so that your thoughts will be easy to follow from sentence to sentence and from paragraph to paragraph.

In addition to being unified and coherent, good paragraphs are *developed*. They contain details and material that fulfill the promise made to the reader in the topic sentence. Several methods of paragraph development are available to you, and they are presented in Chapters 7–13.

WRITING TIPS

According to the dictionary . .

The dictionary is a learning tool that you will use in your college classes and for the rest of your life. A dictionary contains much more than definitions. It tells you the history of a word and how it is spelled, hyphenated, and pronounced. Traditional favorites of college students and instructors include *The American Heritage College Dictionary, Merriam-Webster's Collegiate Dictionary*, and *The Random House College Dictionary*. Ask your instructor for more suggestions.

WRITING WITH THE COMPUTER

Until recent years, writing a composition of any length meant taking notes, writing one or more drafts while revising and correcting at each stage, and typing a final copy. Weakness in content, mistakes in grammar, and even typographical errors were sometimes ignored because the author did not want to type another copy. In recent times, however, the act of writing has changed because of the introduction of computers. Increasing numbers of writers believe that composing on a computer makes the revising and editing process much easier and more efficient. A computer becomes a word processor when a word-processing program is loaded into it. Although computers and word-processing programs may vary in the features they offer, all word processing offers certain benefits for the writer.

The chief advantage of a word processor is that it allows you to rewrite, correct, change, and revise selected portions of your paper without retyping the whole manuscript. The parts that you do not change remain in their original form and do not have to be retyped. As you can imagine, word processors allow and encourage writers to revise their manuscripts more easily and quickly than the traditional way.

Just as there are different writing styles for those who use a pen or typewriter, so there are differing practices for users of word processors. Some writers work directly at the keyboard and compose after they have completed their first draft. Then they revise and edit until they have made all of their modifications and changes. Others write their first draft by hand and then use the word processor for preparing their final copy. Still others write on the screen, print a copy, and then revise with pen or pencil, going back to the word processor for further alterations.

Regardless of the composing style that you adopt, you should not become discouraged at your first attempts to use a computer. For your initial effort, try typing your first draft on the word processor. As you master its keyboard, you will learn that you can move around or delete words, sentences, paragraphs, or entire pages; change words, phrases, or sentences; correct punctuation, mechanics, and misspelled words; and copy part or all of the manuscript to use for other purposes.

In addition to revising and editing, the word processor has other uses. In the preparation and formatting of a manuscript you can change spacing and margins, incorporate boldface, italicize words and titles, center material on a page, and close any spaces left by deletions and substitutions.

The effect of using a word processor will be obvious as you become familiar with its features. The most obvious is that revision is easier: by merely pressing a few keys, you can shift words, sentences, and entire paragraphs. By putting down ideas as they come to you, you will be less worried about forgetting important points and more likely to draft quickly. You can incorporate additional material and insert it in an earlier copy, and because you can get

© 2001 Addison-Wesley Educational Publishers Inc.

Editing Exercise

The sentences below contain some of the most common errors in usage. Rewrite each sentence in standard written English. To help you recognize the errors, you can refer to the appropriate chapter indicated after each sentence.

1. Looking through my high school annual bring back bittersweet memories. (Chapter 4)

2. The prospect of moving to a warmer climate delighted his wife and he. (Chapter 5)

3. Each of the band members had signed their name on the concert program. (Chapter 6)

4. After running in the marathon, Jackie laid down and rested. (Chapter 7)

5. When Don was a freshman in college he had broke three records as a member of the basketball team. (Chapter 7)

6. An old-fashioned remedy for a cough, made by mixing honey, lemon, and hot water. (Chapter 9)

7. Osteoporosis is caused by loss of bone mass and strength, it affects 25 percent of women over age 60. (Chapter 9)

8. Rappelling is a descent used by mountain climbers it employs double ropes rather than picks and shoe cleats. (Chapter 9)

9. Sean bought a motorcycle for his wife with an electric starter. (Chapter 10)

10. Because the sidewalk was covered with ice, I walked very careful to avoid falling. (Chapter 10)

a clean copy whenever you want after making changes, you will probably revise and edit more than if you had to retype continually.

Using the word processor will not make you a good writer. You will still need to arrange your ideas in the most effective and logical order, develop and plan your paragraphs carefully, and use the most appropriate word choice and sentence structure. But for the last, important stage of the writing process—revising and editing—the word processor can be an invaluable tool.

WRITING PARAGRAPHS

This assignment calls for you to write a paragraph of at least six sentences on the topic of your choice. Remember that all of your sentences in the paragraph should deal with a single topic. After you have finished your first draft, look it over for ways to improve it. Will the paragraph be clear and interesting to your reader? Does your paragraph contain any sentences that stray from your topic? Does it have any errors in spelling, usage, or punctuation? Your instructor may ask you to exchange your first draft with another student in your class for his or her suggestions.

a. Describe one of the following:
   - Your favorite hideaway when you want to "get away from it all."
   - Your impressions of a recent movie, concert, or television program.

b. Tell what happened the last time you had an unpleasant encounter with a person in authority. For example, it may have been an argument with a traffic cop, a dispute with your parents, or a run-in with your boss.

Writing Tips

In the Beginning . . .

Unless your instructor says otherwise, your assignments don't need title pages. Instead, provide a simple heading on your first page. Starting one inch from the top of the page, type (or write) your name flush with the left margin. Below it, type your instructor's name, the course number, and the date. Double-space each line. Double-space twice more, indent five spaces (one-half inch), and begin your paper.

Computer Activity

Create a file for each of the computer activities in our text. Each activity will take the form of a stand-alone document created with your word-processing program.

When you begin a new document, give it an appropriate name, using your SAVE AS command.

On the first line of the page, enter a document/subject title and the date, or follow the naming style your instructor advises.

For Chapter 1, list the benefits that you hope to gain from reviewing basic grammar and paragraph writing.

If your class has a projector for displaying computer screens, discuss your comments with your classmates, or exchange your file with a classmate for discussion.

© 2001 Addison-Wesley Educational Publishers Inc.

2

The Parts of Speech: A Review

The Internet. Modem. Hyperlink. E-mail. Cyberspace. These are just a few of the many words from the world of computers that have entered the English language within the last few years. Although our language has more than a half-million words, it is constantly adding thousands of new ones from every field of human activity. Despite their number, all of these words—long or short, familiar or strange—can be divided into only eight categories: the eight parts of speech. When you learn to recognize the parts of speech, you will be on your own way to understanding how the English language works, and you can talk about it intelligently and precisely. Even more important, you will be able to identify the tools that will help you to write clear, interesting, and correct sentences and paragraphs and to become a more confident writer. Our study of grammar and usage continues, therefore, by examining the parts of speech.

THE NOUN

We will start with the noun because every English sentence either contains one or is about one. A **noun** *is a word that names something—a person, a place, a thing, or an idea.*

◆ Jay Leno, Florida, nest, envy

Some nouns refer to a general class of persons, places, or things. They are called **common nouns,** and they are not capitalized unless they are used to begin a sentence.

◆ newscaster, restaurant, sneakers

Some nouns refer to specific persons, places, or things. They are called **proper nouns,** and they are always capitalized.

♦ George Washington Carver, Dallas, Porsche Boxster

As you will see in later chapters, nouns are important because they can work as several parts of the sentence.

TIP FOR SPOTTING NOUNS

If you can put a word in the slot in the following sentence, it is a noun: "A (or *An*)
_____ *is remarkable.*"

Examples: "*An* elephant *is remarkable.*"
"*A* rainbow *is remarkable.*"

THE PRONOUN

We could not get along without nouns. But occasionally, in order to avoid repetition, we use other words in place of nouns. The words that we substitute for nouns are called **pronouns.**

♦ As Paul began to take Paul's biology exam, Paul tried to ignore the beeping sound coming from a cellular phone behind Paul.

This sentence is obviously monotonous because of its overuse of *Paul*. We can improve it by using pronouns:

♦ As Paul began to take *his* biology exam, *he* tried to ignore the beeping sound coming from a cellular phone behind *him*.

The pronouns in this sentence are *his, he,* and *him,* and their *antecedent* (the word to which they refer) is *Paul*. Here is another sentence with pronouns and an antecedent:

♦ The runner waved to her fans as she ran the victory lap around the track, and the crowd cheered her.

What are the pronouns in this sentence? What is their antecedent?

© 2001 Addison-Wesley Educational Publishers Inc.

Unlike a noun, a pronoun does not name a specific person, place, thing, or idea. You will learn more about pronouns and their uses in Chapters 5 and 6. Meanwhile, you should try to recognize the most common pronouns:

I, me, my, mine	we, us, our, ours
you, your, yours	they, them, their, theirs
he, him, his	anybody, everybody, somebody
she, her, hers	everyone, no one, someone
it, its	something, some, all, many, any
who, whose, whom	each, none, one, this, that, these
	those, which, what

Exercise 2-1

Underline the nouns and circle the pronouns.

1. Although he died in 1977, Elvis Presley continues to be the subject of books and documentaries, and he has become one of our country's musical legends.
2. Elvis was born in 1935 in Tupelo, Mississippi, but he later moved with his parents to Memphis, Tennessee.
3. His father and mother were uneducated and "dirt poor," according to friends of the family; nevertheless, they encouraged their son's interest in music and bought him a guitar.
4. While working as a truck driver, Elvis began to sing in church basements, at school, in neighbors' backyards, and for anyone who would listen to him.
5. He was fascinated by Southern gospel songs, country-and-western music, and the musical style of black performers who were popular in the South during the 1950s.
6. To develop his own stage personality and to conceal his nervousness, he wore far-out clothes and combed his hair in a grease-laden pompadour.
7. He made a few records at a local studio and began to tour with a show throughout the South.
8. Those records, whose value today continues to increase, caught the attention of Colonel Tom Parker, who was to become his manager.
9. Parker urged Elvis to emphasize the rhythm-and-blues style of black musicians.
10. In 1956 his first big hit, "Heartbreak Hotel," was released, and its success launched his career.
11. For the next 16 months, his recordings were among the top ten national best-sellers, and their popularity spread to Europe, where they soon dominated the sales charts.
12. His television appearances and concerts attracted mobs of screaming teenagers, but many regarded his gyrations and music as symbols of decay in our society.

13. After a brief Army career, Elvis starred in several movies in the 1960s; they were ridiculed by the critics but praised by his fans.
14. His sudden death in 1977 shocked his millions of fans throughout the world; a common reaction was that one of our national idols had fallen.
15. Today his admirers come to pay their respects at his grave in Graceland, his home in Tennessee.

THE VERB

Every sentence that you speak or write contains a *verb*. Sometimes the verb is only implied; usually, however, it is stated. When you can recognize and use verbs correctly, you have taken a big step toward being a better speaker and writer.

A **verb** is a word that expresses action or a state of being and thereby tells us what a noun or pronoun does or what it is. If the verb tells us what a noun or pronoun does, it is an **action verb.**

- Roberta *paints* beautiful landscapes, which she hides in her attic.
- Neil Armstrong *landed* on the moon in 1969.
- Huang *attends* medical school in California.

If the verb expresses a state of being rather than action, it is a **linking verb.** Linking verbs do not express action; instead, they connect a noun or pronoun with a word or group of words that describe or rename the subject:

- The subject of tonight's debate *is* prayers in public school. (*Subject* is linked by the verb *is* to *prayers*, a word that renames it.)
- I.Q. tests *are* unreliable predictors of academic success, according to many educators. (*Tests* is linked to *predictors* by the verb *are*.)
- My new speakers *sound* much better than my old ones. (*Speakers* is linked to the word that describes it—*better*—by the verb *sound*.)
- Computers were very expensive for the average family to purchase in the 1970s. (What words are linked? What word links them?)
- Belize is a small nation in Central America. (What word renames Belize? How are the two words linked?)

The most common linking verbs are formed from the verb *to be: am, are, is, was,* and *were*. Others often used as linking verbs are *appear, become, grow, remain,* and *seem,* and the "sense" verbs: *feel, look, smell, sound,* and *taste*.

© 2001 Addison-Wesley Educational Publishers Inc.

Verbs are the only words that change their spelling to show *tense*. **Tense** is the time when the action of the verb occurs. Notice in the following sentences how the tense or time of the action is changed by the spelling of the verb:

◆ Our mayor *delivers* an annual message to the citizens of our city. (Present tense)
◆ Last week she *delivered* her message on local television. (Past tense)

You will learn more about the use of tense in Chapter 7.

To show additional differences in meaning, verbs often use helping words that suggest the time at which the action of the verb takes place and other kinds of meaning. These words are called **helping/auxiliary verbs,** and they always come before the main verb. Verbs that consist of helping verbs and a main verb are called *verb phrases*. Look carefully at the following sentences.

◆ I *will* bowl.   ◆ The sisters *were* saddened.
◆ He *had* studied.   ◆ The child *was* photographed.
◆ Cliff *did* not want lunch.   ◆ They *might have been* selected.

Each of the verbs in the preceding sentences consists of a helping/auxiliary verb and a main verb. Here are the common helping/auxiliary verbs. You should memorize them.

◆ *can, could, may, might, must, ought, shall, should, will, would, have, has, had, do, does, did, am, is, are, was, were, been*

Some verbs can be either helping/auxiliary verbs or main verbs. In other words, if they appear alone without a helping/auxiliary verb, they are main verbs. But if they precede a main verb, they are helping/auxiliary verbs. The following verbs can be either helping/auxiliary verbs or main verbs. You should memorize them.

Forms of "to be": *am, is, are, was, were*
Forms of "to do": *do, does, did*
Forms of "to have": *has, have, had*

Look at the following sentences carefully:

◆ Victims of the earthquake *were* unable to drink the water. (*Were* is the main verb in this sentence.)
◆ Victims of the earthquake *were given* food and clothing by the Red Cross. (*Were given* is a verb phrase. The main verb is *given*, and the helping/auxiliary verb is *were*.)

◆ Tanya *has* a new car. (*Has* is the main verb in this sentence.)
◆ She *has* already *driven* it two thousand miles. (*Has driven* is a verb phrase. The main verb is *driven*, and the helping/auxiliary verb is *has*.)

TIPS FOR RECOGNIZING VERBS

An *action verb* is a word that fits in the slot in the following sentence:
"*I* (or *He* or *She* or *They*) *usually* _____."

Examples: *I usually* **jog.**
She usually **snores.**
They usually **help.**

A *linking verb* is a word that fits in the slot in the following sentence:
"*I* (or *He* or *She* or *They*) _____ **happy.**"

Examples: *I* **am** *happy.*
He **is** *happy.*
They **were** *happy.*

Exercise 2-2

If the italicized word in each sentence is an action verb, write "1"; if the italicized word is a linking verb, write "2"; if the italicized word is a helping/auxiliary verb, write "3." Use the space provided on the left.

_____ 1. Horses *have been* pets and helpers to humans for thousands of years.

_____ 2. Although a variety of breeds *exists*, there are some general traits which most horses share.

_____ 3. Most horses *are* social animals who enjoy living and moving with other horses.

_____ 4. They *observe* a hierarchy within their groups.

_____ 5. For example, young horses *will* rarely drink water from a trough until older group members have finished drinking.

_____ 6. Until a new horse's place is determined within the group, many conflicts *may* occur.

_____ 7. Horses *are* natural runners, and they race each other just for fun.

_____ 8. They are also swift learners and *can* master a number of skills to help or amuse their owners.

_____ 9. Like dogs, horses possess acute hearing and *can become* easily frightened by sudden loud noises.

_____ 10. Thanks to equally sharp eyesight, horses *are* able to see distant leaves where another animal is scampering.

_____ 11. Believe it or not, horses *enjoy* music, and some may step in rhythm during parades or shows.

© 2001 Addison-Wesley Educational Publishers Inc.

_____ 12. The position of the horse's eyes *provides* a wide, panoramic view.

_____ 13. If a horse shifts her weight back and forth repeatedly, she probably / exercise.

_____ 14. Horses are highly sensitive to touch, so a light pull of reins *is* eno꜡ ꜱ guide them.

_____ 15. When treated well and trained patiently, horses *will* provide dec꜡ of pleasure and companionship.

THE ADJECTIVE

In your writing you will often want to modify (or describe) a noun or pronc꜡ ꜀he word you will use will be an **adjective,** a word that modifies nouns and pronouns. / ꜀tives usually answer one of the following questions: *How many? What kind? Which c꜡ Vhat color?*

- ◆ How many? Many students believe that the Social Security Syste꜡ ꜀l be bankrupt before they will be old enough to retire. (*Many* ꜀fies *students.*)
- ◆ What kind? Egg bagels gave us energy for our hike. (*Egg* modif꜡ *gels.*)
- ◆ Which one? *This* backpack was found in the cafeteria. (*This* m꜡ ꜀s *backpack.*)
- ◆ What color? His *purple* socks did not complement his red sui꜡ ꜀urple modifies *socks.*)

The adjectives in the sentences above came immediately before the nouns they modified. Some adjectives, however, come after linking verbs and describe the subject of the verb. Adjectives in this position are called **predicate adjectives.** Study the following sentences carefully:

- ◆ We were surprised to learn that old pairs of American jeans in Russia are very *expensive.* (*Expensive* is a predicate adjective because it comes after a linking verb—*are*—and modifies the noun *pairs.*)
- ◆ After waiting in the hot sun for three days, the refugees became *angry.* (*Angry* is a predicate adjective because it comes after a linking verb—*became*—and modifies the noun *refugees.*)

Possessive pronouns (pronouns that show ownership such as *my, your, her, his, our, their*) are adjectives when they come before nouns. Notice the following examples:

- ◆ *our* apartment
- ◆ *their* lunch break
- ◆ *my* employer

Demonstrative pronouns (pronouns that point out or indicate) are adjectives when they come before nouns. Notice the following examples:

- *this* building
- *that* statement
- *these* flowers
- *those* books

A special type of adjective is called the **article.** The English language contains three articles: *a, an* (before words that begin with a vowel sound), and *the*.

- After *an* absence of sixteen years, Maricela returned to *the* city of her birth and *a* parade in her honor.

TIPS FOR SPOTTING ADJECTIVES

1. You can add *-er* and *-est* or *more* and *most* to adjectives:
   Examples: strong, strong*er*, strong*est*
   eager, *more* eager, *most* eager

2. An adjective will fill the blank in this sentence:
   The (noun) *is* _____
   Example: The cupboard is *empty.*

3. Adjectives describe nouns and pronouns:
   Examples: The *tired* surfers paddled back to shore.
   She is *proud* of her degree in math.

4. Adjectives tell *how many, what kind, which one,* and *what color.*
   Examples: Butch has *four* dogs, *three* cats, and *a dozen* goldfish.
   I have a *German* pen-pal and an *Ecuadoran* pen-pal.
   Did you eat the *last* bagel?
   White roses and *yellow* daisies dot her garden.

Exercise 2-3

A. *In the space before each sentence, write the noun or pronoun that is modified by the italicized adjective.*

_____ 1.   A classic example of a *false* rumor that swept the country was the alleged death of Paul McCartney, the Beatle.

_____ 2.   In 1969 a Detroit disc jockey casually mentioned a *fictional* story about McCartney's death.

_____ 3.   Within a *few* days the rumor of his death had spread throughout the world.

_____ 4.   According to one version, McCartney had been killed in an automobile accident *several* years previously.

© 2001 Addison-Wesley Educational Publishers Inc.

_____ 5. His record company had replaced him with a look-alike and persuaded the *remaining* Beatles to conceal the event.

_____ 6. But the Beatles, according to the rumor, had inserted *various* clues about McCartney's death in their records to let others in on the secret.

_____ 7. In the weeks following, their fans searched the Beatles' albums for these *alleged* clues.

_____ 8. They held up Beatles' album covers to mirrors, hoping to find some message in the *reverse* image.

_____ 9. *Repeated* denials by record-company officials failed to have much impact on the rumor.

_____ 10. Finally, Paul McCartney issued a *public* statement disproving the truth of the rumor, adding, "If I were dead, I'd be the last to know about it."

B. *In the space before each sentence, write the predicate adjective that modifies the italicized noun or pronoun.*

_____ 1. The recent *excavation* of an ancient Egyptian tomb is important because it shows how wine was used in ancient rituals.

_____ 2. Until recent times the *tomb* was obscure except to local natives.

_____ 3. Many of its *secrets* remain unknown to archaeologists who continue to search its depths.

_____ 4. The *tomb* became significant because it was the tomb of Scorpion I, one of Egypt's first kings.

_____ 5. Three *rooms* in the tomb are interesting to archaeologists because they are stacked with wine jars.

_____ 6. *Archaeologists* have been able to determine the contents of seven-hundred vessels so far.

_____ 7. If each *jar* was full at the time of Scorpion's death, there may have been nearly twelve hundred gallons of wine.

_____ 8. The *jars* are empty, but at one time were filled with wine.

_____ 9. *Wine* was important in Egyptian burial feasts to celebrate fertility of the fields.

_____ 10. The jars were imported from Israel, suggesting that *trade* between Egypt and Palestine was probable.

THE ADVERB

Adverbs are words that describe or modify verbs, adjectives, and other adverbs. Study these sentences carefully:

◆ The huge chopper transported the soldiers *quickly*. (*Quickly* modifies the verb *transported*.)

◆ The *extremely* tall guard dribbled the basketball *slowly*. (*Extremely* modifies the adjective *tall*, and *slowly* modifies the verb *dribbled*.)

◆ The tall guard dribbled the basketball *very* slowly. (*Very* modifies the adverb *slowly*.)

Adverbs usually answer the following questions: *When? Where? How? To what extent?*

◆ **When?**   Hector *immediately* realized that he had confused Sue with her sister. (The adverb *immediately* modifies the verb *realized*.)

◆ **Where?**   Please wait *here*. (The adverb *here* modifies the verb *wait*.)

◆ **How?**   The deer struggled *unsuccessfully* to escape. (The adverb *unsuccessfully* modifies the verb *struggled*.)

◆ **To what extent?**   The state capitol building was *completely* remodeled after the election. (The adverb *completely* modifies the verb *was remodeled*.)

Adjectives and adverbs are often confused. Remember that *adjectives* describe nouns and pronouns, and that *adverbs* modify verbs, adjectives, and other adverbs. Notice the differences in the following sentences:

◆ Her *loud* hiccups distracted the speaker. (*Loud* is an adjective because it modifies the noun *hiccups*.)

◆ If you sneeze *loudly*, you will distract the speaker. (*Loudly* is an adverb because it modifies the verb *sneeze*.)

Many adverbs are formed by adding *-ly* to the adjective (as in *loudly*, in the sentence above). But keep in mind that some adverbs do not end in *-ly* (*above, never, there, very*, and so on). On the other hand, some words that end in *-ly* are not adverbs (words such as *silly, friendly*, and *lovely*).

TIPS FOR RECOGNIZING ADVERBS

1. Adverbs are words that will fit in the following slot:
   "He will meet us _____."
   Examples: He will meet us *later. (when)*
                    He will meet us *here. (where)*
                    He will meet us *punctually. (how)*
                    He will meet us *briefly. (to what extent)*
2. Adverbs tell *when, where, how,* and *to what extent.*

Exercise 2-4

A. *In the space before each sentence, write the adjective, verb, or adverb modified by the italicized adverb.*

© 2001 Addison-Wesley Educational Publishers Inc.

_____ 1. *Approximately* twenty million Americans attend monster truck spectaculars every year.

_____ 2. Monster trucks have huge tires that enable them to scoot up a ramp, take off and travel through the air 100 feet, 30 feet off the ground, then crash *dramatically* back to earth without being smashed to pieces.

_____ 3. A common feat is to land on a car, *preferably* a Japanese import, and crush it.

_____ 4. Other *very* popular events at truck shows include mud racing and dropping drivers strapped in their cars 170 feet in the air onto several vans.

_____ 5. The appeal of monster trucks *probably* derives from the roar and the mud.

_____ 6. It also stems *partly* from the fantasy most of us have experienced as we have been trapped in traffic, wishing we could push aside the cars around us.

_____ 7. The trucks *inevitably* have colorful names such as Carolina Crusher, Bearfoot, and Grave Digger, among others.

_____ 8. But the *most* famous is Bigfoot, the product of Bob Chandler, the originator of the monster truck.

_____ 9. Bigfoot-licensed products and souvenirs sold at truck shows gross over $300 million *annually*.

_____ 10. Over seven hundred monster truck shows a year are held throughout the world, and the *most* popular drivers enjoy the kind of fame reserved for movie stars.

B. *In the space before each sentence, write the adverb that modifies the italicized word or words.*

_____ 1. Though it is widely thought that Betsy Ross designed the first United States flag in 1776, several other versions *existed* previously.

_____ 2. The oldest predecessor was the Grand Union, which brightly *bore* a red cross and white cross in a background of blue.

_____ 3. Our red and white stripes first *appeared* on the flag in 1776, proudly hoisted by General George Washington's rebel army.

_____ 4. Later that year, a flag *appeared* which featured 13 white stars on a blue field, in addition to the stripes.

_____ 5. At Concord, in 1775, some Minutemen from Massachusetts carried a flag bearing a silver arm and sword *burnished* brightly on a red background.

_____ 6. Other Minutemen waved a very *different* flag, a solid field of red with a green pine tree.

_____ 7. Meanwhile, the Philadelphia Light Horse Troop *carried* a yellow flag bearing a slogan, coat of arms, and 13 blue and silver stripes.

_____ 8. By 1777, most patriots *had* increasingly *adopted* a flag containing 13 red and white stripes, a square of blue with an arch of 11 white stars, and the figure "76."

_____ 9.   After becoming President, Washington ordered the creation of the flag which closely *resembles* today's version: 15 stripes alternating in red and white, and 15 stars on a blue field.

_____ 10.   Today's flag contains 13 stripes to signify the original states, and 50 stars to denote all states, though no star *belongs* specifically to any state.

THE PREPOSITION

Prepositions are connecting words—they do not have any meaning or content in or of themselves. They exist only to show relationships between other words. For this reason they must simply be learned or remembered. Prepositions are words like *at, by, from,* and *with* that are usually followed by a noun or pronoun (*at home, by herself, from Toledo, with you*). The word following the preposition is called its **object;** the preposition and its object are called a **prepositional phrase.**

Here are some prepositional phrases. The object in each prepositional phrase is italicized. Notice that a preposition can have more than one object, and that some prepositions are made up of more than one word.

◆ according to *authorities*
◆ in addition to *requirements in science*
◆ after *the meeting*
◆ through *the final week*
◆ below *the deck*
◆ together with *the director and producer*
◆ between *you and me*
◆ within *the hour*
◆ from *one coast to another*
◆ without *a clue*

Here are some of the most common prepositions. As noted above, some prepositions consist of more than one word.

about	before	due to
above	behind	during
according to	below	except
across	beneath	for
after	besides	from
against	between	in
ahead of	beyond	in addition to
along	but (when it means *except*)	in front of
among	by	inside
around	concerning	instead of
away from	despite	into
because of	down	like

© 2001 Addison-Wesley Educational Publishers Inc.

near	over	under
next to	past	underneath
of	regarding	unlike
off	round	until
on	since	up
onto	through	upon
on account of	to	with
out	together with	within
out of	toward	without
outside		

Prepositional phrases may serve the same function as either adjectives or adverbs in a sentence.

- ◆ **adjective:** News *of an impending rebellion* panicked the government. (The italicized phrase modifies the noun *News*.)
- ◆ **adjective:** The ushers *in blue suits* quieted the crowd. (The italicized phrase modifies the noun *ushers*.)
- ◆ **adverb:** Tod and Jan left *during the intermission*. (The italicized phrase modifies the verb left.)
- ◆ **adverb:** The President spoke *with emotion*. (The italicized phrase modifies the verb *spoke*.)

TIPS FOR RECOGNIZING PREPOSITIONS

1. A preposition is a word that will fill the slot in the following sentence:
   "The airplane flew _____ the clouds."
   "The airplane flew *above, below, beyond, under, around*, or *through* the clouds."

2. A preposition is a word that will fill the slot in the following sentence:
   "A purse was lying _____ street."
   "A purse was lying *in, next to, alongside*, or *beside* the street."
   Some prepositions, of course, will not fit either sentence, and they must be learned.

Exercise 2-5

Underline the prepositional phrases in each sentence; write "adv" above the phrase if it is used as an adverbial modifier, or "adj" if it is used as an adjectival modifier.

1. The first symptom of Alzheimer's disease in most older people is loss of memory.

2. Most patients are not aware of the problem and don't realize the need for an appointment with a doctor.

3. Alzheimer's disease affects the hippocampus, one of the areas of the brain.

4. The hippocampus is involved in learning something initially, and then that information is stored or processed in other areas of the brain.

5. For that reason, most Alzheimer's patients have problems with learning and remembering new things, but are better at remembering old things.

   Billions of cells make up the brain like bricks that make up a house.

   The dendrite is the part of the cell that receives information, and the axon is the part that sends information out.

   The axons and dendrites are important to memory because they connect one brain cell to another.

9. ne of the theories held by scientists is that the axons and dendrites shrink in heimer's patients.

10. result, loss of memory is one of the first effects when these connections are ted.

THE CONJ   ON

A **conjunctic**   word that joins words or groups of words. In a sense, conjunctions are like prepositions.   do not represent things or qualities. Instead, they merely show different kinds of relat   ips between other words or groups of words. There are two kinds of conjunctions you v   ed to recognize: *coordinating* and *subordinating*.

Coordinating co   **tions** join words and word groups of equal importance or rank. You should memorize the   rdinating conjunctions:

◆ *and, but, so, for, :   , yet*

The following sentences show how coordinating conjunctions join single words and groups of words:

◆ Alexi speaks English *and* Russian fluently. (*and* links two words)

◆ Nguyen was born in Vietnam, *but* he moved to the United States at the age of four. (*but* links two independent clauses)

◆ Do you prefer fish *or* chicken? (*or* links two words)

◆ You should talk to a counselor, *or* you might take the wrong courses. (*or* links two independent clauses)

In Chapter 8 you will see how coordinating conjunctions are used in compound sentences. Incidentally, it used to be considered ungrammatical to begin a sentence with one of these words, but this "rule" is no longer observed, even by the best writers.

© 2001 Addison-Wesley Educational Publishers Inc.

Some coordinating conjunctions combine with other words to form **correlative conjunctions.** The most common correlative conjunctions are *both . . . and; either . . . or; neither . . . nor;* and *not only . . . but also.* Notice the following examples.

- *Both* Ty Murray *and* Kristie Peterson are legends of professional rodeo.
- Ray will *either* go to summer school *or* work in his father's store.
- John Kennedy was *not only* the first Roman Catholic President *but also* the first President born in the twentieth century.

Subordinating conjunctions, like coordinating conjunctions, join groups of words. Unlike coordinating conjunctions, however, they join unequal word groups or grammatical units that are "subordinate." You will study subordinating conjunctions in greater detail in Chapters 8 and 9, especially with respect to complex sentences and fragments.

Some conjunctions like *after, before, for, since, but,* and *until* can also function as prepositions:

- The popularity of leisure suits declined *after* the presidency of Richard Nixon. (*preposition*)
- Harold sold his leisure suit *after* Richard Nixon wore one. (*conjunction*)
- Jaime bought flowers *for* his girlfriend. (*preposition*)
- Jaime bought flowers, *for* he knew his girlfriend was angry. (*conjunction*)
- Every member of the General Assembly *but* Cuba voted for the motion. (*preposition*)
- Every member voted, *but* Cuba demanded a recount. (*conjunction*)

Exercise 2–6

Underline the coordinating conjunctions in the sentences below.

1. The savings-and-loan disaster several years ago cost the government millions of dollars, but the greatest loss was to the lives of investors.
2. The relationship between smoking and cancer has been long established, yet many young people continue to smoke.
3. Neither the Israelis nor the Palestinians would comment on the negotiations.
4. Because he had a car alarm and had parked in front of a church, he was surprised and angry to discover that his new Miata was either stolen or towed away.
5. Leon bought a fax machine, but he didn't know how to use it.

THE INTERJECTION

The **interjection** (or *exclamation,* as it is sometimes called) is a word that expresses emotion and has no grammatical relationship with the rest of the sentence.

Mild interjections are followed by a comma:

- *No,* it's too early.

◆ *Oh*, I suppose so.

◆ *Yes*, that would be fine.

Strong interjections require an exclamation mark:

◆ *Wow!* My phone bill is huge!

◆ *Ouch!* That hurts!

◆ *Fire!*

◆ *Yo!* I'm over here!

◆ *Hey!* I think I finally understand physics!

A WORD OF CAUTION

Many words do double or triple duty; that is, they can be (for instance) a noun in one sentence and a verb in another sentence. The situation is much like a football player who lines up as a tight end on one play and a halfback on another. His or her function in each play is different; and so it is with words and parts of speech. A word like *light*, for example, can be used as a verb:

◆ We always *light* our Christmas tree after the children are asleep.

It can also be used as an adjective:

◆ Many beer drinkers spurn *light* beer.

Light can also be used as a noun:

◆ All colors depend on *light*.

What part of speech is *light*, then? It depends on the sentence; no word exists in a vacuum. To determine the part of speech of a particular word, you must determine its function or use in the sentence.

WRITING SENTENCES AND THE PARTS OF SPEECH

This review exercise gives you a chance to show that you can recognize the parts of speech. It also lets you show your originality by writing sentences of your own. When writing your sentences, do not hesitate to review the appropriate pages in this chapter as needed.

1.   Write two original sentences; in each sentence use a common noun and a proper noun. Circle the nouns.

© 2001 Addison-Wesley Educational Publishers Inc.

2. Write two original sentences; in each sentence use at least one pronoun from the list on page 9. Circle the pronouns.
3. Write a sentence containing an action verb. Circle the action verb.
4. Write a sentence containing a linking verb. Circle the linking verb.
5. Write a sentence containing a helping/auxiliary verb and a main verb. Circle the helping verb.
6. Write a sentence containing a predicate adjective. Circle the predicate adjective.
7. Write a sentence containing at least one adverb. Circle the adverb.
8. Write a sentence containing at least two prepositional phrases. Circle each prepositional phrase.

Editing Exercise

Identify the part of speech of each italicized word in the following paragraph.

A quinceañera is a *young* woman's fifteenth-birthday religious *celebration in* both Mexico and the United States, and *it* symbolizes her transition *from* childhood to adulthood. In the small villages of Mexico the emphasis *is* on the *religious* nature of the ceremony. In Chicano communities in the United States, it is *often* followed *by* a dinner and dance in the gym *of* the local church *or* community center. Not *all* 15-year-olds *have* quinceañeras. Many *families* cannot afford *them*. Food for several hundred guests, *printed* invitations, flowers, paying *for* a band for dancing, *rental* of a hall, *and* hiring a professional photographer are *among* the expenses that *the* parents of the *young* honoree must *necessarily* assume for this occasion.

© 2001 Addison-Wesley Educational Publishers Inc.

►Review Test 2-A

Parts of Speech

A. *Identify the parts of speech of the italicized words by using the appropriate letter in the space provided.*

a. noun   b. pronoun   c. adjective   d. adverb

_____ 1. Nintendo continues to reign as the decade's *top-selling* maker of computer games.

_____ 2. Actress Cameron Diaz is a *native* of San Diego.

_____ 3. Women own about one-third of all *companies* in the United States.

_____ 4. Rottweilers are *increasingly* popular among dog owners.

_____ 5. *We* will hold an auction to benefit the home for battered women.

_____ 6. Diana's husband Mark can narrate the career of any *present* or past member of the Los Angeles Dodgers.

_____ 7. The Big Dipper is *actually* part of a larger constellation, Ursa Major.

_____ 8. In Antarctica, *there* is a huge peak named for President Andrew Jackson.

_____ 9. We agreed to meet at the Main Street *drawbridge* in Jacksonville, Florida.

_____ 10. Jupiter is the *largest* planet in our solar system.

B. *Identify the parts of speech of the italicized words by using the appropriate letter in the space provided.*

a. preposition   b. conjunction   c. interjection

_____ 11. Tran and Keisha enjoyed golfing on Cape Cod *despite* the thick fog.

_____ 12. I wonder whether my '67 Beetle would survive a trek *across* Death Valley.

_____ 13. *Look!* Your dog is wearing your baseball cap!

_____ 14. Julie played point guard in high school *but* started as center at Princeton.

_____ 15. *Between* you and me, my secretary makes terrible coffee.

C. *Identify the italicized words by using the appropriate letter in the space provided.*

a. action verb   b. linking verb   c. helping/auxiliary verb

_____   16.   The report of the Surgeon General *listed* three main causes of lung cancer.
_____   17.   My conversations with Theresa *were* brief but amiable.
_____   18.   By arriving early I *was* able to find a convenient parking space.
_____   19.   She *regrets* her decision to resign, but has already been replaced.
_____   20.   By exercising regularly, you *can* reduce your risk of heart disease.
_____   21.   Kent and Jason *are* exhausted from their backpacking trip through Bali.
_____   22.   No one without tickets *will be* allowed into the laserium show.
_____   23.   As a child, I *slept* through even the loudest portions of *Mary Poppins*.
_____   24.   We *were* impressed by the new paint job on Miguel's '49 Mercury.
_____   25.   Rob *collects* posters of Toni Braxton.

© 2001 Addison-Wesley Educational Publishers Inc.

▶Review Test 2-B

Parts of Speech

A. *Identify the parts of speech of the italicized words by using the appropriate letter in the space provided.*

   a. noun   b. pronoun   c. adjective   d. adverb

_____   1.   I wonder how Bart Simpson would score on the *Scholastic Aptitude Test*.

_____   2.   The *meager* supply of food was soon consumed by the refugees.

_____   3.   Although I played soccer in high school, I *rarely* watch it on television.

_____   4.   Grace has wanted a horse ever since *she* first attended the races at Belmont Park.

_____   5.   The largemouth *bass* which Tyrell caught last week weighed almost twenty pounds.

_____   6.   Jeff Bagwell is *one* of baseball's most impressive players.

_____   7.   *Democracy* originated in Greece during the fifth century B.C.

_____   8.   Actor Alec Baldwin was born in the *small* town of Massapequa, New York.

_____   9.   Susan likes to have her blue jeans *professionally* dry-cleaned.

_____   10. Naomi's peach tree has shed its leaves and rotten *fruit* on her neighbor's roof.

B. *Identify the parts of speech of the italicized words by using the appropriate letter in the space provided.*

   a. preposition   b. conjunction   c. interjection

_____   11. The driver and four passengers were injured *in* the bus accident.

_____   12. *No*, thank you, I don't care for another serving of pasta.

_____   13. We found the cat hiding *under* Kurt's bed.

_____   14. He's not very good at chemistry, *but* in math he is superior.

_____   15. *Between* you and me, I thought that the Yankees were outplayed in the last Series.

C. *Identify the italicized words by using the appropriate letter in the space provided.*

a. action verb   b. linking verb   c. helping/auxiliary verb

_____ 16. My uncle *loves* to talk about having seen Ted Williams play at Fenway Park.

_____ 17. Proteins *are* crucial because they build, repair, and maintain the body.

_____ 18. Artifacts from Chile show that humans *lived* in the Americas as long as 12,500 years ago.

_____ 19. Mild burns *can be* treated by placing the area in ice water until the pain diminishes.

_____ 20. Marcus *will* eat catfish only if it is from the Mississippi River.

_____ 21. Buying and opening a fast-food franchise *can* cost almost four hundred thousand dollars.

_____ 22. Recovered from his fever, Pedro *slept* throughout the night.

_____ 23. A beam of the sun's light *reaches* Earth in about eight minutes.

_____ 24. Marco loves the Grateful Dead, and he *has* a collection of all of their CDs.

_____ 25. William Henry Harrison *was* President for only 31 days before dying of pneumonia.

© 2001 Addison-Wesley Educational Publishers Inc.

Writing Paragraphs

The Topic Sentence and Unity in the Paragraph

Every good paragraph deals with a single topic or an aspect of a topic. The sentence that states the paragraph's topic is the *topic sentence*. It is the sentence that alerts the reader to the central idea. It also reminds the writer of that central idea so that he or she does not include sentences that wander off the topic. For this reason, the topic sentence is frequently placed at the beginning of the paragraph, although it can appear in other parts of the paragraph. Regardless of its location, the topic sentence is usually the most general sentence in the paragraph, and it is developed and supported by the specifics in the sentences that follow or precede it.

In your reading you will occasionally notice paragraphs by experienced writers that do not include a topic sentence. In such instances the topic sentence is implicit—that is, the controlling or central idea is implied because the details in the paragraph are clear and well organized. But until you become an adept writer and are certain that your paragraphs stick to one idea, you should provide each paragraph with a topic sentence.

Topic Sentence First

The following paragraph was written by Frederick Douglass, a former slave who gained fame as a gifted speaker for voting rights for African Americans in the nineteenth century. The first sentence in the paragraph is the topic sentence, and it announces the main idea in a general way: "Everybody has asked the question, and they learned to ask it early of the abolitionists, 'What shall we do with the Negro?'" The sentences that follow give examples of possible actions which Douglass says should be avoided; they explore and answer the question posed in the topic sentence. Like most well-written paragraphs, this one begins with a general point and then supports it with specific details.

◆ Everybody has asked the question, and they learned to ask it early of the abolitionists, "What shall we do with the Negro?" I have had but one answer from the beginning. Do nothing with us! Your doing with us has already played the mischief with us. Do nothing with us! If the apples will not remain on the tree of their own strength, if they are wormeaten at the core, if they are early ripe and disposed to fall, let them fall! I am not for tying or fastening them on the tree in any way, except by nature's plan, and if they will not stay there, let them fall. And if the Negro cannot stand on his own legs, let him fall also. All I ask is, give him a chance to stand on his own legs! Let him alone! If you see him on his way to school, let him alone, don't disturb him! If you see him going to the dinner table at a hotel, let him go! If you see him going to the ballot-box, let him alone, don't disturb him! If you see him going into a work-shop, just let him alone,—your interference is doing him a positive injury. Let him fall if he cannot stand alone!

—Frederick Douglass, "What the Black Man Wants"

The topic sentence in the above paragraph is clear. It tells the reader what to expect in the sentences that follow, and it reminds the writer of the central idea of the paragraph so that he or she is unlikely to stray from the topic.

Topic Sentence in the Middle

Sometimes the topic sentence is placed in the middle of the paragraph. In such cases the sentences that precede the topic sentence lead up to the main idea, and the sentences that follow the main idea explain or describe it.

◆ There are 1,500 species of bacteria and approximately 8,500 species of birds. The carrot family alone has about 3,500 species, and there are 15,000 known species of wild orchids. *Clearly, the task of separating various living things into their proper groups is not an easy task.* Within the insect family, the problem becomes even more complex. For example, there are about 300,000 species of beetles. In fact, certain species are disappearing from the earth before we can even identify and classify them.

—Wallace, *Biology: The World of Life*, p. 283

Notice that the writer begins his paragraph with examples of living things with many species. Then he announces his main idea: separating living things into their proper species is not an easy task. The rest of the paragraph gives another example and additional information to support his topic sentence.

Topic Sentence Last

Many writers lead up to the main point of a paragraph and then conclude with it at the end.

◆ Is there a relationship between aspects of one's personality and that person's state of physical health? Can psychological evaluations of an individual be used to predict physical as well as psychological disorders? Is there such a thing as a disease-prone personality? *Our response is very tentative, and the data are not all supportive, but for the moment we can say yes, there does seem to be a positive correlation between some personality variables and physical health.*

—Gerow, *Psychology: An Introduction*, p. 700

© 2001 Addison-Wesley Educational Publishers Inc.

In this paragraph the writer poses a series of questions about the relationship between one's personality and physical health. Then he concludes at the end of the paragraph that they are related.

Exercise A   Locating Topic Sentences

Underline the topic sentence in each of the following paragraphs. Be ready to explain your choice.

a. The offices of most doctors today are overloaded with people who are convinced that something dreadful is about to happen to them. At the first sign of pain they run to a doctor, failing to realize that pain is rarely an indication of poor health. We are becoming a nation of pill-grabbers and hypochondriacs who regard the slightest ache as a searing ordeal. Instead of attacking the most common causes of pain such as tension, worry, boredom, frustration, overeating, poor diets, smoking, or excessive drinking, too many people   reach almost instinctively for the painkillers—aspirins, barbiturates, codeine, tranquilizers, sleeping pills, and dozens of other desensitizing drugs.

b. Reasons for the popularity of fast-food chains appear obvious enough. For one thing, the food is generally cheap as restaurant food goes. A hamburger, french fries, and a shake at McDonald's, for example, cost about one-half as much as a similar meal at a regular "sit-down" restaurant. Another advantage of the chains is their convenience. For busy working couples who don't want to spend the time or effort cooking, the fast-food restaurants offer an attractive alternative. And, judging by the fact that customers return in increasing numbers, many Americans like the taste of the food.

c. The dolphin's brain generally exceeds the human brain in weight and has a convoluted cortex that weights about 1,100 grams. Research indicates that, in humans, 600 to 700 grams of cortex is necessary for a vocabulary. Absolute weight of the cortex, rather than the ratio of brain weight to total body weight, is thought to be indicative of intelligence potential. The dolphin's forehead is oil-filled and contains complex sound-generating devices. Tests indicate that the dolphin is sensitive to sound at frequencies up to 120 kilocycles, whereas human vocal cords pulsate at 60 to 120 cycles per second with a choice of many more harmonics. These facts provide convincing argument for possible dolphin intelligence.

Focusing the Topic Sentence

Keep in mind that a topic sentence must be focused and limited enough to be discussed fully within a single paragraph. Notice the difference between the following pairs of topic sentences:

◆ **(Too broad)**   The United States has many museums with excellent collections of art.

◆ **(Focused)**   The St. Louis Art Museum has an outstanding collection of Expressionist paintings and prints.

◆ **(Too broad)**   Cultures vary throughout the world with respect to body language.

◆ **(Focused)**   Hand gestures that are seemingly innocent in the United States are frequently obscene or insulting in certain Latin countries.

◆ **(Too broad)**   Shakespeare's plays indicate that he was familiar with many areas of knowledge.

◆ **(Focused)**   Shakespeare's *Merchant of Venice* suggests that he was familiar with the law.

Another requirement of the topic sentence is that it must be capable of being developed. If the main idea is merely factual, it does not permit development. Notice the differences between the following sentences:

◆ **(Factual)**   St. Petersburg is a major city in Russia.

◆ **(Revised)**   St. Petersburg reminds its visitors of the Italian city of Venice.

◆ **(Factual)**   California has more than one hundred community colleges.

◆ **(Revised)**   Many California college freshmen prefer the community college for its many unique features.

◆ **(Factual)**   Some school systems in our country do not have music appreciation courses in their grade schools.

◆ **(Revised)**   Students should be introduced to the pleasures of music while still in the lower grades.

Exercise B   Revising Topic Sentences

The topic sentences below are either too broad or too factual. Revise each so that it will make an effective topic sentence.

1. The All-Star baseball game is held every July.
2. The Great Depression of the 1930s had a series of traumatic consequences for our nation.
3. The debate over the Vietnam War has raged for many years.
4. High blood pressure increases the risk of serious illness.
5. John Lennon was born in 1940.
6. The annual Cotton Bowl is held in Dallas.
7. Many reforms have been proposed for America's public schools.
8. The real name of "Dr. Seuss," the writer, is Theodore Geisel.
9. Admission of women to the service academies began in the fall of 1976.
10. Astronomy is a fascinating subject.

© 2001 Addison-Wesley Educational Publishers Inc.

The best way to be certain that your paragraphs have unity is to construct a specific, focused topic sentence and then develop it through the entire paragraph. If the paragraph sticks to what is promised in the topic sentence, it has unity. Any sentence that does not develop the topic violates the unity of the paragraph and should be omitted.

In the following paragraph, notice how the sentence in bold type introduces another idea and violates the unity of the paragraph:

◆ It is within the power of the citizens of this country to make their schools once more a place to develop their children's intellectual and physical talents rather than a stage for the performance of athletic heroes. First, they can compare the amount of money spent on teams, bands, uniforms, transportation, and maintenance of facilities with the amount of money spent on books and laboratory equipment. Second, they should compare the amount of time spent practicing during the week for a forthcoming athletic spectacle with the amount of time spent on homework and time in class. **Many high school athletes win scholarships that enable them to attend college.** Third, they should ease the pressure on the coaches for winning. Finally, they should demand to know what the schools' athletic departments are doing for those students who are not athletically inclined, and they should insist that all boys and girls are included.

The topic sentence in the preceding paragraph announced the main idea: the citizens of this country can make their schools a place to develop their children's intellectual and physical talents rather than a stage for the performance of athletic heroes. The fact that some high school athletes win scholarships to college is irrelevant and does not support the topic sentence. Therefore the bold type sentence should be deleted from the paragraph.

Writing Tips

First impressions . . .

Make sure the appearance of your assignments matches the quality of their content. Most instructors expect papers which employ the following:

- a standard typeface if prepared on a computer;
- use of one side of the paper only;
- 1-inch margins at the top, bottom, and both sides;
- black or dark blue ink if handwritten;
- indentation of the first word of each paragraph (one-half inch, or five spaces if typed);
- double-spacing of the text when typing or word-processing.

Exercise C   Focusing Topics

The topics below are too general to be the subjects of single paragraphs. Select five from the list and, for each, write a tightly focused topic sentence that could be adequately developed in one paragraph.

- heavy metal music
- the Olympics
- teenage marriages
- the Internet
- daily exercise

- the warming of the planet
- Social Security
- Wal-Mart stores
- late-night television
- being an only child

Writing Paragraphs

Read each of the following professionally written paragraphs carefully. Then follow the directions for each paragraph.

a. Although each tribe or peoples has its own unique system of spiritual beliefs and practices, there are some commonly held philosophical ideas that are generally shared by Native American people throughout the hemisphere. The natural world is the focal point of American Indian spirituality. From this foundation springs a number of understandings regarding the nature of the world and the cosmos generally, as well as the appropriate role of human beings in it. Humans are viewed as intimately linked, and morally bound, to the natural world in such a way that one's individual, family and community past are intertwined with the Old Stories that teach how things came to be as they are today, as well as right behavior for ensuring that future generations will continue to rely on a balanced relationship with the natural world. All creatures—the two-legged (humans), the four-legged, the winged ones, the green things, creatures that swim in the rivers and seas, even rocks and things that from a non-Indian philosophical perspective are considered inanimate—are part of this spirituality or sacred life force. For many Indians living today, this circle of the sacred to which we human beings are connected, ideally in balance and harmony with nature, also includes the life-giving sun, the many stars of the night sky, and Mother Earth herself. Because this perspective encompasses all time, all places, and all beings, Native Americans generally prefer the word *spirituality* of the *sacred* rather than religion.

—Lobo and Talbot, eds., *Native American Voices*, pp. 266–67

Notice that this paragraph begins with a topic sentence that signals to the reader what he or she can expect to find in the sentences that follow: "there are some com-

© 2001 Addison-Wesley Educational Publishers Inc.

monly held philosophical ideas that are generally shared by Native American people throughout the hemisphere." The rest of the paragraph gives examples of those "commonly held philosophical ideas." Develop one of the following subjects into a topic sentence that can be adequately developed in at least six supporting sentences. Remember that a good topic sentence is narrow enough to be developed in one paragraph.

- ocean pollution
- honesty
- careers
- credit cards

- shopping malls
- women's sports
- censorship
- teenage parents

b. Oprah Winfrey—actress, talk-show host, and businesswoman—epitomizes the opportunities for America's entrepreneurs. From welfare child to multimillionaire, Ms. Winfrey—resourceful, assertive, always self-assured, and yet unpretentious—has climbed the socioeconomic ladder by turning apparent failure into opportunities and then capitalizing on them.

With no playmates, Oprah entertained herself by "playacting" with objects such as corncob dolls, chickens, and cows. Her grandmother, a harsh disciplinarian, taught Oprah to read by age 2½, and as a result of speaking at a rural church, her oratory talents began to emerge.

At age 6, Winfrey was sent to live with her mother and two half-brothers in a Milwaukee ghetto. While in Milwaukee, Winfrey, known as "the Little Speaker," was often invited to recite poetry at social gatherings, and her speaking skills continued to develop. At age 12, during a visit to her father in Nashville, she was paid $500 for a speech she gave to a church. It was then that she prophetically announced what she wanted to do for a living: "get paid to talk."

Her mother, working as a maid and drawing available welfare to make ends meet, left Oprah with little or no parental supervision and eventually sent her to live with her father in Nashville. There Oprah found the stability and discipline she so desperately needed. "My father saved my life," Winfrey reminisces. Her father—like her grandmother—a strict disciplinarian, obsessed with properly educating his daughter, forced her to memorize 20 new vocabulary words a week and turn in a weekly book report. His guidance and her hard work soon paid off, as she began to excel in school and other areas.

—Mosely, Pietri, and Megginson, *Management: Leadership in Action*, p. 555

Select one of the following topics and write a paragraph of at least six sentences. Underline your topic sentence and be certain that your paragraph does not contain any sentences that do not support or develop the topic sentence.

1. What is Oprah Winfrey's success based on? How did she turn disadvantages into opportunities and then capitalize on them?

2. Do you know of someone else—perhaps a person not as famous as Oprah Winfrey and known to only a small group—who has overcome similar handicaps and has also climbed the socioeconomic ladder? You might consider a person in your community, or a relative.

Writing Tips

Topic sentences . . .

Be sure that your paragraph contains a topic sentence that tells the reader what he or she can expect to find in the paragraph.

- Is your topic sentence too broad and general to be covered in just one paragraph? If so, narrow your topic.

- Do all of the facts and details in your paragraph follow logically to the end?

- Does any sentence wander off the topic? If so, get rid of it!

Computer Activity

Choose one of the topics from the list in Exercise 2-9 on page 34 and narrow its focus so that you can write about it in one paragraph. When finished with your paragraph, SAVE your document.

Exchange your electronic document with a classmate. Read your classmate's paragraph and italicize its topic sentence by using the ITALICIZE command.

If your classmate did not recognize your topic sentence, discuss the reason. You may need to rewrite your topic sentence.

© 2001 Addison-Wesley Educational Publishers Inc.

3

Finding the Subject and the Verb in the Sentence

Sentences are the building blocks of writing. To improve your writing you should master the sentence and its two main parts, the *subject* and the *verb*.

THE SUBJECT AND THE VERB

The **subject** of a sentence names a person, place, thing, or idea; it tells us *who* or *what* the sentence is about. The **verb** describes the action or state of mind of the subject; it tells us what the subject *does*, what the subject *is*, or what the subject *receives*.

      (subject)   (verb)
◆ *Francis Scott Key wrote* the words to our national anthem.

      (subject) (verb)
◆ *Baton Rouge is* the capital of Louisiana.

      (subject)   (verb)
◆ *Gertrude Ederle was* the first woman to swim the English channel.

      (subject)   (verb)
◆ *Martin Luther King, Jr. received* the Nobel Prize for Peace in 1964.

   (subject) (verb)
◆ *I rarely eat* this much licorice.

Each of the above sentences contains a subject and a verb, and each makes a complete statement. In other words, they convey a sense of completeness. In conversations, sentences often lack stated subjects and verbs, but their contexts—the words and sentences that surround them—make clear the missing subject or verb. For example:

◆ "Studying your sociology?"

◆ "Yes. Big test tomorrow."

◆ "Ready for it?"

◆ "Hope so. Flunked the last one."

If this conversation were written in formal sentences, the missing subjects and verbs would be supplied, and the exchange might look something like this:

◆ "Are you studying your sociology?"

◆ "Yes. I have a big test tomorrow."

◆ "Are you ready for it?"

◆ "I hope so. I flunked the last one."

All sentences, then, have subjects, either stated or implied. Before proceeding further, therefore, it is important that you be able to locate the subject and the verb in a sentence. Because it is usually the easiest to locate, the verb is the best place to begin.

FINDING THE VERB

You will remember from Chapter 2 that the verb may be a single word (He *sleeps*) or a verb phrase of two, three, or even four words (He *had slept*, He *had been sleeping*, He *must have been sleeping*). Remember, too, that parts of the verb can be separated by adverbs (He *must* not *have been sleeping*).

Action Verbs

As you saw in Chapter 2, **action verbs** tell what the subject does:

◆ Carbohydrates provide energy for body function and activity by supplying immediate calories. (What action takes place in this sentence? What do carbohydrates do? They *provide*. Therefore, the verb in this sentence is *provide*.)

◆ Taiwan holds the record for most Little League World Series titles. (What does Taiwan do? It *holds*. The verb in this sentence is *holds*.)

◆ The students boarded the plane for San Juan. (What did the students do? They *boarded*. The verb in this sentence is *boarded*.)

© 2001 Addison-Wesley Educational Publishers Inc.

◆ Oceans cover three-quarters of the earth's surface. (What action takes place in this sentence? What do the oceans do? They *cover*. Therefore, the verb in this sentence is *cover*.)

◆ Blood returning from the body tissues enters the right atrium. (What does the blood do? It *enters*. The verb in this sentence is *enters*.)

◆ Visitors to Disneyland buy souvenirs for their friends at home. (What do visitors do? They *buy* souvenirs. The verb is *buy*.)

Exercise 3-1

Each of the following sentences contains one or more action verbs. Circle them.

1. When the siren of an ambulance wails, sound waves vibrate in all directions.
2. Scientists describe the effect as an acoustical sphere.
3. If the ambulance moves forward, the sound waves in front of it compress as new waves pile up behind older waves.
4. Behind the ambulance, the opposite happens, as individual waves expand.
5. The frequency of these sound waves changes their pitch.
6. As the ambulance comes toward you, the frequency of the waves increases.
7. This creates a higher pitch.
8. It reaches its pinnacle as the ambulance passes close to you.
9. After that, the pitch declines as the sound waves stretch out until they no longer reach your ear.
10. Scientists call this phenomenon the Doppler effect.

Linking Verbs

Some verbs do not show action. Instead, they express a condition or state of being. They are called **linking verbs,** and they link the subject to another word that renames or describes the subject. You will recall from Chapter 2 that most linking verbs are formed from the verb "to be" and include *am, are, is, was,* and *were.* Several other verbs often used as linking verbs are *appear, become, feel, grow, look, remain, seem, smell, sound,* and *taste.*

The verbs in the following sentences are linking verbs. They link their subjects to words that rename or describe them.

◆ My parents *seem* happy in their new apartment. (The linking verb *seem* connects the subject *parents* with the word that describes them: *happy.*)

◆ French *is* the language of the province of Quebec in Canada. (The linking verb *is* connects the subject *French* with the word that renames it: *language.*)

◆ The first-graders *remained* calm during the earthquake. (The verb *remained* connects the subject *first-graders* with the word that describes them: *calm.*)

◆ Chris Rock *has become* an actor as well as comedian. (The linking verb *has become* connects the subject *Chris Rock* with the word that renames it: *actor*.)

◆ Lord Kelvin *was* a founder of the science of thermodynamics. (The linking verb *was* connects the subject *Lord Kelvin* with the word that renames it: *founder*.)

Exercise 3-2

Each of the following sentences contains a linking verb; circle it.

1. Few people realize how bad conditions were for the Pilgrims who came to Massachusetts on the *Mayflower* in 1620.
2. The *Mayflower* was a cargo ship, not designed to carry people.
3. There was not enough sleeping space for everyone, so 80 passengers slept on the deck, and others slept inside a rowboat stored below deck.
4. The passengers could not bathe during the 66-day voyage because there were no bathrooms on the boat.
5. Bugs and mold were often in their food.
6. After standing in oak barrels for several weeks, the drinking water tasted bitter, so both adults and children began to drink beer.
7. Despite games and the presence of a cat and two dogs aboard the ship, the journey probably seemed boring for the children.
8. One of the women passengers became a mother during the voyage and named her son Oceanus.
9. Upon seeing land at last, the Pilgrims grew joyful at the lonely and wild look of the thickly forested shore.
10. While the men explored the countryside, the women were on the beach.

When looking for the verb in a sentence, you should remember that it sometimes consists of more than one word. In such cases, they are called **verb phrases,** and they consist of a main verb and a helping verb, sometimes called a **helping/auxiliary verb** (see Chapter 2). Any helping/auxiliary verbs in front of the main verb are part of the verb, as in the following examples:

◆ *may have* disappeared
◆ *should be* avoided
◆ *might* stay
◆ *did* guarantee
◆ *is* speaking
◆ *could have* objected

For a complete list of the words that serve as helping/auxiliary verbs, see page 11 in Chapter 2.

© 2001 Addison-Wesley Educational Publishers Inc.

Exercise 3-3

Circle the verbs in the following sentences, including any helping/auxiliary verbs.

1. We have decided to return to our favorite city, Oaxaca, Mexico, for our summer vacation.
2. One of Mexico's oldest cities, Oaxaca has been inhabited by Zapotec and Mixtec Indians for nearly ten thousand years.
3. Able astronomers and mathematicians, they are reputed to have developed the oldest system of writing on the North American continent.
4. Descendants of the early Indians can be heard speaking their ancient dialects in villages which surround the city.
5. Many of Oaxaca's buildings are made of a green volcanic stone that can appear a glistening gold at sunset.
6. Other buildings are painted bright turquoise or pink.
7. I will abandon my diet when I see the tamales that are steamed in banana leaves and the spicy mole sauces.
8. My husband has been dreaming of the fried grasshoppers which are served with a dash of lime juice.
9. I could spend a month's salary on Oaxaca's colorful jewelry and hand-loomed clothing, but I have vowed to keep a strict budget.
10. Because Oaxaca has carefully preserved its spotless beaches, ancient architecture, and cultural celebrations, it is no surprise that the entire city has been named a National Historic Monument by the Mexican government.

Exercise 3-4

Circle the verbs in the following sentences; be sure to include any helping/auxiliary verbs. Some sentences have more than one verb.

1. Normal red blood cells look round and plump, something like jelly doughnuts.
2. In about eight percent of American blacks, however, some red blood cells are much smaller than normal and have a sickle, or crescent, shape.
3. Sickling of the red blood cells is an inherited trait that has been traced to a mutation in a single gene.
4. A person who has inherited two sickling genes has sickle-cell anemia.
5. Sickle cells carry much less oxygen than normal cells, and such a person frequently suffers from insufficient oxygen.
6. In addition, the cells often clog blood vessels, cause severe pain, damage tissue, and even cause death if vessels that supply the brain or lungs are blocked.
7. People with sickle-cell anemia frequently die at an early age.
8. Certain African populations contain a high incidence of the sickling gene.
9. These populations live in areas with a high incidence of malaria.

10. People with the sickle-cell trait (one sickling gene and one normal gene) have a substantially lower incidence of malaria than the rest of the population.
11. Scientists have concluded that having one sickle-cell gene improves a person's chances of surviving malaria.
12. Because having a single sickling gene is an advantage in areas with malaria, the gene remains in the population.
13. The sickling trait is destructive to blacks with two sickling genes, but it survives in many people with only one.
14. Malaria kills many individuals in Africa, but those with one sickle-cell gene are more likely to survive.
15. For American blacks, the sickling gene has no adaptive function because malaria is no longer a medical problem.

Words Mistaken for the Verb

You may sometimes be confused by two forms of the verb that may be mistaken for the main verb of the sentence. These forms are the *infinitive* and the *present participle*.

The **infinitive** is the "to" form of the verb: *to leave*, *to write*, *to start*, and so on. The infinitive is the base form of the verb—in other words, it merely names the verb. It does not give us any information about its person, its tense, or its number. The infinitive by itself is never the verb of the sentence. Note how the following word groups fail to make sense because they use only the infinitive form—the "to" form—of the verb:

◆ Homeowners *to install* new roofs because of the damage from hail.
◆ My reading comprehension *to improve* by 15 percent.
◆ Missionaries from Spain *to arrive* in California in the 1760s.
◆ Ornithologists *to study* the mating habits of condors.
◆ Contractors *to build* cheaper and smaller homes in the future.

These word groups are not sentences because they try to make an infinitive do the work of a main verb. They can be corrected by placing a verb before the infinitive:

◆ Homeowners *had* to install new roofs because of the damage from hail.
◆ I *wanted* to improve my reading comprehension by 15 percent.
◆ Missionaries from Spain *began* to arrive in California in the 1760s.
◆ Ornithologists *plan* to study the mating habits of condors.
◆ Contractors *vow* to build cheaper and smaller homes in the future.

Of course, these word groups could also have been converted to sentences merely by changing the infinitives to main verbs: *installed*, *improved*, *arrived*, *study*, and *will build*.

© 2001 Addison-Wesley Educational Publishers Inc.

The other form of the verb that sometimes looks as though it is the main verb is the **present participle,** the "-ing" form of the verb. It is the result of adding *-ing* to the verb, as in the following: *leaving, starting, writing,* and so on. Like the infinitive, the present participle can never stand by itself as the verb in a sentence. Notice how the following groups of words fail to make sense because they attempt to use the present participle—the "-ing" form—as their verb:

- Homeowners *installing* new roofs because of the damage from the hail.
- My reading comprehension *improving* by 15 percent.
- Missionaries from Spain *arriving* in California in the 1760s.
- Ornithologists *studying* the mating habits of condors.
- Contractors *building* cheaper and smaller homes in the future.

These word groups can be corrected by placing a form of the verb *to be* in front of the present participle:

- Homeowners *were* installing new roofs because of the damage from the hail.
- My reading comprehension *has been* improving by 15 percent.
- Missionaries from Spain *were* arriving in California in the 1760s.
- Ornithologists *have been* studying the mating habits of condors.
- Contractors *will be* building cheaper and smaller homes in the future.

A final warning: You will never find the verb of a sentence in a prepositional phrase. The reason for this rule is simple. Prepositional phrases are made of prepositions and their objects, which are either nouns or pronouns—never verbs. Therefore, a prepositional phrase will never contain the verb of a sentence.

TIPS FOR FINDING THE VERB

1. Find the verb by asking what action takes place.
2. Find the verb by asking what word links the subject with the rest of the sentence.
3. If a word fits in the following slot, it is a verb:
   "*I* (or *He* or *They*) _____."
   Examples: I *hunt* elk.
   He *swims* every morning.
   They *bring* us flowers each time they visit.
4. Remember that the verb in a sentence will never have "to" in front of it.
5. The *-ing* form (the present participle) can be a verb only if it has a helping verb in front of it.
6. The verb will never be in a prepositional phrase.

Exercise 3-5

Identify the italicized words by writing the appropriate letter in the space provided.

a. verb   b. present participle   c. infinitive

_____   1.   If you are a musician who dreams of fame and fortune, *making* an album is the first step.

_____   2.   Your own album *opens* avenues of publicity through radio airplay and record reviews.

_____   3.   It also offers a way *to make* money through off-stage sales, mail order, and retail outlets.

_____   4.   Most important, an album *is* more impressive than a demo tape when you are negotiating with clubs and getting good gigs.

_____   5.   *Producing* a marketable tape or CD is a multistep process.

_____   6.   First, you *must decide* what percentage of your new release is cassette or CD.

_____   7.   Most managers *recommend* a 50–50 mix, with an initial run of 1,000 units.

_____   8.   Regardless of the format, you *should plan* the order of the cuts on the album.

_____   9.   It is important to try out tracks in different orders and *to pay* attention to the pacing of the cuts.

_____   10.   *Noticing* how the musical keys of songs blend together when they are back-to-back is also important.

_____   11.   On a cassette tape release, you *should try* to make both sides approximately the same length.

_____   12.   On a CD release, you should try *to keep* the total running time under 70 minutes and the total number of tunes under 20.

_____   13.   Your next job *is* to locate a duplicator or replicator that suits your budget.

_____   14.   By *looking* in one of the many directories that list mastering, pressing, and duplication facilities that are available, you can find one that best suits your project.

_____   15.   After you receive the finished album, you are ready *to begin* the next stage of your journey to stardom: to make sure the right people hear your album.

FINDING THE SUBJECT

A sentence is written about something or someone—the **subject** of the sentence. The verb, as you have learned, tells what the subject *is* or *does*. Every grammatically complete sentence has a subject. Sometimes, as in the case of commands, the subject is not directly stated but implied:

© 2001 Addison-Wesley Educational Publishers Inc.

◆ Please return all overduc library books by next Friday. (Although the subject *you* is not stated, it is implied.)

The rule for finding the subject of a sentence is actually very clear. To find the subject of a sentence, first find the verb. Then ask, "Who?" or "What?" The answer will be the subject. Read the following sentences carefully to see how the rule works.

◆ The invoice was paid on February 10. (By asking "What was paid?" you can easily determine the subject of this sentence: *invoice*.)

◆ Lou follows a strict diet because of his high blood pressure. (As in the sentence above, you can find the subject in this sentence by locating the verb and asking "Who?" or "What?" *Lou* follows a strict diet, and therefore is the subject.)

◆ Several cracks in the kitchen ceiling appeared after the last earthquake. (What appeared? *Cracks*, the subject.)

Subjects and Other Words in the Sentence

Do not be confused if a sentence has several nouns or pronouns in it. Only the word that answers "Who?" or "What?" before the verb can be the subject. In the following sentence notice that only *mayor* answers the question, "*Who* blamed?"

   (*subject*)
◆ The *mayor* blamed himself, not the city manager, the council, or the voters, for the defeat of the bond issue.

Do not mistake phrases beginning with such words as *along with, in addition to, including, rather than, together with,* and similar terms for a part of the subject of the sentence. Note the following sentences:

◆ The summary, as well as the chapters, contains several important terms to memorize. (Although *chapters* might appear to be the subject because it is closer to the verb, the subject is *summary* because it answers the question "*What* contains?")

◆ The basketball players, together with their coach, are featured in this week's sports special. (The subject is *players* because it answers the question "*Who* are featured?")

Simple and Complete Subjects

The main noun or pronoun without any of its modifiers that answers the questions "Who?" or "What?" before the verb is the **simple subject.** The **complete subject** is composed of the simple subject and its modifiers—the words and phrases that describe it.

In the sentence below, "waiter" is the *simple subject;* "A tall, gracious, smiling waiter" is the *complete subject.*

◆ A tall, gracious, smiling waiter seated us at our table.

In the sentence below, what is the simple subject? What is the complete subject?

◆ The woman in the green dress and high heels is my sister.

When you are asked to identify the subject of a sentence, you normally name the simple subject.

Compound Subjects

A sentence can have more than one subject, just as it can have more than one verb. Two or more subjects are called **compound subjects.**

◆ *Athletes and celebrities* are frequently seen on television endorsing products.
◆ *Polluted water and smog* made the city unattractive to tourists.
◆ *Either hamburgers or hot dogs* will be served at the picnic.

Exercise 3-6

Underline the simple subject of each sentence. Some sentences have more than one simple subject.

1. The daring life and unexplained death of an American pilot, Amelia Earhart, have intrigued people for decades.
2. Her love affair with airplanes bloomed when Amelia attended an air show in California with her father.
3. Amelia received a parade and a medal from President Herbert Hoover in 1932 after she became the first woman to fly alone across the Atlantic Ocean.
4. Her most treasured goal, however, was to be the first pilot ever to circle the earth at the equator.
5. Amelia, along with her copilot, Fred Noon, took off from Miami in June, 1937.
6. Articles and photographs for American newspapers, together with letters to her husband, were sent by Amelia throughout her journey.
7. The public followed Amelia and Fred's progress eagerly.
8. Everyone was stunned when their airplane suddenly vanished one month after their quest began.
9. The two flyers had completed 22,000 miles of the mission.
10. A final message from Amelia to a Coast Guard ship indicated that her plane was near New Guinea, in the South Pacific.
11. Neither the plane nor its pilots were ever found, though squads of Army planes and Navy ships searched thoroughly.
12. Numerous adventurers, scholars, and Earhart fans have launched their own unsuccessful searches.
13. Rumors about the pilots' disappearance continue to circulate today.

© 2001 Addison-Wesley Educational Publishers Inc.

14. Some say that Earhart dove into the ocean deliberately, while others claim she was on a spy mission and was captured by the Japanese.
15. Nevertheless, many modern female pilots cite Earhart's courage and achievements among their reasons for learning to fly.

Subjects in Inverted Sentences

Most sentences follow the subject-verb pattern. In **inverted sentences,** however, the pattern is reversed: the subject generally comes *after* the verb. Read the following inverted sentences carefully:

♦ Across the street stood the abandoned schoolhouse. (The abandoned *schoolhouse* stood across the street; *schoolhouse* is the subject, although street is in the subject position before the verb.)
♦ On her desk is a new word processor. (What is the verb? What is the subject?)

Questions are usually inverted, with the subject coming after the verb:

♦ Was Charles Lindbergh the first man to fly across the Atlantic? (The verb *Was* precedes the subject *Charles Lindbergh.*)
♦ Where are the keys to the car? (The subject *keys* follows the verb *are.*)
♦ What is the best time to call you? (The subject *time* follows the verb *is.*)

In sentences that begin with *here is, here are, there is,* or *there are,* the real subject follows the verb. To find the subject in such sentences, use the method you learned earlier. Ask "Who?" or "What?" before the verb.

♦ Here is a map of the subway route to the Bronx. (What is here? The subject, *map,* is here.)
♦ There are several reasons to explain his refusal. (What are there? Several *reasons,* the subject.)

Subjects with Verbs in Active and Passive Voice

The sentences that we have examined so far have contained subjects that performed actions indicated by action verbs, or they contained subjects that were connected by linking verbs to words that described or renamed them. Occasionally, however, we may encounter or write sentences in which the subjects receive the action.

If the subject of the sentence performs the act, the verb is in the **active voice:**

♦ Dale repaired his tractor.
♦ Burl's poodle attacked Bob.

In the **passive voice** the subject is replaced by the object:

◆ The tractor was repaired by Dale.

◆ Bob was attacked by Burl's poodle.

As you can see, in the active voice the emphasis is on the *subject*, which performs the action of the verb. In the passive voice the emphasis is shifted to the *object* instead of the subject, which is "passive" or acted upon. The passive voice of a verb always consists of a form of the helping/auxiliary verb *be* (such as *is, was, has been*, and so on) plus the **past participle** of the main verb. (The past participle of a regular verb is the form that ends in *-ed*.)

To change a sentence from active to passive voice, we turn the sentence around and use a form of *be* as a helping/auxiliary verb:

◆ Active: The intruder *surprised* the hotel guests.

◆ Passive: The hotel guests *were surprised* by the intruder.

◆ Active: Chiang *threw* the winning touchdown.

◆ Passive: The winning touchdown *was thrown* by Chiang.

To change a sentence from passive to active voice, we substitute a new subject for the previous one:

◆ Passive: Tides *are caused* by the moon.

◆ Active: The moon *causes* tides.

◆ Passive: The soldiers *were wounded* by the snipers.

◆ Active: The snipers *wounded* the soldiers.

You will often be able to choose between active and passive voice when composing sentences. The active voice is usually more direct and forceful. For this reason you should use active verbs except in cases when you have good reason to use passive ones.

Exercise 3-7

Revise the following sentences by changing passive verbs to active voice when possible.

1. The law regarding term limits has been strongly supported by Senator Torres.
2. The winner of the marathon was surprised by the number of autograph-seekers.
3. My brother has been cursed with asthma since his childhood.
4. We are astounded by the news that Kareem will move to Alaska next month.
5. The silken fiber that is spun by spiders is twisted into an endless variety of patterns.
6. Helen's corneas were damaged by the sun.

© 2001 Addison-Wesley Educational Publishers Inc.

7. The effects of television violence on children's behavior have been studied by psychologists for generations.
8. If you visit Sea World, you will be splashed repeatedly by the whale Shamu.
9. We gasped when we were told by our son that his new role model is Bart Simpson.
10. Video cameras were installed by bank officials after a series of frightening robberies.
11. When summer arrives, I am always reminded of childhood memories of watching the Cardinals play baseball at Busch Stadium.
12. Neither earthquakes nor volcanic eruptions can be predicted accurately by scientists.
13. The "wind chill factor" and "comfort index" are often cited by television weathercasters.
14. Our dog had been abandoned by her previous owners after she was hit by a car and they could not afford veterinary treatment.
15. Your letter was postmarked last Thursday, and it was received yesterday, but it has been decided by the admissions committee that they are prohibited from making an exception.

Subjects and Prepositional Phrases

The subject of a sentence will never be in a prepositional phrase. The reason for this rule is simple. Any noun or pronoun in a prepositional phrase will be the object of the preposition, and the object of a preposition cannot also be the subject. Examine the following sentences, in which the subjects can be confused with objects of prepositions.

◆ Thousands of tourists from countries throughout the world visit Chesapeake Bay in Maryland. (*Tourists*, *countries*, and *world* are in the subject position before the verb *visit*, but they are all objects of prepositions, and therefore cannot be the subject. By asking "Who visits?" you can determine the subject: *Thousands* visit. *Thousands* is the subject.)

◆ The author of *Adam Bede* was better known as George Eliot, rather than by her real name, Mary Anne Evans. (Although *Adam Bede* is in the subject position, it is the object of a preposition and cannot therefore be the subject of this sentence. Who was virtually ignored? The *author* of Adam Bede. The subject is *author*.)

◆ One of the Beatles continues to produce records. (*Beatles* is the object of a preposition and therefore is not the subject. Who continues to produce records? The subject is *One*.)

By placing parentheses around the prepositional phrases in a sentence, you can more easily identify the subject and verb. Examine the sentence below:

◆ The warden (of a jail) (in the northern part) (of Minnesota) explained (in an interview) (on television) (during the past week) his position (on the death penalty.)

By discarding the prepositional phrases, we can easily see the subject ("The warden") and the verb ("explained").

TIPS   FOR FINDING THE SUBJECT IN A SENTENCE

1. The subject will answer the questions *Who?* or *What?* before the verb.
2. In questions or inverted sentences the subject will usually come after the verb.
3. The subject of a sentence will never be "here" or "there."
4. The subject of the sentence will never be in a prepositional phrase.

Exercise 3-8

Underline the simple subject and circle the verb in these sentences. Some sentences have more than one subject or verb.

1. Many animals are friendly, helpful, or amusing, but others possess venom that can cause their victims pain or even death.
2. Rattlesnake bites, for example, can cause severe pain, swelling, and temporary paralysis.
3. Several old horror movies feature Gila monsters, a type of venomous lizard that frequents the southwestern United States and Mexico.
4. Bites from Gila monsters can bring horrible pain and dangerously low blood pressure.
5. Many people are allergic to bites from bees, wasps, hornets, and even ants.
6. Allergic reactions can include swelling and rashes.
7. Some victims are so allergic that they may die of shock within minutes of being bitten.
8. Though most spiders' bites cause only itching and swelling, others are much more harmful.
9. Black widow spiders cause severe pain, weakness, and convulsions, though survival from their bites is likely.
10. The brown recluse spider is often called a "fiddleback" because of its oblong body.
11. Bites from brown recluse spiders produce flu-like symptoms of fever and nausea and can be fatal.
12. Several people in the Southwest have died from brown recluse spider bites because they did not seek medical treatment quickly enough.
13. The oceans, too, host creatures with dangerous bites.
14. Housed in beautiful cone shells, mollusks shoot barbs which can paralyze their victims.
15. A number of summer beach vacations have been ruined by stingray bites, which usually bring pain, nausea, and vomiting.

© 2001 Addison-Wesley Educational Publishers Inc.

SUBJECTS AND VERBS IN COMPOUND AND COMPLEX SENTENCES

You have seen that sentences may have more than one subject and more than one verb:

        (s)   (v)   (v)

a. Mark Twain piloted a riverboat and later wrote several novels.

        (s)   (s)   (v)

b. Cynthia Cooper and Lisa Leslie are two of the WNBA's best players.

        (s)   (s)   (v)   (v)

c. Nelson Mandela and Vaclav Havel were political prisoners and later became elected leaders of their countries.

Sentence "a" above has one subject and two verbs; sentence "b" has two subjects and one verb; sentence "c" has two subjects and two verbs. All three sentences are **simple sentences** because they each contain only one **independent clause.** An independent clause is a group of words with a subject and verb capable of standing alone. As we saw above, the subject and the verb may be compound.

We will now look briefly at two other kinds of sentences: the compound sentence and the **complex sentence.** Both kinds of sentences are discussed in detail in Chapter 8 ("Compound and Complex Sentences"). At this point we need to learn only enough to recognize their subjects and verbs.

A **compound sentence** consists of two or more independent clauses containing closely related ideas and is usually connected by a **coordinating conjunction.** In other words, it is two or more simple sentences connected by one of the following conjunctions:

◆ *and, but, for, nor, or, so, yet*

The following are simple sentences because each contains one independent clause:

◆ The violin has only four strings.

◆ It is difficult to play.

By combining these two simple sentences with the conjunction *but,* we can create a *compound sentence:*

◆ The violin has only four strings, *but* it is difficult to play.

Each of the independent clauses in the preceding sentence has its own subject (*violin* and *it*) and verb (*has* and *is*) and is capable of standing alone. A compound sentence, therefore, has at least two subjects and two verbs. Of course, a compound sentence can have more than two independent clauses. But regardless of the number of clauses, a compound sentence remains the same: two or more independent clauses usually connected by a coordinating conjunction. (In Chapter 8 you will see that semicolons may also connect independent clauses to form compound sentences.)

Notice that the conjunction *but*, which connected the two independent clauses in the compound sentence above, was preceded by a comma. In general, a coordinating conjunction linking two independent clauses in a compound sentence should be preceded by a comma. Chapter 8 will give you greater practice in the punctuation of compound sentences.

Exercise 3-9

In each of the following compound sentences, underline the simple subjects and circle the verbs in each independent clause.

1. Acupuncture is a method of inhibiting or reducing pain impulses, but it is also used to abandon habits like smoking and nail-biting.
2. The word comes from two Latin words meaning "needle" and "to sting," but most acupuncture treatments are virtually painless.
3. Needles are inserted through selected areas of the skin, and then they are twisted gently by the acupuncturist or by a battery-operated device.
4. The location of the needle insertion depends on the patient's ailment, and each part of the body corresponds to certain illnesses.
5. Acupuncture is routinely used in China as an anesthetic; in an operation for the removal of a lung, one needle is placed in the forearm, midway between the wrist and the elbow.
6. To pull a tooth, the acupuncturist inserts a needle in the web between the thumb and the index finger; for a tonsillectomy, one needle is inserted about two inches above the wrist.
7. There is no satisfactory explanation to account for the effects of acupuncture; according to one theory, however, the twisting of the acupuncture needle stimulates two sets of nerves.
8. One very narrow nerve is the nerve for pain, and the other, a much thicker nerve, is the nerve for touch.
9. The impulse passing along the touch nerve reaches the spinal cord first, and it "closes the gate" to the brain, blocking the pain impulse.
10. Acupuncture still encounters much skepticism in the United States; nevertheless, increasing numbers of Americans, including medical doctors, are investigating its claims.

A **complex sentence** is a sentence containing a **dependent clause.** A dependent clause is a group of words containing a subject and verb but is not capable of standing alone as a sentence. (An independent clause, you remember, has a subject and a verb and can stand alone to form a sentence.) A dependent clause always needs to be attached to an independent clause in order to complete its meaning. Examine carefully the following sentence:

◆ Because a cure for cancer does not exist, some patients resort to bizarre diets and remedies.

© 2001 Addison-Wesley Educational Publishers Inc.

This sentence is made up of two clauses, each containing a subject and a verb. The first clause ("Because a cure for cancer does not exist") will not stand alone to form a sentence, and therefore it is a *dependent clause*. The second clause ("some patients resort to bizarre diets and remedies") is capable of standing alone as a sentence, and therefore it is an *independent clause*. The entire sentence is a *complex sentence* because it contains a dependent clause.

You can recognize dependent clauses because they do not express complete thoughts. You can also spot them because they usually begin with **subordinating conjunctions.** Here are some of the most common subordinating conjunctions:

◆ after, although, as, because, if, since, though, unless, until, when, while, why

In Chapter 8 you will learn how to recognize and form compound and complex sentences so that your writing will have variety and will not consist only of simple sentences.

Exercise 3-10

Place parentheses around the dependent clause in each of the following complex sentences. Then underline all of the subjects in the sentences and circle the verbs.

1. Although autism is rare, the disorder has been the subject of much research.
2. Because it appears in early childhood, clinicians have used four major symptoms to identify autism.
3. Autistic infants do not seek social interaction, although they may respond to social situations.
4. The second symptom is prolonged, repetitive behavior when they are alone, such as rocking in their cribs or spinning the wheels of a toy car for hours at a time.
5. The third symptom is a terrible temper tantrum if there is even a slight change in their environment.
6. The fourth characteristic of autistic children is their inability to communicate when they want or need something.
7. Although some autistic children do eventually use language, many never do it normally.
8. Autism is caused by some biological factor, although no one has yet been able to identify it.
9. If an autistic child has a nonverbal I.Q. score below 50, his or her future is very gloomy.
10. Those with more normal intelligence have a fair chance of overcoming many of their childhood deficits if they are shown appropriate social and conversational behavior.

Editing Exercise

The following paragraph consists of a series of choppy simple sentences. By chang-ing the structure of the sentences, revise the paragraph in order to make it flow more smoothly. For example, you might combine two simple sentences into a com-pound sentence or into a simple sentence with a compound subject and compound verb. Other changes could include creating complex sentences by converting simple sentences into dependent clauses and attaching them to independent clauses, or changing passive verbs to active voice.

For nearly two centuries the Alamo has symbolized Texans' pride. It has also symbolized Texans' independent spirit. The Alamo was established as a Catholic mission in 1718. Mexican general Martin Perfecto de Cos converted it into a fort in 1835. He was attempting to squelch a revolt by white settlers. They had wanted to separate from Mexico. Cos's effort failed. Mexico's ruler, General Antonio Lopez de Santa Ana, sent 4,000 troops to attack the Alamo and subdue the settlers. Texas general Sam Houston ordered Colonel James Bowie to destroy the fort rather than let it suffer attack by Santa Ana's huge army. Determined to fight for Texas's independence, Bowie ignored Houston's orders. He had fewer than two hundred soldiers to help him. The famous fight for the Alamo started on February 23, 1836. It lasted 13 days. Meanwhile, Bowie died of pneumonia. On the morning of March 6, Santa Ana's troops stormed the Alamo's north wall. They killed all of the Texan soldiers, including famed adventurer Davy Crockett. Today, visitors can explore the Alamo, including its chapel, Long Barracks, and a research library. Displays of artifacts and slain soldiers' personal items can also be seen.

WRITING SENTENCES

Identifying Subjects and Verbs

This review exercise asks you to identify the subjects and verbs in sentences that you write. When writing your sentences, do not hesitate to review the appropriate pages in this chapter as needed.

© 2001 Addison-Wesley Educational Publishers Inc.

1. Write two original sentences; each sentence should contain a compound subject. Circle the subjects.
2. Write two inverted sentences. Circle the subject and verb in each sentence.
3. Write a sentence in which the verb is in the active voice. Circle the verb.
4. Using the same verb used in the preceding sentence, write a sentence with the verb in the passive voice. Circle the verb.
5. Write three compound sentences. Circle the subject and the verb in each independent clause.
6. Write three complex sentences. Circle the subject and the verb in each dependent (subordinate) and independent clause.

© 2001 Addison-Wesley Educational Publishers Inc.

▶Review Test 3-A

Finding the Subject and the Verb in the Sentence

A. *Identify the italicized word or words by writing the appropriate letter in the space before each sentence.*

   a. action verb   b. linking verb   c. helping/auxiliary verb   d. none of the above

_____   1.   Norman *felt* powerless to correct the situation.
_____   2.   Yo-Yo Ma *is* one of the world's greatest cellists.
_____   3.   Termites *have* destroyed the floor of the toolshed.
_____   4.   Soccer seems *to be* more popular today than a decade ago.
_____   5.   Cindy *runs* a mile after school every day.
_____   6.   Forrest *has* failed the driving test three times.
_____   7.   A couple of fish tacos *sound* delicious right now.
_____   8.   She *plays* practical jokes on her coworkers.
_____   9.   The survivors *were* reluctant to talk about their experiences.
_____   10. Tony Wood owns an exact replica of James Dean's Porsche convertible.

B. *In the space before each sentence, write the letter that corresponds to the simple subject of the sentence. Some sentences have more than one subject.*

_____   11.   Only a small percentage of the population is born with perfect pitch.
               a. Only   b. percentage   c. population   d. pitch

_____   12.   Members of the ethics committee will present their findings tomorrow.
               a. Members   b. ethics   c. committee   d. findings

_____   13.   Here are the books that I ordered.
               a. Here/I   b. books/I   c. I/ordered   d. Here/books

_____   14.   The painting, not the sculpture, is my best work.
               a. painting   b. sculpture   c. best   d. work

_____   15.   Complaining as we drove home, Raul regretted buying such expensive shoes.
               a. Complaining   b. we/Raul   c. Raul/shoes   d. Complaining/Raul

_____   16.   Spectators were warned by police of the dangerous condition of the road.
               a. Spectators   b. police   c. condition   d. road

_____   17.   According to medical authorities, the epidemic was caused by unsanitary conditions at the meat-packing plant.
               a. authorities   b. epidemic   c. conditions   d. plant

_____ 18. Admitting his guilt, the robber blamed his behavior on his childhood.
a. guilt   b. robber   c. behavior   d. childhood

_____ 19. After a day at the amusement park, we returned home penniless.
a. day   b. park   c. we   d. home

_____ 20. Having won the lottery, I gladly told my boss goodbye.
a. lottery   b. I   c. boss   d. goodbye

_____ 21. Last semester I stayed in a room at the dorm across from the library.
a. semester   b. I   c. room   d. dorm

_____ 22. Because of changes in the tax law, we will owe less money this year.
a. changes   b. law   c. we   d. money

_____ 23. Air pollens, as well as smog, can aggravate allergies.
a. pollens   b. smog   c. aggravate   d. allergies

_____ 24. Are you ready for more cake or pizza, Maria?
a. you   b. cake   c. pizza   d. Maria

_____ 25. At one time Los Angeles was under 100 feet of water, according to scientists.
a. time   b. Los Angeles   c. water   d. scientists

© 2001 Addison-Wesley Educational Publishers Inc.

▶Review Test 3-B

Finding the Subject and the Verb in the Sentence

A. *Identify the italicized word or words by writing the appropriate letter in the space before each sentence.*

> *a. action verb   b. linking verb   c. helping/auxiliary verb   d. none of the above*

_____ 1. Instead of *playing* jazz, the band decided to feature show tunes.
_____ 2. Many of the statements about him *were* false, claimed his attorney.
_____ 3. *Is* there anything to be gained by leaving now, rather than later?
_____ 4. The dark clouds *obscured* the sun, suggesting an approaching storm.
_____ 5. After Raymond *joined* the YMCA, he learned to swim.
_____ 6. Learning to play the piano *has* helped Clarence learn to type.
_____ 7. By *purchasing* a reliable car, you will avoid repair bills later.
_____ 8. The ringing of the doorbell *announced* Jo Ann's arrival.
_____ 9. What *is* the difference between longitude and latitude?
_____ 10. Many immigrants from Southeast Asia *have* become successful business people in this country.

B. *In the space before each sentence, write the letter that corresponds to the simple subject of the sentence. Some sentences have more than one subject.*

_____ 11. Declaring his love for Muriel, Don asked her to marry him and move to Iowa.
　　　　　a. Muriel   b. Don   c. him   d. Iowa
_____ 12. Doesn't your car have a CD player or radio?
　　　　　a. car   b. CD   c. player   d. radio
_____ 13. The walls of the cave are painted red, and the floor is made of clay.
　　　　　a. walls/cave   b. floor/clay   c. walls/floor   d. cave/clay
_____ 14. A pitcher of iced tea near his desk, Mitchell prepared the report for his supervisor.
　　　　　a. pitcher   b. tea   c. Mitchell   d. report
_____ 15. Among the five survivors of the massacre was a nun from Detroit.
　　　　　a. survivors   b. massacre   c. nun   d. Detroit
_____ 16. Despite his tendency to exaggerate, Roy's story about the fish was true.
　　　　　a. tendency   b. story   c. exaggerate   d. fish

_____ 17. Here are some of the reasons for my decision to leave.
           a. Here   b. some   c. reasons   d. decision

_____ 18. Many years ago there were flowers and trees on this land.
           a. years   b. there   c. flowers and trees   d. land

_____ 19. The convertible, not the van, was fully insured by its owner.
           a. convertible   b. van   c. insured   d. owner

_____ 20. Because of his high blood pressure, Dave no longer skis in Colorado.
           a. pressure   b. Dave   c. skis   d. Colorado

_____ 21. The insurance company, as well as the restaurant owner, was sued by the
           customer.
           a. company   b. restaurant   c. owner   d. customer

_____ 22. One of the most popular radio programs in our city is about car repair.
           a. One   b. programs   c. city   d. car

_____ 23. Beyond the bright facade of the building was concealed its decay.
           a. Beyond   b. facade   c. building   d. decay

_____ 24. For her birthday Maxine was given a subscription to _National Geographic_.
           a. birthday   b. Maxine   c. subscription   d. _National Geographic_

_____ 25. Neither of the twins could be identified by their teachers or friends.
           a. Neither   b. twins   c. teachers   d. friends

© 2001 Addison-Wesley Educational Publishers Inc.

WRITING PARAGRAPHS

COHERENCE IN THE PARAGRAPH

Coherence means "sticking together," and in a *coherent* paragraph, all the ideas stick together. You have seen that when a paragraph is unified, all the other sentences support or develop the topic sentence. By placing the sentences in the right order with the right connecting words so that the reader is never confused, the writer's thought is easy to follow from sentence to sentence and from paragraph to paragraph.

Good writers make their paragraphs coherent in two ways: they arrange their ideas in an *order* that best fits their subject, and they use *linking words or phrases* between their sentences to help the reader understand how the ideas are related.

Coherence Through Chronological Order

To tell a story, give directions, explain a process, summarize historical events, or report on the steps or actions taken by an individual, paragraphs are usually arranged in *chronological order*—they present their ideas in the order in which they happened.

In the following paragraph notice that all of the details are presented in the order in which they happened:

◆ After his arrival in Illinois at the age of 21, Abraham Lincoln tried his hand at a variety of occupations. In 1830 he worked as a flatboatman, making a voyage down the Mississippi River to New Orleans. On his return he worked as a storekeeper, postmaster, and surveyor. With the coming of the Black Hawk War in 1832, he enlisted as a volunteer. After a brief military career he was elected to the state assembly. In 1836, having passed the bar examination after private study, he began to practice law. The next year he moved to Springfield and began a successful career. By the time he started to become prominent in national politics in 1856, he had made himself one of the most distinguished lawyers in Illinois.

When you use chronological order to organize your paragraphs, it is important that you relate the events in the order in which they occurred. The paragraph above would have been confusing to readers if the writer had started with Lincoln's career in national politics, then detailed his early days as a storekeeper, then jumped ahead to his practice of law, and so on. You can avoid confusion by including all points or incidents as they happened.

Chronological order can also be used in personal narrative writing. A personal narrative is simply a story taken from your life. It is organized chronologically—that is, it moves along in time from one event to another as they happened. Whenever writers want to tell what happened they rely on narration, sometimes in combination with description and other kinds of writing.

A personal narrative is easy to write because it is about someone you are an authority on: yourself. A personal narrative has a beginning, a middle, and an end. If it is brief, it should be about one main point or incident. By arranging the details and incidents chronologically, you can help your reader see and feel the experience, as well as read about it.

Exercise A   ## Chronological Development

Select one of the topics from "a" or "b" below and develop it into a paragraph in which the ideas are arranged chronologically. Underline your topic sentence. Before writing your final copy, make certain that you have asked yourself the following questions:

1. Are all of my ideas and details in the right order or sequence?
2. Have I stayed with the main idea as stated in my topic sentence, or have I included sentences that wander off the topic?
3. Did I read my paragraph carefully, looking for any errors in spelling, punctuation, or usage?

a. • meeting my boyfriend's or girlfriend's parents
    • a childhood memory
    • getting lost in a strange city
    • how a friend took advantage of my trust
    • my first attempt to play a musical instrument

b. • changing the oil in an automobile
    • downloading a software program
    • selecting the right dress or suit for a formal affair
    • preparing a favorite dish
    • planning a hiking trip

Writing Tips

Timely Transitions . . .

Paragraphs arranged chronologically should have words that signal the order in which events happen in the paragraphs. Words like *first, second, next, then, before, after, during, finally,* and *while* help the reader follow the ideas in a paragraph. Be sure to include them in your chronologically arranged paragraphs.

© 2001 Addison-Wesley Educational Publishers Inc.

Exercise B   Chronological Development

The paragraphs below are developed in chronological order. Read both paragraphs carefully and then follow the directions in either "a" or "b."

Inman watched the woman cook. She was frying flatbread from cornmeal batter in a skillet over the one stove lid. She dipped out batter into sputtering lard and cooked piece after piece. When she had a tall stack in a plate, she folded a flap of the bread around a piece of roast goat and handed it to Inman. The bread was shiny with lard and the meat was deep reddish brown from the fire and the rub of spices.

—Charles Frazier, *Cold Mountain*, p. 213

a. Narrate in chronological order an event which occurred in a short time span—perhaps even a matter of seconds, as in the above excerpt from the novel *Cold Mountain*. Remember that brief narratives can be enriched with the use of descriptions based on the five senses (sight, sound, touch, taste, smell). Some possible topics:

- a practical joke
- receipt of good or bad news
- a family gathering
- an awards ceremony
- a frightening experience
- a memorable date

The collapse of the Berlin Wall virtually overnight was one of the most important and unanticipated events in recent memory. The fall of the wall that had long separated the German city, as well as a nation, really began with the advent of Mikhail Gorbachev's policies of *glasnost* and *perestroika*. Gorbachev visited East Germany, and eleven days later, Egon Krenz was named as party chief, ending decades of tyrannical rule by Erich Honecker, who was too ill to rule. Soon, East Germans began sneaking across the border to Hungary and Czechoslovakia, eventually making their way into West Germany. When it became clear that the Hungarians and Czechs felt no desire to stop the East Germans, what started as a stream threatened to turn into a flood. Krenz gambled that if the government opened the way directly to West Germany, the long suppressed East Germans would feel less compelled to leave East Germany permanently, would visit the West, and then willingly return. That opening was all the East Berliners needed. On November 9, 1989, Berliners from both sides met at the wall, and in a dramatic scene, they embraced each other, climbed on top of the wall, danced and celebrated, and even began tearing the wall down. This was a day to remember, a day many never expected to live to see.

—R. Yarber and A. Hoffman, *Writing for College*, p. 42

b. Presenting your ideas in chronological order, write a paragraph of at least 150 words on an event which unfolded over several days, months, or years. Use an event from world history, current news, or your own life. Some possible topics:

- the origins of a war
- a natural disaster
- an unforgettable vacation

Writing Tips

Better than an X File . . .

Keep a separate notebook or file to jot down assignments and record problems and questions that arise during the semester. Many students also keep a journal as a source for ideas that can be used later in essays and reports.

Journal writing is a superb way to improve the speed and ease with which ideas and images strike your mind. Try writing for ten minutes each day without proofreading your work or worrying about grammar and spelling. To get started, try writing about the day's events, a current quagmire, a new goal or dream, or a recent conversation. Write without letting your pen or typing fingers stop. You will soon be surprised at how many ideas you can develop.

Computer Activity

Using your word processor can make an easy task of correcting errors in paragraphs written in chronological order. Choose a topic from "a" or "b" on page 62 and write a paragraph in which the chronology or sequence is important.

Exchange your paragraph with a writing partner.

Use SAVE, COPY, and PASTE commands to move any sentences that are out of chronological order in your classmate's paragraph. Ask a classmate to do the same for your paragraph.

© 2001 Addison-Wesley Educational Publishers Inc.

CHAPTER 4

Making the Subject and Verb Agree

Mistakes in subject-verb agreement are among the most common writing and speaking errors, and they are particularly irritating to readers. The rule on subject-verb agreement is obvious:

◆ The subject and the verb must agree in number and in person.

Agreement in **number** means that a singular subject takes a singular verb and a plural subject takes a plural verb. The singular form of all verbs except *be* and *have* is formed by adding *-s* or *-es: goes, takes, writes, fishes, brings, drives*. The singular forms of *be* and *have* are *is* and *has*. The singular form of the verb is used when the subject is *he, she, it*, a singular indefinite pronoun (such as *anyone* or *somebody*), or a singular noun. Plural verbs do not have these endings, and they are used when the subject is *I, you, we, they*, or a plural noun.

A singular subject with a singular verb:

◆ Gricelda's *father makes* delicious empanadas.

A plural subject with a plural verb:

◆ Gricelda's *parents maintain* their Salvadoran customs.

Notice that adding an *-s* or *-es* to a noun makes the noun **plural,** but adding *-s* or *-es* to a verb in the present tense makes the verb *singular*.

Agreement in *person* means that a subject and its verb must both be in the same person (*first, second, third*). The following sentences illustrate this rule.

First person (*I, we*)

◆ I *work* (not *works*) during the summer to pay for the courses that I *take* (not *takes*) in the fall.

◆ We *stay* (not *stays*) with my brother-in-law in San Jose when we *take* (not *takes*) a trip to northern California.

Second person (*you*)

◆ You *are* (not *be* or *is*) required to pass a stringent physical examination when applying for a job with the fire department.

◆ You *receive* (not *receives*) one day of vacation for each month you *work* (not *works*).

Third person (*he, she, it, they*)

◆ The Colonial Parkway *connects* (not *connect*) the towns of Jamestown, Williamsburg, and Yorktown.

◆ Jazz and the blues *are* (not *is*) American contributions to music, and they *appeal* (not *appeals*) to listeners of all ages and races.

Exercise 4–1

Circle the verbs that can be used with the following subjects. There may be more than one verb.
Example: *She   bring, (walks,) study, (plays)*

1. She   knows, sing, skates, treat
2. The beaver   run, sit, bite, sleeps
3. They   join, tries, flee, travel
4. You   says, leap, count, watches
5. We   shudder, listens, laughs, sigh
6. He   go, say, takes, bows
7. My sons   ski, climbs, squint, tell
8. Madonna   dance, acts, ask, sing
9. It   remain, wants, proves, mean
10. The teachers   meets, explain, protest, shout
11. The rain   soak, streaks, chills, inconveniences
12. I   asks, say, remind, plants
13. You   hums, exercise, lifts, yawn
14. The reader   thinks, question, groans, respond
15. Movies   frighten, entertains, educate, record

© 2001 Addison-Wesley Educational Publishers Inc.

If the rule given above is so simple, why are there so many errors in subject-verb agreement? Probably because of the writer's or speaker's uncertainty about the identity of the real subject of the sentence and confusion about whether the subject and verb are singular or plural.

Here are three steps to ensure subject-verb agreement. *First,* find the subject of the sentence. (You may want to review Chapter 3.) *Second,* determine whether the subject is singular or plural. *Third,* select the appropriate singular or plural form of the verb to agree with the subject. The suggestions below will help you follow these steps.

1. Remember that a verb must agree with its subject, not with any words that follow the subject but are not part of it. These include terms such as *as well as, including, such as, along with, accompanied by,* and *rather than.* If the subject is singular, use a singular verb; if the subject is plural, use a plural verb.

    ◆ A tape-recorded confession by the suspects, as well as statements by eyewitnesses, *has* (not *have*) been read to the jury.
    ◆ Stuffed grape leaves, often accompanied by strong Turkish coffee, *are* (not *is*) featured in many Armenian restaurants.
    ◆ The ambassadors from the West African countries, accompanied by a translator, *intend* (not *intends*) to meet with the President this afternoon.
    ◆ The plan for the new convention center, together with proposals for raising tax revenues, *is* (not *are*) to be debated by the city council members today.

2. Do not confuse the subject with words that rename it in the sentence.

    ◆ The referee's only reward *was* (not *were*) taunts and threats.
    ◆ A transcript of the Senator's remarks *is* (not *are*) available on the Internet.
    ◆ Automobile accidents *are* (not *is*) the chief cause of death on New Year's Eve.

3. Do not be confused by sentences that are not in the usual subject-verb pattern.

    ◆ Where *is* (not *are*) the box of paper clips that was on my desk?
    ◆ *Are* (not *Is*) cumulus clouds a sign of rain?
    ◆ Under the sofa *were* (not *was*) found the missing cuff links.
        BUT: Under the sofa *was* (not *were*) the set of missing cuff links.
    ◆ There *are* (not *is*) many reasons for her success.
    ◆ There *is* (not *are*) one particular reason for her success.

Exercise 4–2

Draw a line under the simple or compound subject. Then choose the correct verb and write the appropriate letter in the space provided.

_____ 1. The subject of the lecture (a. was   b. were) Israel, as well as its neighbors.
_____ 2. Goalies, rather than defensive players, often (a. receive   b. receives) most of the publicity.
_____ 3. In the newspaper (a. was   b. were) several stories about the famine in Africa.
_____ 4. On the curb (a. was   b. were) sitting several young men.
_____ 5. (a. Has   b. Have) the results of the election been announced yet?
_____ 6. A problem facing the area (a. was   b. were) killer bees.
_____ 7. Car alarms (a. are   b. is) a source of irritation for many.
_____ 8. Around the bend (a. was   b. were) seen the outlaws on their horses.
_____ 9. The expectations of the people (a. has   b. have) caused disappointment.
_____ 10. There (a. are   b. is) a good reason for the many divorces that occur among young people today.

4. Subjects connected by "and" or by "both . . . and" usually require a plural verb.

◆ Following the proper diet *and* getting enough exercise *are* important for maintaining one's health.

◆ *Both* Al Unser *and* his son *have* raced in the Indianapolis 500.

   Exceptions: Use a singular verb when a compound subject refers to the same person or thing:

◆ Vinegar and oil *is* my favorite salad dressing.

◆ The best hunter and fisherman in town *is* Joe Patterson.

Use a singular verb when a compound subject is preceded by *each, every, many a,* or *many an:*

◆ *Each* owner and tenant *has* been given a copy of the new zoning regulations.

◆ *Every* cable and pulley *receives* a monthly inspection.

Use a plural verb when a compound subject is followed by *each:*

◆ The tenor and the soprano *each wear* different costumes in the final act.

5. If the subject consists of two or more words connected by *or, either . . . or, neither . . . nor,* or *not only . . . but also,* the verb agrees with the subject that is closer to it. This rule presents few problems when both subjects are plural or singular:

© 2001 Addison-Wesley Educational Publishers Inc.

◆ *Neither* the politicians *nor* the voters *show* much interest in this year's election. (Both subjects are plural, and therefore the verb is plural.)

◆ *Not only* the car *but also* the greenhouse *was* damaged by the tornado. (Both subjects are singular, and therefore the verb is singular.)

When one part of the subject is singular and the other is plural, the verb agrees with the part that is closer to it:

◆ *Either* the frost *or* the aphids *have* killed my roses. (The plural noun *aphids* is closer to the verb, and therefore the verb is plural.)

Sentences with singular and plural subjects usually sound better with plural verbs. Notice the difference between the following sentences:

◆ Neither the players nor the coach *doubts* they will win the Stanley Cup. (Although technically correct, this sentence would sound less awkward if the subjects were reversed and a plural verb used.)

◆ Neither the coach nor the players doubt they will win the Stanley Cup. (This version is less awkward and has not sacrificed the meaning of the sentence.)

REMEMBER . . .

1. Adding an *-s* or *-es* to a *noun* makes the noun *plural*.
    Adding an *-s* or *-es* to a *verb* makes the verb *singular*.
2. If the subject is singular, the verb must be singular; if the subject is plural, the verb must be plural.
3. The verb must agree with its *subject*, not with any other words in the sentence. Do not be confused by sentences not in the usual subject-verb pattern.

Exercise 4-3

Write the letter of the correct verb in the space before each sentence.

_____ 1. Mars (a. is   b. are) Earth's closest neighbor.
_____ 2. Mars (a. travel   b. travels) 15 miles per second, circling the sun every 687 days.
_____ 3. The thin atmosphere of Mars (a. have   b. has) been determined to contain mostly carbon dioxide.
_____ 4. Therefore, humans (a. is   b. are) unable to breathe on Mars unless specially equipped.

_____   5.   More than half of Mars' surface (a. is   b. are) desert.
_____   6.   No wonder, then, that Mars (a. appear   b. appears) red to observers on Earth.
_____   7.   Some green patches on Mars (a. have   b. has) been observed by astronomers.
_____   8.   Scientists used to think that these green areas (a. is   b. are) fields of vegetation.
_____   9.   Recent discoveries, however, have shown that neither oxygen nor water (a. exist   b. exists) on the planet, and therefore the green patches cannot be vegetation.
_____   10.   The patches of green (a. remain   b. remains) a mystery.

6. Indefinite pronouns that are singular take singular verbs, and indefinite pronouns that are plural take plural verbs. Some pronouns may be either singular or plural in meaning, depending on the noun or pronoun to which they refer. An indefinite pronoun is one that does not refer to a specific thing or person.

   When used as subjects or as adjectives modifying subjects, the following indefinite pronouns are always singular and take singular verbs:

another	each
anybody	each one
anyone	either
anything	every
everybody	no one
everyone	nothing
everything	one
much	somebody
neither	something
nobody	someone

   ◆ Everybody *is* eligible for the drawing tonight.
   ◆ Much of the work on the engine *has* been done.
   ◆ Something *tells* me that I am wrong.
   ◆ Each dismissed worker *receives* two weeks' pay.

   When used as subjects or as adjectives modifying subjects, the following indefinite pronouns are always plural and take plural verbs:

both
few

© 2001 Addison-Wesley Educational Publishers Inc.

many

others

several

- ◆ *Few* of the passengers on the tragic cruise of the Titanic *are* living today.
- ◆ *Many* of the parts in an American car *are* manufactured in other countries; *several come* from Japan.

When used as subjects or as adjectives modifying subjects, the following indefinite pronouns may be singular or plural, depending on the nouns or pronouns to which they refer:

all

any

more

most

some

- ◆ Unfortunately, *all* of the rumors *were* true.
- ◆ *All* of the snow *has* melted.
- ◆ *Most* of the food *tastes* too spicy for me.
- ◆ *Most* of my freckles *have* disappeared.

Note: *None* is considered a singular pronoun in formal usage. According to informal usage, however, it may be singular or plural, depending on the noun to which it refers. Note the difference in the following sentences:

- ◆ (formal usage)   None of the babies *has* learned to speak yet.
- ◆ (informal usage)   None of the babies *have* learned to speak yet.

Exercise 4-4

In the space before each sentence write the letter corresponding to the correct verb.

_____   1.   No motorcycle (a. has   b. have) enjoyed more fame or mystique than the Harley-Davidson.

_____   2.   The motorcycle company's history of innovations and achievements (a. span   b. spans) nearly a century.

_____   3.   The main goal of founders William Harley and Arthur Davidson (a. was   b. were) "to take the work out of bicycling."

_____   4.   A total of three motorcycles (a. was   b. were) produced in 1903, Harley-Davidson's first year of manufacturing.

_____   5.   One of the company's many unique features, the V-Twin engine, (a. was b. were) introduced in 1909.

_____   6.   Sixty miles per hour (a. was   b. were) the 1909 model's top speed, a pace considered amazing at the time.

_____   7.   More than a hundred thousand Harleys (a. has   b. have) been used in American military efforts, including World Wars One and Two.

_____   8.   Even border skirmishes with Pancho Villa, the Mexican revolutionary, (a. was   b. were) won on Harley-Davidson motorcycles.

_____   9.   One of Harley-Davidson's 1921 models (a. was   b. were) the first bike ever to win a race at speeds averaging one-hundred miles an hour.

_____   10. Over the next few years, a spate of innovations, including the Teardrop gas tank and front brake, (a. was   b. were) boosting Harley-Davidson's appeal even more.

_____   11. Harley-Davidson's 1980 Tour Glide, with its five-speed transmission, hidden rear chain, and vibration-isolated engine, (a. was   b. were) nicknamed "King of the Highway."

_____   12. Today's touring bikes (a. are   b. is) derived from the Tour Glide.

_____   13. The Harley Owners Group (a. has   b. have) organized local and even cross-country rides, often to raise money against diseases such as breast cancer and muscular dystrophy.

_____   14. Many unofficial riding clubs, consisting of friends or residents from a specific region, (a. has   b. have) blossomed throughout the country.

_____   15. Though some people think that the typical Harley-Davidson owner is an outlaw, the majority (a. are   b. is) quiet citizens who may wear business suits and drive family vans when they are not enjoying their motorcycles.

REMEMBER . . .

Some indefinite pronouns always take *singular* verbs; some always take *plural* verbs; still other indefinite pronouns may be singular or plural, depending on the nouns or pronouns to which they refer. Look over the lists on pages 70–71 if you are not sure.

7. If the subject is *who*, *which*, or *that*, be careful: all of these relative pronouns can be singular or plural, depending on their antecedents. When one of them is the subject, its verb must agree with its antecedent in number.

   ◆ Rick is one of those musicians *who are* able to play music at first sight. (*Who* refers to *musicians*; several musicians are able to play music at first sight, and Rick is one of them.)

© 2001 Addison-Wesley Educational Publishers Inc.

◆ Franz is the only one of the musicians *who has* forgotten his music. (*Who* refers to *one*. Among the musicians, only one, Franz, has forgotten his music.)

◆ I ordered one of the word processors *that were* on sale. (*That* refers to *word processors* and therefore takes a plural verb.)

◆ I also bought a desk *that was* reduced 40 percent. (*That* refers to *desk* and therefore takes a singular verb.)

Exercise 4-5

In the space before each sentence write the letter corresponding to the correct verb.

_____ 1. Josephine Baker (a. was   b. were) one of the hottest and most intriguing stars of the jazz world.

_____ 2. Baker's flamboyant life (a. has   b. have) been as widely discussed as her music.

_____ 3. Born in an East St. Louis ghetto, Baker as a child sometimes (a. live   b. lived) in cardboard boxes.

_____ 4. At the age of 13 she (a. work   b. worked) as a waitress.

_____ 5. The beginning of many daring adventures (a. was   b. were) her move to Paris in 1925.

_____ 6. Besides singing in a Paris revue, Baker (a. help   b. helped) the French army fight the German Nazis in World War Two.

_____ 7. The French people (a. has   b. have) considered her a national hero ever since.

_____ 8. Baker (a. was   b. were) appalled by the racism against blacks in the United States and lived most of her life outside her native country.

_____ 9. In 1963 Baker (a. returned   b. returns) to the United States to speak at Martin Luther King, Jr.'s March on Washington.

_____ 10. American blacks (a. looked   b. looks) to Baker for her willingness to go boldly against stereotypes and promote the beauty of black women.

_____ 11. Painter Pablo Picasso (a. speak   b. spoke) of her "coffee skin" and "ebony eyes."

_____ 12. Baker (a. was   b. were) an international symbol of glamour and daring.

_____ 13. Baker wore bright, glittery dresses and (a. was   b. were) often seen walking her pet leopard down Parisian avenues.

_____ 14. Upon her death in 1975, the nation of France (a. gave   b. give) Baker a lavish state funeral.

_____ 15. Baker (a. had   b. has) always claimed Paris her home city.

8. Collective nouns take singular verbs when the group is regarded as a unit, and plural verbs when the individuals of the group are regarded separately.

A **collective noun** is a word that is singular in form but refers to a group of people or things. Some common collective nouns are *army, assembly, committee, company, couple, crowd, faculty, family, flock, group, herd, jury, pair, squad,* and *team.*

When the group is thought of as acting as one unit, the verb should be singular:

- The faculty *is* happy that so many students are volunteering for community service.
- The committee *has* published the list of finalists.
- The couple *was* married last week.

If the members of the group are thought of as acting separately, the verb should be plural:

- The faculty *have* been assigned their offices and parking spaces.
- The committee *are* unable to agree on the finalists.
- The couple constantly *argue* over their jobs and their children.

9. Some nouns appear plural in form but are usually singular in meaning and therefore require singular verbs. The following nouns are used this way: *athletics, economics, electronics, measles, mathematics, mumps, news, physics, politics, statistics.*

- Mathematics *frightens* many students.
- The news from the doctor *is* encouraging.
- Politics *is* the art of the possible.
- Electronics *is* an intriguing field offering relative job security.

When the items they refer to are plural in meaning, these words are plural.

- The economics of the your plan *sound* reasonable.
- My measles *are* spreading.
- The statistics *indicate* that little progress has been made.

10. Subjects plural in form that indicate a quantity or number take a singular verb if the subject is considered a unit, but a plural verb if the individual parts of the subject are regarded separately. Such expressions include *one-half of* (and other fractions), *a part of, a majority of,* and *a percentage of.*

If a singular noun follows *of* or is implied, use a singular verb:
- Two-thirds of her fortune *consists* of stock in computer companies.
- Part of our intelligence, according to geneticists, *depends* on our genes.
- A majority of the herd of sick cattle *has* to be destroyed.

If a plural noun follows *of* or is implied, use a plural verb:

© 2001 Addison-Wesley Educational Publishers Inc.

- Three-fourths of the students in the third grade *speak* a foreign language.
- A large percentage of the film actors *live* in either Los Angeles or New York.
- A majority of the lawyers *want* to make the law exam more difficult.

11. Words that refer to distance, amounts, and measurements require singular verbs when they represent a total amount. When they refer to a number of individual items, they require plural verbs.

- More than six hundred dollars *was* spent on my dental work.
- Many thousands of dollars *were* collected for Thanksgiving meals for the poor.
- Two miles *is* the maximum range of his new rifle.
- The last two miles *were* paved last week.
- Six months *is* a long time to wait for an answer to my complaint.
- Six months *have* passed since we last heard from you.

12. When *the number* is used as the subject, it requires a singular verb. *A number* is always plural.

- The number of students who work part-time *is* increasing.
- A number of students *receive* financial support from government loans.

13. Some words taken from foreign languages, especially Greek and Latin, keep their foreign plural forms, but others have acquired English plural forms. As a result, it is not always obvious when to use the singular or the plural form of the verb. For example, "Data are available" is preferred to "Data is available." If you are not sure about their plural form, consult your dictionary. Here are some of the more common words from Greek and Latin and their plural forms.

singular	plural
alumnus	alumni
alumna	alumnae
criterion	criteria
crisis	crises
medium	media
memorandum	memoranda
parenthesis	parentheses
phenomenon	phenomena
stimulus	stimuli
thesis	theses

REMEMBER . . .

Collective nouns take singular verbs if you consider the group as a unit; they take plural verbs if you regard the individuals in the group separately.

A number are, but *the number* is.

Exercise 4-6

In the space before each sentence write the letter corresponding to the correct verb.

_____ 1. The couple (a. was   b. were) awarded prizes for their costumes.
_____ 2. Every year the board of education in most school districts (a. recognize   b. recognizes) the outstanding high school graduates.
_____ 3. Four miles (a. was   b. were) the distance that he ran every week last year.
_____ 4. Approximately $1,200 (a. remain   b. remains) in my bank account to pay my expenses next semester.
_____ 5. About half of the drivers on the road (a. has   b. have) no liability insurance.
_____ 6. The cab driver decided that 15 minutes (a. was   b. were) long enough to wait for his fare.
_____ 7. Statistics (a. are   b. is) a required course for psychology majors.
_____ 8. Approximately two-thirds of last semester's graduates (a. has   b. have) been unable to find jobs.
_____ 9. Statistics (a. reveal   b. reveals) that women are still paid less than men for doing the same work.
_____ 10. The last two miles of the marathon (a. was   b. were) the most difficult.
_____ 11. The faculty at our college (a. tend   b. tends) to be very helpful to students who seek advice outside the classroom.
_____ 12. A number of scholarships available last fall (a. are   b. is) still available to students.
_____ 13. The number of representatives that a state may send to Congress (a. depend   b. depends) upon its population.
_____ 14. One-half of the questions on the test (a. was   b. were) on the previous chapter.
_____ 15. The freshman class (a. take   b. takes) a sequence of courses in Western civilization.

WRITING SENTENCES

Subject and Verb Agreement

In this exercise you are asked to write original sentences in which the subject and verb agree in number and person. Refer to the appropriate section of the chapter as needed.

© 2001 Addison-Wesley Educational Publishers Inc.

1. Write an original sentence with two subjects connected by "both . . . and" and requiring a plural verb.
2. Write a sentence in which the subject consists of two or more words connected by "either . . . or," "neither . . . nor," or "not only . . . but also."
3. Write two sentences that use an indefinite pronoun as a singular subject in each sentence. Circle the pronoun and the verb.
4. Write two sentences that use an indefinite pronoun as a plural subject in each sentence. Circle the pronouns and the verbs.
5. Select two of the following pronouns and use them as subjects of two sentences: *all, any, more, most, none, some*
6. Write a sentence in which you use a collective noun as a singular subject. Circle the noun and its verb.
7. Write a sentence in which you use a collective noun as a plural subject. Circle the noun and its verb.

Editing Exercise

The paragraph below describes a famous tourist stop in Belfast, Northern Ireland. The paragraph contains a series of errors in subject-verb agreement. Improve the paragraph by correcting the errors. Revise the sentences when necessary.

There is many interesting shops and restaurants along the Golden Mile in Belfast, Northern Ireland. Among the most popular stops are a Victorian gin palace called the Crown Liquor Saloon. Deemed a National Trust property, it has an exterior consisting of amber, pink, green, blue, and smoke-gray tiles which glitters in the sun. Inside, none are able to resist the beauty of the scrolled ceilings and patterned floors. The seating is divided into snugs, which is a small enclosed booth. The door of each snug ensure privacy and makes visitors feel as though they're in a private railway compartment. Huge beasts, carved into each oaken doorway, guards each snug. Clients pining for a strong cup of coffee or a beverage pushes a button and soon one of the waiters, dressed in a crisp white shirt and black tie, appear. A little rest, conversation, and refreshment is all that is needed before strolling back out to the Golden Mile, where a wealth of bookstores, gift shops, and nightclubs await the visitor.

© 2001 Addison-Wesley Educational Publishers Inc.

▶Review Test 4-A

Making the Subject and Verb Agree

Identify the correct verb by using the appropriate letter.

_____ 1. Stephanie and Julie (a. make   b. makes) sure that every volunteer receives a Certificate of Appreciation.

_____ 2. Whether viewing violence on television (a. encourage   b. encourages) violence among children is a topic that is widely debated.

_____ 3. Sergio always (a. surf   b. surfs) when he visits Hawaii.

_____ 4. Most waiters (a. rely   b. relies) on tips, and therefore they often tolerate rude customers.

_____ 5. The faculty (a. are   b. is) arguing among themselves over the location of their parking spaces.

_____ 6. Fish (a. breathe   b. breathes) through gills, not nostrils.

_____ 7. New Orleans frequently (a. host   b. hosts) national conventions.

_____ 8. Laverne (a. unwind   b. unwinds) by jogging along the beach after work.

_____ 9. Sheila and Patrick (a. was   b. were) married on the campus of their alma mater.

_____ 10. Each of my favorite television shows (a. feature   b. features) doctors.

_____ 11. A sport such as polo or skiing (a. are   b. is) often expensive.

_____ 12. Coach Talsky and her team (a. plan   b. plans) to watch the Sparks game tomorrow night.

_____ 13. The gardener and his assistant (a. are   b. is) responsible for the lawn's beautiful appearance.

_____ 14. Rob is one of those lucky musicians who (a. has   b. have) perfect pitch.

_____ 15. Marty claims that a pair of his socks (a. has   b. have) been eaten by my chihuahua.

_____ 16. A number of the players (a. has   b. have) asked me to arrange our games for Saturday afternoons.

_____ 17. Anyone who avoids junk food and desserts (a. face   b. faces) constant temptation.

_____ 18. Two tracks of train rail (a. carries   b. carry) as many passengers in an hour as sixteen lanes of freeway can.

_____ 19. Although books can be read on the Internet, libraries (a. report   b. reports) that their circulation of books continues to rise.

_____   20.   Two rolls of film (a. are   b. is) adequate for our trip to the amusement park.

_____   21.   A cup of blueberries (a. do not   b. does not) seem to be enough for this pie recipe.

_____   22.   The pictures of Anne's wedding (a. was   b. were) taken by her brother-in-law.

_____   23.   My brother, not my sisters, (a. are   b. is) familiar with the art of macrame.

_____   24.   There (a. exist   b. exists) an endless stream of statistics for baseball fans to master.

_____   25.   Connecticut, along with Minnesota, (a. rank   b. ranks) high among states with good public-school systems.

© 2001 Addison-Wesley Educational Publishers Inc.

▶Review Test 4-B

Making the Subject and Verb Agree

Identify the correct verb by using the appropriate letter.

_____ 1. A number of bomb threats (a. has   b. have) caused panic and fear among the populace.

_____ 2. The frequency of his absences from meetings of the city council (a. has   b. have) triggered rumors that he will resign.

_____ 3. Members of the band (a. travel   b. travels) together in a large bus.

_____ 4. Politics often (a. attract   b. attracts) those who merely seek fame.

_____ 5. Rita is one of those drivers who (a. take   b. takes) unnecessary chances.

_____ 6. Across the river (a. was   b. were) three hunting dogs that were stranded.

_____ 7. Soccer, rather than football and other sports, (a. appeal   b. appeals) to many European athletes.

_____ 8. Every tile and shingle (a. was   b. were) blown loose by the storm.

_____ 9. On the last page of the manuscript (a. was   b. were) the signature of the author.

_____ 10. Everyone who volunteered (a. has   b. have) experience at the job.

_____ 11. Mrs. Saunders is one of those instructors who (a. are   b. is) easy to speak to outside of the classroom.

_____ 12. One of the ladders (a. has   b. have) a broken rung.

_____ 13. Mel is the only one of the players who consistently (a. practice   b. practices) every day.

_____ 14. The chief disadvantage of her new job (a. are   b. is) the long hours.

_____ 15. The President, not the cabinet officers, (a. believe   b. believes) that the treaty should be signed.

_____ 16. Emil insisted that it was Barbara's personality, not her riches, that (a. fascinate   b. fascinates) him.

_____ 17. Michael Jackson, along with his brothers and sisters, (a. has   b. have) become wealthy as a result of musical fame.

_____ 18. There (a. remain   b. remains) two additional problems to solve.

_____ 19. Here (a. was   b. were) the site of the first home built in this area.

_____ 20. When practicing golf, there (a. are   b. is) several things that you must consider besides merely hitting the ball.

_____ 21. A hobby such as chess or checkers (a. require   b. requires) hours of one's time.

_____ 22. Dr. McCormick is one of those people who (a. possess   b. possesses) a photographic memory.

_____ 23. One of the benefits of the new computers (a. are   b. is) their reduced price.

_____ 24. Here is a photograph of the only survivor of the tragedy who (a. reside   b. resides) in Chicago.

_____ 25. Anyone who studies bees and wasps soon (a. learn   b. learns) how to handle them without fear.

© 2001 Addison-Wesley Educational Publishers Inc.

Writing Paragraphs

Coherence Through Spatial Order

If the purpose of your paragraph is to tell how something looks, the most effective organization pattern is usually *spatial*. Spatial order presents a visual effect: through your careful attention to detail, word choice, and organization, a paragraph organized in this way draws a mental picture for your readers. This means that in order for your reader to see your subject, you have to select details that make the subject clear, and you have to present those details in a pattern that your reader can follow. The arrangement often used in this kind of paragraph follows the sequence in which you would look at a scene or an object: from top to bottom, side to side, front to back, or near to far.

The following description, written by a student, describes a museum containing a replica of a street scene in the early 1930s. Notice that she begins her paragraph with a topic sentence that presents the main idea. Notice, too, that she supplies details in a spatial order to support that topic sentence.

◆ As you open the doors of the museum, you will think that you have stumbled onto the main street of a small Western town as it was in the early 1930s. Hitched to a wagon immediately in front of you are four huge black mules, standing fetlock-deep in gray mud. The wagon is piled high with suitcases, children's toys, and mattresses. Through the open doors of a drugstore on your left come the big-band sounds of a Nickelodeon and the chatter of young people clustered around the soda fountain. On the right a couple stands hand in hand gazing at a poster featuring a movie starring Myrna Loy and Gary Cooper. In the muddy street a Model A Ford clugs patiently, unable to move, its wheels stuck in the ooze. Suddenly the sky darkens, and lightning cracks the gathering clouds. Everyone stops and looks up, expecting another downpour that will turn the street into a river of mud.

Spatial order presents a *visual effect*. Notice how the use of specific details helps to make clear the image of the newborn baby.

◆ Babies right after birth are not beautiful. The trip through the birth canal compresses the unfused bones of the skull, and many babies' heads are temporarily cone-shaped. The pressure also pastes back their ears. Newborns are covered with vernix, a white protective skin coating that looks like cheese, and are splotched with their mothers' blood. Some have virtually no hair on their heads, and some are born with a coat of fine hair (lanugo) all over their bodies. Even after they're cleaned up, most have mottled red skin from their arduous passage to birth. The struggle to be born is so exhausting that most newborn babies fall asleep within a couple of hours and stay fast asleep for many hours afterward.

Exercise A   Spatial Order

Arranging your ideas in spatial order, write a paragraph of at least one hundred words on one of the following topics. Underline your topic sentence.

- my roommate's closet
- my grandparent
- the ugliest building in town
- my city from the air
- a favorite restaurant
- a favorite painting

After you write your first draft, answer the following questions:

1. Does my paragraph concentrate on describing one thing, scene, person, or object, or does it try to describe too much?
2. Have I given my reader specific details so that he or she can see what I am describing, or is my paragraph just a series of general and vague statements?
3. Does my paragraph have a plan, or does it jump around, confusing my reader?
4. Does my paragraph reflect the care I put into it, or is it filled with careless spelling mistakes or other errors?

Writing Tips

Tell Me the Truth!

After you've revised your paragraph the best you can, let a friend or classmate read it to make sure it conveys exactly the points you intend. Ask him or her to consider the following questions:

- What is the point of the paper?
- Do you accept the writer's argument or point of view? Why or why not?
- Could any ideas be expanded? Omitted?
- Are some sentences unclear?
- Are there any grammatical or spelling errors?
- What is the paragraph's strongest quality?
- Does the paragraph stick to its topic?
- Does the author avoid slang, vagueness, repetition, and careless word choice?

© 2001 Addison-Wesley Educational Publishers Inc.

WRITING PARAGRAPHS

These paragraphs, the first written by a well-known American writer of the nineteenth century, and the second written by a modern American novelist, are both based on spatial order. Read each paragraph carefully and then write a response to "a" or "b" in the exercises that follow.

a. The most foreign and picturesque structures on the Cape, to an inlander, not excepting the salt-works, are the wind-mills,—gray-looking octagonal towers, with long timbers slanting to the ground in the rear, and there resting on a cart-wheel, by which their fans are turned round to face the wind. These appeared also to serve in some measure for props against its force. A great circular rut was worn around the building by the wheel. The neighbors who assemble to turn the mill to the wind are likely to know which way it blows, without a weathercock. They looked loose and slightly locomotive, like huge wounded birds, trailing a wing or a leg, and reminded one of pictures of the Netherlands. Being on elevated ground, and high in themselves, they serve as landmarks,—for there are no tall trees, or other objects commonly, which can be seen at a distance in the horizon; though the outline of the land itself is so firm and distinct that an insignificant cone, or even precipice of sand, is visible at a great distance from over the sea. Sailors making the land commonly steer either by the wind-mills or the meeting-houses.

    —Henry David Thoreau, *Cape Cod*, p. 39

b. The county seat was not a town of great refinement. On one side there were four clapboard store buildings in a row, then a hog pen and a mud pit, then two more stores, a church, and a livery. On the other side, three stores, then the courthouse—a cupolaed white frame building set back from the road with a patchy lawn in front—then four more storefronts, two of them brick. After that, the town trailed off into a fenced field of dried cornstalks. The streets were cut deep by narrow wagon wheels. Light glinted off water pooled in the numberless basins made by horse tracks.

    —Charles Frazier, *Cold Mountain*, p. 139

Exercise B   ## Spatial Order

Presenting your ideas in spatial order, write a paragraph of at least 150 words on one of the following:

- a campus hangout
- your best friend's appearance
- a popular vacation spot

- your neighborhood
- your favorite room in your house
- a cherished possession
- a favorite article of clothing
- an "offbeat" place

Writing Tips

Now Hear This!

One of the best ways to revise your paper is to hear it. Seeing your writing is usually not enough. As you read it silently, you unconsciously fill in missing punctuation marks, letters, and even words. You might even miss rough sentences or clumsy expressions. When you read it aloud, however, you use different cognitive and critical skills that will expose the errors that might escape a silent reading.

Computer Activity

Follow the directions for writing a paragraph in Exercise A or B. Use SAVE, COPY, and PASTE commands to make a second copy.

Exchange your file with a classmate.

Italicize words or phrases that refer to spatial order such as to the left (or right), behind, in front of, to one side, under, beyond, or next to.

Ask your classmate to do the same for your paragraph.

© 2001 Addison-Wesley Educational Publishers Inc.

5

Using the Correct Form of the Pronoun

Most of us—unless we were just beginning to learn the English language or were babies—would not be likely to say or write sentences like "Me am tired" or "Her is my sister." We instinctively know that "I" is the subject for "am" and that "She" is used with "is." Unfortunately, the choices we face in our writing and speaking are not always so obvious. For example, do we say "between you and I" or "between you and me"? What about "he and myself"? Is there any way to keep "who" and "whom" separate? Pronouns can cause a great deal of uncertainty, even among the most educated writers and speakers.

One probable reason for confusion over pronouns is the existence of so many classes and forms to choose from. Unlike prepositions or conjunctions and most other parts of speech, pronouns have the distracting habit of changing their form or spelling depending on the way they are used in a particular sentence. To use them with confidence, therefore, it is important to recognize the various kinds of pronouns and to learn the specific way each kind is used in a sentence.

We will begin our study of this confusing part of speech with an overview of the most important classes of pronouns and then examine them more closely. The chart on page 89 gives a summary of the classes of pronouns.

THE CLASSES OF PRONOUNS

Pronouns can be classified according to their form (the way they are spelled) and their function (the way they are used in a sentence).

1. **Personal Pronouns**
   Personal pronouns refer to specific individuals, and they are the pronouns most frequently used in writing and speaking. Personal pronouns can be singular or plural, and

they can be classified by **gender** (*masculine*, *feminine*, or *neuter*) and by *function* or **case** (*subjective*, *possessive*, and *objective*).

2. **Indefinite Pronouns**
Although they function as nouns, **indefinite pronouns** do not refer to specific individuals. Because of their importance in pronouns agreement and reference, they are treated in detail in Chapter 6 ("Common Errors in Pronoun Agreement and Reference").

3. **Demonstrative Pronouns**
Demonstrative pronouns point out persons or things, as in the following:

   ◆ *This* is the house I was born in. *Those* are the trees my father planted.

4. **Relative Pronouns**
These pronouns connect or relate groups of words to nouns or other pronouns, as in the following sentences:

   ◆ A Vietnam veteran *who* is suffering from cancer testified *that* it was caused by chemicals *that* were used during the war.

Because **relative pronouns** are used to introduce dependent clauses in complex sentences, they are discussed in Chapter 8 ("Compound and Complex Sentences").

5. **Intensive Pronouns**
Intensive pronouns strengthen or intensify the subject of a verb:

   ◆ I did it *myself*.
   ◆ You *yourself* are guilty.

6. **Reflexive Pronouns**
Reflexive pronouns are used to direct the action of a verb toward its subject:

   ◆ He helped *himself* to the cake.
   ◆ They let *themselves* into the apartment.

7. **Interrogative Pronouns**
These pronouns introduce questions:

   ◆ *Who* can identify Michael Crichton?
   ◆ *Whose* boomerang is this?
   ◆ *What* is the anticipated population of the United States in 2025?

Because personal pronouns are used most often—and because they cause most of the problems in pronoun usage—we will begin with them.

© 2001 Addison-Wesley Educational Publishers Inc.

CLASSES OF PRONOUNS

Personal

I, you, he she, it, we, they, me, her, him, us, them, my, mine, your, yours, hers, his, its, our, ours, their, theirs

Indefinite

all, another, any, anybody, anyone, anything, both, each, either, everybody, everyone, everything, few, many, more, most, much, neither, nobody, none, no one, nothing, one, other, several, some, somebody, someone, something, such

Demonstrative

this, that, these, those

Relative

who, whose, whom, which, what, that

Reflexive and Intensive

myself, yourself, himself, herself, itself, ourselves, yourselves, themselves

Interrogative

who, whose, whom, which, what

PERSONAL PRONOUNS

The Subject Pronouns

Subject pronouns are used as the *subject of a verb*, as a *predicate pronoun*, or as an *appositive identifying a subject*. They are sometimes called *nominative pronouns*.

As the Subject of a Verb

◆ Donny and *I* [not *me*] rowed until we were exhausted.

◆ Either *she* or *I* [not *her* or *me*] can explain the equation to you.

Note: In some sentences a pronoun will be the subject of an implied verb. This occurs often in comparisons introduced by *than* or *as*. In such cases the subject form of the pronoun should be used. In the following sentences, the implied verbs are in parentheses.

◆ He is fourteen pounds heavier than I *(am)*.

◆ She is not as tall as *he (is)*.

◆ They work longer hours than *we (do)*.

As a Predicate Pronoun   A pronoun that comes after some form of the verb *to be* and describes or renames the subject is called a **predicate pronoun.** It must be a subject pronoun.

◆ That is *she* [not *her*] in the front row. (*She* is a predicate pronoun because it follows the linking verb *is* and renames or identifies the subject *That.*)

◆ The last ones to cross the line were Larry and *I* [not *me*]. (*I* follows the linking verb *were* and, with *Larry*, means the same as the subject *ones*. Therefore, the subject form *I* is needed.)

◆ Everyone knew that it was *they* [not *them*]. (Like the two sentences above, the pronoun following the linking verb identifies the subject and is therefore in the subject form.)

Note: Some exceptions to this rule are allowed. *It is me, It is her,* and *It is them,* for example, are widely used and accepted in informal situations. In formal speaking and writing, however, the preferred forms are *It is I, It is she,* and *It is they.* Follow the advice of your instructor.

As an Appositive Identifying the Subject   An **appositive** is a word or group of words that renames or identifies an immediately preceding noun.

                          appositive
◆ Cleveland, *the city of my birth,* is the home of nine universities and colleges.

                    appositive
◆ Her brother *Phil* was wounded in Bosnia.

Occasionally a pronoun will serve as an appositive renaming the subject of a sentence or a **predicate noun.** In such cases the pronoun should be in the subject form. Note carefully the following sentences:

◆ Only two members, Dean and *I* [not *me*], voted for an increase in dues. (*I*, a subject pronoun, in an appositive phrase renaming the subject, *members.*)

◆ The exceptions were the two new members, Ron and *she* [not *her*]. (*She* is in an appositive phrase renaming the predicate noun, *members.*)

TIPS FOR USING SUBJECT PRONOUNS

1. Memorize the subject pronouns: *I, you, he, she, it, who, whoever, we,* and *they.*
2. Remember that only subject pronouns can be subjects of verbs.

© 2001 Addison-Wesley Educational Publishers Inc.

3. If a pronoun is part of a compound subject, break the sentence into two parts: "My brother and me get along well" is incorrect, as revealed by the following test: "My brother gets along well. I get along well. My brother and *I* get along well."

Exercise 5-1

In the following sentences underline every pronoun used as the subject of a verb and write "A" above it. Underline all pronouns used as a predicate pronoun and write "B" above them. Underline all pronouns used as an appositive identifying the subject and write "C" above them. Ignore all pronouns not used in these three ways.

1. As we watched in horror, the pit bull terriers ran toward us.
2. Because of Tony's gravelly voice, we knew it was he who answered the telephone.
3. They were startled to see themselves on videotape.
4. Nikita and I saw the guide ahead of us, but we were reluctant to follow him.
5. The three top students—Myra, you, and I—will not have to take the final examination.
6. It was Paul's father who taught him to play the cello when he was a child.
7. Frankly, it was you who disappointed me the most.
8. We reluctantly admitted that if we had worked as hard as they, we would have finished the job by now.
9. The three alumni who had come the farthest distance—Bernie, Emil, and Tom— were given prizes by the homecoming committee.
10. Josh has taken more data processing courses than Roberta or I.

The Object Pronouns

As their name suggests, **object pronouns** are used as objects: *objects of prepositions*, *objects of verbs*, and *indirect objects*.

As the Object of a Preposition   In Chapter 2 you saw that a preposition is followed by a noun or pronoun, called the **object of the preposition.** When the object of the preposition is a pronoun, it must be from the list of object pronouns.

- Between you and *me* [not *I*], his singing is off-key.
- Her smiling parents stood next to *her* at the capping ceremony.
- Solar energy is a possible answer to the energy problems faced by *us* [not *we*] Americans.

When the objects of a preposition are a noun and a pronoun, there is a mistaken tendency to use the subject form of the pronoun, as in the following sentence:

◆ **(Incorrect)**   Ruth's parents gave their concert tickets to her and I. (*I* is incorrect because it is a subject pronoun; after a proposition, an object pronoun should be used.)

The best way to correct sentences like this is to break them up into separate sentences. Study the following carefully.

Ruth's parents gave their concert tickets to *Ruth*.

Ruth's parents gave their concert tickets to *me*.

◆ **(Correct)**   Ruth's parents gave their concert tickets to *Ruth and me*.

As Direct Objects   A **direct object** is the word that receives the action of the verb. It can follow only an action verb, never a linking verb. When a pronoun is used as a direct object, it must be an object pronoun.

◆ The falling tree missed *him* by only a few feet.
◆ My big brother took *me* with him on his first date.
◆ Please call *us* if you get lost.
◆ Reggie married *her* before going to boot camp.

As in the case of prepositions, when both a noun and a pronoun are the direct objects of the same verb, the object form for the pronoun is used. Notice the following:

◆ **(Incorrect)**   Sheila surprised Garfield and I with her answer.

By breaking up this sentence into two separate sentences, you can determine the correct form:

Sheila surprised *Garfield* with her answer.

Sheila surprised *me* with her answer.

◆ **(Correct)**   Sheila surprised *Garfield and me* with her answer.

In some sentences a pronoun will be the object of an implied verb. This occurs frequently in comparisons introduced by *than* and *as*. In such cases the object form of the pronoun should be used. (Compare this construction with pronouns used as the subject of implied verbs, as explained on pages 89–90.) In the following sentences, the implied subjects and verbs are in parentheses.

◆ Lorraine knows my brother much better than (*she knows*) me.
◆ The nurse said the shot would hurt her as much as (*it hurt*) him.

© 2001 Addison-Wesley Educational Publishers Inc.

Using the correct pronoun after *than* and *as* is important, as the following sentences show. What is the difference in meaning between these sentences?

◆ My girlfriend likes pizza more than *I*.

◆ My girlfriend likes pizza more than *me*.

As Indirect Objects   An **indirect object** is the person or thing to whom or for whom something is done. The indirect object may be thought of as the recipient of the direct object, and it almost always comes between the action verb and the direct object. When a pronoun is used as an indirect object, the object form of the pronoun should be used.

◆ The mail carrier gave *me* a registered letter.

◆ The dealer offered *Bill and her* a discount on the tires.

◆ Our neighbors sent *us* a postcard from England.

TIPS FOR USING OBJECT PRONOUNS

1. **Memorize the object pronouns:** *me, you, him, her, it, whom, whomever, us, them.*
2. **Use object pronouns when they follow action verbs and propositions.**
3. **Never say or write "between you and *I*." The correct form is "between you and *me*."**

Exercise 5-2

In the following sentences underline every object pronoun and above it write the letter appropriate to its use in the sentence:

a. object of preposition   b. direct object   c. indirect object

1. Because Mary Kay did not want to talk to the reporters, she ignored them.
2. Arlene married him despite the advice of her girlfriends and me.
3. The car dealer offered me a rebate if I bought a car from his inventory.
4. The social worker explained to us the consequences of alcoholism.
5. Between you and me, the paisley tie looks terrible on Fred.
6. I like that store because the clerks give me advice in selecting the best colors for me.
7. Jason moved from the farm because hard work and long hours did not agree with him.
8. The apartment manager told us that we would have to pay a cleaning deposit in order for us to move in.
9. Lou's former girlfriend sat behind him and me at the rock concert last night.
10. The pet shop owner gave Jim and me some advice for training our dogs.

Exercise 5-3

Write the letter which corresponds to the correct pronoun in the space provided.

_____ 1. Ana and (a. I   b. me) have shared the same locker all semester.

_____ 2. The Bagbys and (a. us   b. we) have lived next door to each other for many years.

_____ 3. The woman in the jogging suit standing in front of Tom and (a. I   b. me) is Louise.

_____ 4. Ken was happy to do the favor for Kathy and (a. I   b. me).

_____ 5. Ms. Williams was proud of (a. us   b. we) staff members of the newspaper.

_____ 6. Juanita helped Caroline and (a. I   b. me) fill out the application forms for summer school.

_____ 7. The travel agency sent Brad and (a. I   b. me) some brochures describing Hawaii.

_____ 8. The responsibility for keeping the swimming pool clean will be shared by Carl and (a. I   b. me).

_____ 9. Because of the road conditions, Max will be arriving much later than (a. us   b. we).

_____ 10. The governor claimed that (a. us   b. we) voters were more prosperous than ever.

_____ 11. Everyone but Sharon and (a. he   b. him) thought the joke was funny.

_____ 12. It's difficult for strangers to tell the difference between Nell and (a. her   b. she).

_____ 13. I wish I were as confident as (a. her   b. she) about the results of the interview.

_____ 14. Please keep this a secret between you and (a. I   b. me).

_____ 15. The custodian left the door of the gymnasium unlocked for Pete and (a. I   b. me).

The Possessive Pronouns

The **possessive pronouns** are used to show ownership or possession of one person or thing by another. Most pronouns have two possessive forms:

◆ my, mine, our, ours, his, her, hers, its, their, theirs, your, yours

Use *mine, yours, his, hers, its, ours,* or *theirs* when the possessive pronoun is separated from the noun that it refers to:

◆ The decision was mine.
◆ The problem became theirs.

© 2001 Addison-Wesley Educational Publishers Inc.

◆ The car keys that were found were hers.

Use *my, your, his, her, its, our,* or *their* when the possessive pronoun comes immediately before the noun it modifies:

◆ It was *my* decision.
◆ It became *their* problem.
◆ She lost *her* car keys.

The possessive form is usually used immediately before a noun ending in *-ing.* (Such nouns are called **gerunds,** and they are formed by adding *-ing* to verbs: *walking, riding, thinking,* and so on.)

◆ The team objected to *his* taking credit for the win.
◆ *Our* bombing of the harbor was protested by the Cuban delegation.
◆ Everyone was glad to hear of *your* winning a scholarship.

The possessive forms of *it, who,* and *you* cause problems for many writers. Remember that the apostrophe in *it's, who's* and *you're* indicates that these words are contractions, not possessive forms. In Chapter 11 we will look closely at the use of the apostrophe in contractions and possessive nouns. Notice the difference between the following pairs of words:

◆ *It's* [It is] important to follow a program of regular exercise.
◆ A cardiologist spoke to our physical education class on jogging and *its* effects on the cardiovascular system.
◆ She thinks that she knows *who's [who is]* responsible for this mess.
◆ *Whose* idea was this, anyway?
◆ *You're [You are]* expected to be ready by five o'clock.
◆ Have you memorized *your* account number?

TIPS FOR USING POSSESSIVE PRONOUNS

The possessive pronouns do not contain apostrophes.
  It's means "it is" or "it has."
  Who's means "who is" or "who has."
  You're means "you are."

Exercise 5-4

Write the letter corresponding to the correct word in the space provided.

_____ 1. (a. Its   b. It's) a good idea to know what you will use a computer for before you buy one.

_____ 2. A chef (a. whose   b. who's) recipe won the contest later admitted that he had read it in a cook book.

_____ 3. My dog enjoys chasing (a. its   b. it's) own tail.

_____ 4. What are (a. your   b. you're) chances of receiving a scholarship?

_____ 5. Don't you realize what (a. your   b. you're) getting into?

_____ 6. Did Richard offer an excuse for (a. him   b. his) arriving late for his own wedding?

_____ 7. Professor Dwyer presented a slide show on Ireland and (a. its   b. it's) history.

_____ 8. My wife objects to (a. me   b. my) playing Salt N'Pepa songs early in the morning.

_____ 9. (a. Whose   b. Who's) the author of *The Autobiography of Benjamin Franklin?*

_____ 10. Annie Oakley is the nineteenth-century riflewoman (a. who   b. whom) thrilled audiences by shooting the ends off cigarettes held in her husband's mouth.

_____ 11. (a. Its   b. It's) horrible to even think of missing one day of Mrs. Corliss's exciting physiology class.

_____ 12. The "Elvis Is Alive" club will have a surprise speaker at (a. its   b. it's) next meeting.

_____ 13. (a. Whose   b. Who's) going to pay for the damage to my car?

_____ 14. My brother laughed at (a. me   b. my) dancing a cha-cha while the band played the "Dog Catcher."

_____ 15. If you study hard, practice honesty, and marry the boss's son, (a. your   b. you're) going to go far in your career.

THE RELATIVE PRONOUNS

Relative pronouns can be used in two ways in a sentence: they can connect one clause with another, and they can act as subjects or objects in their own clauses.
As connecting words:

◆ Famine is one of the major problems *that* Africa faces.

◆ He usually accomplishes *whatever* he tries to do.

© 2001 Addison-Wesley Educational Publishers Inc.

As subjects or objects in their own clauses:

- Bob Beamon's record for the long jump, *which* has never been surpassed, was set in Mexico City in 1968.
- Two pedestrians *who* were walking near the curb were hit by flying glass.
- A woman *who* spoke French helped the couple from Paris.

Who, Which, and That: Special Uses

As relative pronouns, *who, which,* and *that* each have particular uses. Use *who* and *whom* only for people:

- Neil Armstrong was the first man *who* set foot on the moon.
- She is one of those natural athletes *who* can play any sport.
- Kate Smith was a singer *whom* everyone admired.
- Muhammad Ali is an athlete *whom* the whole world recognizes.

Use *which* only for animals and things:

- Her dog, *which* is a dachshund, sleeps under her bed.
- The proposal *which* I have offered will not cost more than the other plans.

Use *that* for animals, people, and things:

- A letter *that* does not have sufficient postage will be returned to its sender.
- A desk *that* belonged to Thomas Jefferson was sold recently for six thousand dollars.
- Every cat *that* does not have a license will be put in the animal pound.
- A stranger *that* claimed he was lost seized Todd's wallet and ran.

INTENSIVE AND REFLEXIVE PRONOUNS: PRONOUNS ENDING IN –self AND –selves

Several pronouns end in *-self* or *-selves:*

- myself, yourself, himself, herself, itself, ourselves, yourselves, themselves

As **reflexive pronouns,** these pronouns are used when the action of the sentence is done by the subject to himself or herself:

- They helped *themselves* to the cookies.

◆ I tried to bathe *myself* despite my broken arm.

As **intensive pronouns,** these words stress or emphasize another noun or pronoun:

◆ She tuned the engine *herself*.
◆ You *yourself* are to blame.
◆ The President *himself* awarded the medals to the members of the color guard.

These pronouns should not be used in place of a subject or object pronoun:

◆ **(Incorrect)**   My wife and *myself* would be happy to accept your invitation.
◆ **(Correct)**   My wife and *I* would be happy to accept you invitation.
◆ **(Incorrect)**   On behalf of my family and *myself*, I could like to express our gratitude to all of you.
◆ **(Correct)**   On behalf of my family and *me*, I would like to express our gratitude to all of you.
◆ **(Incorrect)**   Kevin helped Linda and *myself* install a new carburetor in my Chevrolet.
◆ **(Correct)**   Kevin helped Linda and *me* install a new carburetor in my Chevrolet.

Never use forms like *hisself, theirself, theirselves,* or *ourself*. These are nonstandard in both informal and formal speech and writing, and they should always be avoided.

TIPS ON PRONOUNS

1. *Who* is the subject form; *whom* is the object form.
2. Do not use pronouns ending in *-self* or *-selves* as subjects or objects.
3. Never use *hisself, theirself, theirselves,* or *ourself.*

SOME PROBLEMS WITH PRONOUNS: WHO AND WHOM

The difference between *who* and *whom* is a trap into which some writers and speakers occasionally fall. "Whom" has nearly disappeared from informal English, whether spoken or written. In formal English, however, the differences between the two words are still important and should be learned.

The first step to take when selecting the correct form is to determine which word is the subject and which is the object. *Who* is the *subject* form:

© 2001 Addison-Wesley Educational Publishers Inc.

- *Who* is at the door? (*Who* is the subject of *is*.)
- *Who* did he say was at the door? (Notice that *"did he say"* does not affect the subject pronoun *Who* as the subject of the verb *was*.)
- *Who* wants to help me wash the car? (*Who* is the subject of *wants*.)
- *Who* do you think wants to help me wash the car? (*Who* is still the subject of *wants* and is not affected by the words that separate it from the verb.)

Whom is the object form:

- *Whom* did you see? (If you turn this question around, you can see that *Whom* is the object of the verb *did see:* "You did see *whom?*")
- With *whom* do you study? (*Whom* is the object of the preposition *With*.)
- *Whom* you know sometimes seems to be more important than what you know. (*Whom* is the object of the verb *know*.)

If you are uncertain about the correct form, substitute a personal pronoun (*he, him; they, them*). If *he* or *they* fits, use *who*; if *him* or *them* fits, use *whom*. Study the following examples:

- I don't know (*who, whom*) he wanted. (Substitute *him:* He wanted *him*.) The correct form: I don't know *whom* he wanted.
- (*Who, Whom*) shall I say is calling? (Substitute *he:* He is calling.) The correct form: *Who* shall I say is calling?

Don't be misled by expressions like "he said" and "I think" that can follow *who* when it is the subject of a verb.

- My aunt is the person *who* I think has been most influential in my life. (Who is the subject of the verb *has been*, not the object of *think*.)

By deleting or omitting the interrupting words you can easily decide whether the pronoun is the subject or the object.

Many people use *who* at the beginning of a question in cases when *whom* would be the grammatically correct form, as in the following:

- *Who* did he ask for?
- *Who* should I send the thank-you note to?

Such usage is a matter of debate, however, and many careful writers and speakers would object to such a construction. Follow the advice of your instructor in this matter.

Exercise 5-5

In the space before each sentence write the appropriate letter.

_____   1. (a. Who   b. Whom) do you believe will win the National League championship?

_____   2. It is not possible to predict (a. who   b. whom) will benefit from the new tax laws passed by Congress.

_____   3. Norman helped Mitchell and (a. me   b. myself) move into our new apartment.

_____   4. The President (a. himself   b. hisself) greeted the astronauts.

_____   5. By the gestures you used, I knew (a. who   b. whom) you were imitating.

_____   6. The villagers (a. who   b. whom) were living in the earthquake areas were left homeless.

_____   7. I will speak to the person (a. who   b. whom) answers the telephone.

_____   8. We have no one to blame but (a. ourself   b. ourselves).

_____   9. Sylvia was the only adult (a. who   b. whom) the children trusted.

_____   10. Patrick helped (a. himself   b. hisself) to a fresh towel.

_____   11. Manuel and (a. I   b. myself) dressed up as clowns for the party.

_____   12. A cousin (a. who   b. whom) Lakisha has not seen for twenty-five years is coming to visit her.

_____   13. (a. Who   b. Whom) the President will nominate as ambassador to Mexico is difficult to predict.

_____   14. (a. Who   b. Whom) is brave enough to wear this tie?

_____   15. Mr. Gradgrind, (a. who   b. whom) you all know, will be our new supervisor.

WRITING SENTENCES

Using the Correct Form of the Pronoun

Choosing the correct form of the pronoun can be confusing. This exercise lets you demonstrate that you know how to use the right form of the pronoun when you have to make a choice.

1. Write a sentence in which you use "you and I" correctly.
2. Write a sentence using "you and me" correctly.
3. Write a sentence using "who" correctly.
4. Write a sentence using "whom" correctly.
5. Write a sentence using "you" as the subject of a verb.
6. Write a sentence using "you" as the predicate pronoun.

© 2001 Addison-Wesley Educational Publishers Inc.

7. Write a sentence using "me" in an appositive.
8. Write a sentence using "us" as the object of a preposition.
9. Write a sentence using "whom" as a direct object.
10. Write a sentence using "them" as an indirect object.

Editing Exercise

The paragraph below describes the preparations involved in planning a trip into the woods. The paragraph contains a series of errors in pronoun usage. Improve the paragraph by correcting the errors. Revise the sentences when necessary.

Before stepping into the woods for a hike, my brother and me always make sure we have several important supplies. I am usually more concerned about getting lost than him, so I'm in charge of bringing a good map of the trail area. Storms and vandals can uproot trail signs, so us adventurers cannot count on using them to find our way. Most parks and wilderness areas feature a visitors' center or kiosk who offers free maps. My brother is better at reading a compass than myself, so he handles that task. He laughs about me bringing a cellular phone into a rustic setting, but it could help if him and I get lost or injured. Its important to dress properly for hiking; we both wear at least a couple layers of clothing since I am not someone whom predicts weather changes very well. Him and I plan for a nutrition break by bringing ample water and snacks. Many sports equipment stores sell protein bars and small packages of nuts or dried fruit, but between you and I, I think that an apple or orange from home works just as well. Depending on the weather and how we plan to amuse ourselfs, we sometimes also bring field glasses for bird-watching, as well as bathing suits, towels, and a jar for toads whom we may catch for pets. With some easy planning, my brother and myself get to taste adventure without sacrificing safety.

© 2001 Addison-Wesley Educational Publishers Inc.

▶Review Test 5-A

Using the Correct Form of the Pronoun

A. Write the appropriate letter corresponding to the use of the italicized pronoun in each sentence. Use the space provided.

a. object of a preposition   b. direct object   c. indirect object

_____ 1. Julie decided to give her extra concert tickets to Norm and *me*.
_____ 2. The real-estate agent showed *us* houses that cost over a million dollars.
_____ 3. The district attorney charged *him* with spousal rape and battery.
_____ 4. While he was in Paris, Nicholas sent postcards to Denise and *me*.
_____ 5. Because of the rain, my father gave *me* an umbrella.

B. Write the appropriate letter corresponding to the use of the italicized pronoun in each sentence. Use the space provided.

a. subject of a verb   b. predicate pronoun   c. an appositive identifying the subject

_____ 6. Because our father died when *we* were infants, my sister and I do not remember him.
_____ 7. To the surprise of his estranged son, the sole heir to the estate was *he*.
_____ 8. The committee decided to award the prize to *whoever* gave the best impromptu performance.
_____ 9. Three unsuspecting contestants—Maria, Lois, and *I*—were asked to come up to the stage.
_____ 10. Emil watches much more television than *I*.

C. Write the appropriate letter corresponding to the correct pronoun. Use the space provided.

_____ 11. The quarterback was distracted by the fans because of (a. their   b. them) taunting.
_____ 12. Although I had studied longer than Chris and Earl, they received higher grades than (a. I   b. me).
_____ 13. The nurse explained to Eva and (a. I   b. me) the benefits of a low-fat diet.

_____ 14. Professor Douglass described the experiments that Dr. Cohen and
            (a. her   b. she) had performed while in Australia.

_____ 15. The beneficiaries of the new regulations are Roberta and (a. I   b. me).

_____ 16. The insurance agent offered my brother and (a. I   b. me) a discount on
            our car insurance.

_____ 17. The losing candidate blamed (a. himself   b. hisself) for his defeat.

_____ 18. As every planner of a picnic knows, (a. its   b. it's) impossible to predict
            the weather with complete accuracy.

_____ 19. That was Luis and (a. her   b. she) in the front row of the auditorium.

_____ 20. Raymond and (a. I   b. myself) will be leaving for Chicago tomorrow
            morning.

_____ 21. They should have been ashamed of (a. theirselves   b. themselves) for
            their behavior.

_____ 22. Scientists claim that tests taken in childhood can predict
            (a. your   b. you're) chances of suffering from certain diseases in old age.

_____ 23. (a. Its   b. It's) a good idea to know what you will use sneakers for before
            you buy them.

_____ 24. The peace treaty between Jordan and Israel pleased Michael and
            (a. I   b. me).

_____ 25. A poet (a. whose   b. who's) work won first prize admitted that it was
            based on his mother's nursery rhymes.

© 2001 Addison-Wesley Educational Publishers Inc.

▶Review Test 5-B

Using the Correct Form of the Pronoun

A. Write the appropriate letter corresponding to the use of the italicized pronoun in each sentence. Use the space provided.

a. object of a preposition   b. direct object   c. indirect object

_____   1.   Rafael prefers to play tennis with George rather than with *me.*
_____   2.   Tamara sent *us* some postcards while she was in London.
_____   3.   The housemother at the dorm caught Tina, Jennifer, and *me* as we were climbing through the window.
_____   4.   As he passed our car, the driver made an obscene gesture at Sheila and *me.*
_____   5.   After the clothing drive, Mr. Goddard thanked *us* volunteers for our help.

B. Write the appropriate letter corresponding to the use of the italicized pronoun in each sentence. Use the space provided.

a. subject of a verb   b. predicate pronoun   c. an appositive identifying the subject

_____   6.   For years Patrick and *I* have been in love with the same girl.
_____   7.   The most confident couple on the dance floor was Elton and *she.*
_____   8.   *Whoever* told you that was wrong.
_____   9.   Three students—Fred, Mark, and *you*—have been selected to represent us.
_____ 10.   Katie plays chess much better than *I.*

C. Write the appropriate letter corresponding to the correct pronoun. Use the space provided.

_____ 11.   It was difficult to concentrate because of (a. their   b. them) whispering.
_____ 12.   Although Charlotte is older than (a. I   b. me), she is not as tall.
_____ 13.   Dentists try to make (a. us   b. we) patients relax before they examine us.
_____ 14.   While driving to New Orleans, Arnold and (a. her   b. she) stopped in Lafayette to visit their parents.
_____ 15.   The only students who were able to interview the mayor were Paul and (a. I   b. me).

_____   16.   Will offered my wife and (a. I   b. me) a chance to invest in his company.

_____   17.   Mr. Andrews did most of the work (a. himself   b. hisself), although he is eighty years old.

_____   18.   I found out the hard way that (a. its   b. it's) better to review each night rather than at the last minute.

_____   19.   The last ones to leave the playing field—Jess and (a. I   b. me)—were the first to leave the locker room.

_____   20.   Gilbert and (a. I   b. myself) have looked forward to this moment for many months.

_____   21.   When the hostess wasn't looking, the children helped (a. themselves b. theirselves) to the soda.

_____   22.   What are (a. your   b. you're) chances of receiving a scholarship?

_____   23.   (a. Its   b. It's) not always easy to predict my father's behavior.

_____   24.   Calvin offered Naomi and (a. I   b. me) a piece of his birthday cake.

_____   25.   A runner (a. whose   b. who's) shoe came off had to drop out of the race.

© 2001 Addison-Wesley Educational Publishers Inc.

WRITING PARAGRAPHS

THE ORDER OF IMPORTANCE

One of the most useful ways of arranging ideas in a paragraph is *in their order of importance*. To organize your ideas in this pattern, you should first list the ideas that support your topic sentence. The most important ideas should come first, then the next important, and so on. In writing the paragraph, take your ideas from the list in reverse order. Not every paragraph can be constructed in this pattern, of course, but it can be a very emphatic way to arrange ideas.

The advantages of building up to the most important ideas stem from the suspense involved and the tendency for readers to remember best what they read last. The paragraph that concludes with a surprise, a clever comment, an appeal for action, or with some other strong ending is more likely to be successful.

In the paragraph below, written by a student, notice how the writer introduces the least important ideas first and then presents the most important idea in the last sentence, which serves as the topic sentence.

◆ Before a 100-inch telescope was built on Mount Wilson near Los Angeles, astronomers had difficulty in studying the stars. But in 1923 the American astronomer Edwin Hubble, using the new telescope, could pick out stars and calculate distances within our Milky Way. Through his measurements of the stars he calculated that the Andromeda nebula is approximately two million light-years away, a fact that places it far outside our Milky Way. As a result of his discoveries, we now realize that our galaxy is only one among billions of galaxies in the universe, each with billions of stars.

In the next paragraph, also written by a student, notice a similar structure: a series of facts about bulimia paves the way for the most important fact at the conclusion of the paragraph.

◆ Until recently, physicians and scientists have been unable to provide a reliable cure for bulimia, a syndrome of gorging on food followed by voluntary vomiting. The illness, which affects up to two million American women, had been treated by a variety of remedies. Some patients tried hypnosis, but without success. Others tried radical changes in diet, with limited success. Still others tried therapy or large doses of vitamins, but without notable improvement. But a scientist from Harvard Medical School announced recently that ninety percent of the women treated with an antidepressant reported that they "binged" on food half as frequently when on the medication. This finding suggests that bulimia has a chemical and hereditary basis and gives researchers hope that a complete cure will be found soon.

Writing Tips

Last, But Not Least . . . .

When writing a paragraph based on the order of importance, you have to give signals to your reader to indicate the progression of your ideas. Use words like the following:

Consequently, thus, therefore, as a result, in the end, finally, consequently, most important.

WRITING PARAGRAPHS

The ideas in this paragraph are arranged in their order of importance. Read the paragraph carefully and then write a response to "a" or "b" below.

◆ My friend Paul has created enormous problems for himself. First, he neglected to study for a test because he was afraid of failure, thereby ensuring that he would not pass. Since Paul was already on academic probation, this failing grade was the final straw and he was dismissed from school. Because he had borrowed money to pay for school, he now had to find work with no degree. All he could find were low-paying, low-skills jobs that were very tiring and somewhat demeaning. Depressed, he began to drink heavily and injured himself by falling off a ladder at work. However, because he had been drunk at work when he injured himself, he received no worker's compensation and was fired instead. The last I heard, Paul was seen downtown walking with a limp, a bottle of fortified wine in hand, accosting women and yelling obscenities at passersby.

—R. Yarber and A. Hoffman, *Writing for College*, p. 40

Exercise A   Order of Importance

Arranging your ideas in the order of importance, write a paragraph of at least one hundred words on one of the following topics. Underline your topic sentence.

- the effects of exercise
- reasons for majoring in . . .
- the benefits of travel
- the advantages of a long engagement
- the advantages of going away to school
- the benefits of meditation
- preparing for a job interview

© 2001 Addison-Wesley Educational Publishers Inc.

Exercise B   Order of Importance

Presenting your ideas in their order of importance, write a paragraph of at least 150 words on one of the following:

a. Listing them in their order of importance, describe three or four of your goals for the next ten years.
b. Describe the three most admirable traits of one of your friends or relatives.
c. Describe your concept of the ideal mate, boss, or politician.

Writing Tips

Who's Out There, Anyway?

Knowing your audience—the readers you are writing for—is crucial to the success of your assignment. Consider your readers:

- Who is going to read my paragraph?
- How much do my readers already know about my topic?
- What new information or novel angle can I offer?
- How can I keep their attention and make them continue reading?

 ## Computer Activity

Certain words are clues to the relative importance of ideas in a paragraph. Write a paragraph according to the instructions in Exercise A or Exercise B.

Re-read your paragraph and italicize clue words such as *first, second, more important, nevertheless, however, perhaps, finally, above all*. How many of these signposts did you use?

6

Common Errors in Pronoun Agreement and Reference

In the last chapter we noted that even the most educated speakers and writers are occasionally uncertain about the correct form of the pronoun to use. Another area of usage that causes confusion is pronoun agreement and reference.

Pronouns should agree with the words to which they refer. In other words, if a pronoun refers to a plural antecedent, the pronoun should be plural; if the antecedent is singular, the pronoun should also be singular; and if the antecedent is a pronoun in the third person, the pronoun should also be in the third person. (An **antecedent** is the word or term referred to by the pronoun.)

The rules for pronoun agreement and reference are usually easy to follow. However, there are several situations when the choice of pronoun is not clear or when the antecedent is not obvious. Such cases can result in confusion or ambiguity on the part of the reader as well as the writer. Because pronoun agreement and reference are necessary if your writing is to be logical and effective, this chapter will examine the situations when they are most critical.

AGREEMENT IN NUMBER

A pronoun must **agree** with its antecedent *in number*. If the antecedent is singular, the pronoun is singular. If the antecedent is plural, the pronoun is plural. This rule poses no problems in sentences in which the pronoun and its antecedents are close, as in the following examples:

◆ *Elizabeth* wanted to buy a used *car,* but *she* did not want to pay more than nine thousand dollars for *it.* (This sentence has two singular pronouns, each matched with its singular antecedent: she [*Elizabeth*] and it [*car*].)

◆ Her *parents* told Elizabeth that *they* would be willing to lend her an additional two thousand dollars. (The plural pronoun *they* matches its plural antecedent *parents.* Do you see another pronoun in this sentence? What is its antecedent?)

◆ *Richard* purchased *his* tickets yesterday for the Janet Jackson concert. (The singular pronoun *his* matches its singular antecedent *Richard.*)

Problems in pronoun agreement occur when the writer loses sight of the antecedent or confuses it with other nouns in the sentence, as in the following sentence:

◆ **(Incorrect)**   The faculty committee presented *their* recommendations for new graduation requirements to the deans of the college.

This sentence is incorrect because the plural pronoun *their* does not agree with its singular antecedent *committee.* How many committees were there? Only one. Therefore, the pronoun referring to it should be singular: *its.* The writer of this sentence may have been thinking of the individuals on the committee or of the recommendations that were submitted, or even of the deans, and therefore wrongly selected *their,* a plural pronoun.

Here, then, is the correct version:

◆ **(Correct)**   The faculty committee presented *its* recommendations for new graduation requirements to the deans of the college.

The following rules will help you to use pronouns in your sentences that will agree with their antecedents in number:

1. In general, use a *singular pronoun* when the antecedent is an *indefinite* pronoun. (For a review of indefinite pronouns, see Chapter 5.) Some indefinite pronouns present exceptions to this rule—they are always plural, or they can be singular or plural depending on the kind of noun they represent.

   a. The following indefinite pronouns are always *singular,* which means that other pronouns referring to them should be singular:

   another, anybody, anyone, anything, each, each one, either, every, everybody, everyone, everything, many a, much, neither, nobody, no one, nothing, one, other, somebody, someone, something

   Notice that in the following sentences the indefinite pronouns are accompanied by singular pronouns:

© 2001 Addison-Wesley Educational Publishers Inc.

- *Anyone* planning a trip to Russia should apply for a visa before *he* leaves this country.
- *Each* of the girls told me *her* name.
- When I returned, *everything* was in *its* place.
- *Many a* son belatedly wishes he had listened to *his* father's advice.
- *Everyone* was asked to contribute as much as *he* could.
- *Everyone* is responsible for making *his* own bed.
- *Neither* of the girls wanted *her* picture taken.

You probably noticed the use of masculine pronouns (*he* and *his*) in the first, fifth, and sixth sentences above. Many writers and readers object to the exclusive use of masculine pronouns with indefinite pronouns such as *anybody, everyone, someone,* and *everybody*. Note carefully the following sentence:

- Everyone took *his* seat.

This is traditional usage, with *his* used to refer to humanity in general. To avoid the sole use of masculine pronouns, some writers would word the sentence like this:

- Everyone took *his or her* seat.

Because this form can be awkward, some writers prefer the following method to avoid only masculine pronouns:

- Every took *their* seats.

While avoiding the exclusive use of the masculine pronoun, this sentence combines a plural pronoun (*their*) with a singular antecedent (*Everyone*). Those who prefer this version should be aware that it is not yet accepted in formal written English.

What is the answer to this dilemma? An increasingly popular solution is to reword the sentence, making the subject plural:

- The members of the audience took *their* seats.

For additional suggestions for avoiding sexism in pronoun usage, see pages 121–23.

b. The following indefinite pronouns are always *plural:*

both, few, many, others, several

When they are used as antecedents, pronouns referring to them are always *plural*. Note their use in the following sentences:

- *Many* of his customers transferred *their* accounts to another company.

◆ A *few* of the students admitted *they* had not studied.
◆ *Several* of the golfers said *they* wanted to bring their own caddies.
◆ *Both* of the cars had *their* mufflers replaced.

c. The following indefinite pronouns can be either singular or plural:

all, any, more, most, none, some

Antecedents referring to them will be either singular or plural, depending on their meaning and the noun they represent:

◆ **(Plural)**   *Most* fast-food customers want less fat in *their* hamburgers.
◆ **(Singular)** *Most* of the hamburger has less fat in *it*.
◆ **(Plural)**   *All* of the leaks have been traced to *their* sources.
◆ **(Singular)** *All* of the water has leaked from *its* container.
◆ **(Plural)**   *Some* of the customers want *their* money refunded.
◆ **(Singular)** *Some* of the money was found in *its* hiding place.

Exercise 6–1

In the space before each sentence, write the letter indicating the correct pronoun.

_____   1. At a recent public meeting of battered wives, each woman told
             (a. her   b. their) story.
_____   2. Anyone who buys a used car in California must get a smog certificate
             before (a. he or she   b. they) can purchase new license plates.
_____   3. Many of the early settlers passed laws as intolerant as those
             (a. he or she   b. they) had previously suffered.
_____   4. Some of the immigrants from Ethiopia are learning Hebrew in
             (a. his or her   b. their) new homeland.
_____   5. Each of the girls put (a. her   b. their) toys away.
_____   6. The faculty of the business school were praised for
             (a. its   b. their) publications.
_____   7. Anyone who claims (a. his or her   b. their) bill was incorrect may
             speak to the manager.
_____   8. Each magazine and book was cataloged according to (a. its   b. their)
             subject.
_____   9. Both the painter and the plumber have submitted (a. his   b. their) esti-
             mates.
_____   10. Neither of the sisters could afford (a. her   b. their) own attorney.
_____   11. Every player on the girls' lacrosse team must furnish (a. her   b. their)
             own uniform and shoes.
_____   12. Most of the disputes (a. has   b. have) been settled out of court.

© 2001 Addison-Wesley Educational Publishers Inc.

_____   13.   Most of the blame (a. has   b. have) been attributed to the driver of the red truck.

_____   14.   Many a professional baseball player wishes (a. he   b. they) had invested their huge salaries more wisely.

_____   15.   After the concert every instrument was placed in (a. its   b. their) proper place.

2.   Antecedents joined by *and* usually take plural pronouns:

◆ *Prince Charles and Prince Edward of England* are more famous for *their* private lives than for *their* political views.

◆ *West Germany and East Germany* voted to unite *their* peoples in 1990.

When the antecedents are joined by *and* but refer to a single person or thing, tʰ pronoun may be singular:

◆ The physicist and Nobel Prize winner was able to present *her* ideas in te that the students could understand.

◆ The largest tree and oldest living thing on earth, the *Sequoiadendron ɟ teum*, is better known by *its* familiar name, the Giant Sequoia.

When the compound antecedent is preceded by *each* or *every*, a singular pr   ın should be used:

◆ *Each* team player and substitute received a certificate recognizing *heɪ*   ici- pation.

◆ *Every* father and son was assigned to *his* table.

3.   Collective nouns (see Chapter 4) usually take singular pronouns if the group is re- garded as a unit:

◆ The *couple* was honored for *its* contribution to the church.

◆ The *faculty* was renowned for *its* research and scholarship.

If the members of the group are acting separately, a plural pronoun should be used:

◆ The *couple* disagreed over the amount of money *they* should pay for a new car.

◆ The *faculty* were paid various amounts, depending on *their* education, experi- ence, and publications.

4.   When two or more antecedents are joined by *or* or *nor*, the pronouns should agree with the nearer antecedent:

◆ Neither Millard Fillmore *nor* James Polk is remembered for the brilliance of *his* presidency.

◆ Neither the defendant *nor* the witnesses changed *their* testimony.

◆ Neither the roofers *nor* the carpenters finished *their* work on schedule.

When the antecedent closer to the pronoun is singular, the result can sometimes be awkward:

◆ Neither the sopranos *nor* the tenor could sing his part without looking at *his* music. (Though technically correct, this sentence is confusing.)

Such a sentence should be revised:

◆ Neither the tenor nor the sopranos could sing *their* parts without looking at *their* music.

5.   Pronouns that are used as *demonstrative adjectives (this, that, these, those)* must agree in number with the nouns they modify. Do not say or write "these kind," "these sort," "those kind," "those type," and so on. The correct forms are "these kinds," "these sorts," "this kind," "this sort," "that kind," "those kinds," and so on.
The following sentences illustrate the use of pronouns as demonstrative adjectives:

◆ **(Incorrect)**   These kind of trees are common throughout the South.

◆ **(Correct)**   This kind of tree is common throughout the South. [**Or:** These kinds of trees are common throughout the South.]

◆ **(Incorrect)**   These type of ball bearings never need lubrication.

◆ **(Correct)**   This type of ball bearings never needs lubrication. [**Or:** These types of ball bearings never need lubrication.]

TIPS   ON PRONOUN AGREEMENT

Pronouns should agree in number with the nouns for which they stand.
   1.   **Determine which noun is the real antecedent.**
   2.   **Determine whether the antecedent is singular or plural in meaning.**
   3.   **Remember that singular pronouns must refer to singular antecedents and that plural pronouns must refer to plural antecedents.**

Exercise 6-2

In the space before each sentence, write the letter corresponding to the correct pronoun.

_____   1.   The Olympic medalist and American hero was greeted by (a. his   b. their) coach and wife.

_____   2.   Senator Calderon told the panel that (a. that   b. those) kind of change in the law would raise taxes.

© 2001 Addison-Wesley Educational Publishers Inc.

PRONOUN REFERENCE

Pronouns depend on other words—their antecedents—for their meaning. If their relationship to their antecedents is unclear, their meaning or identity will be confusing. For this reason, you should make certain that every pronoun in your writing (except for indefinite pronouns like *anyone* and *somebody,* and idioms like "*It* is two o'clock") refers specifically to something previously named—its antecedent. In doing so, you will avoid the two most common kinds of problems in pronoun reference: *vagueness* because the writer did not furnish a specific antecedent, and *ambiguity* because the writer supplied too many antecedents.

Here is an example of each kind of error:

◆ **(Vague)**   Several minor political parties nominated presidential candidates every four years. This is one of the characteristics of the American political system. (*What* is one of the characteristics of the American political system?)

◆ **(Ambiguous)**   Gore Vidal wrote a biography of Abraham Lincoln that demonstrates his knowledge and sensitivity. (*Who* demonstrates his knowledge and sensitivity: Gore Vidal or Abraham Lincoln?)

By following the suggestions given below, you can make clear the relationship between pronouns and their antecedents:

The antecedent of a pronoun should be specific rather than implied. Avoid using *that, this, which,* and *it* to refer to implied ideas unless the reference is unmistakably clear.

◆ **(Vague)**   Juana was so impressed by the lecture given by the astronomer that she decided to major in it. (Major in what? *It* has no antecedent in this sentence.)

◆ **(Revision)**   Juana was so impressed by the lecture given by the astronomer that she decided to major in astronomy.

◆ **(Vague)**   Brad consumes huge quantities of potatoes, spaghetti, and ice cream every day, and it is beginning to be noticeable. (What is beginning to be noticeable?)

◆ **(Revision)**   Brad consumes huge quantities of potatoes, spaghetti, and ice cream every day, and the increase in his weight is beginning to be noticeable.

◆ **(Vague)**   Helen enjoys singing with music groups at school, and she would like to be a professional one someday. (A professional what?)

◆ **(Revision)**   Helen enjoys singing with music groups at school, and she would like to be a professional singer someday.

Such vague sentences are corrected by supplying the missing antecedent. Some sentences, however, are confusing because they have more than one possible antecedent, and the result is ambiguity.

To avoid ambiguity, place pronouns as close as possible to their antecedents. Revise sentences in which there are two possible antecedents for a pronoun.

- ◆ **(Confusing)**   Jackie's new car has leather seats, a sunroof, a digital dash with graphic readouts, a vocal warning system, power window, and an eight-speaker stereo. It is power-driven. (What does *It* refer to? What is power-driven?)

- ◆ **(Revision)**   Jackie's new car has leather seats, a sunroof that is power-driven, a digital dash with graphic readouts, a vocal warning system, power windows, and an eight-speaker stereo.

- ◆ **(Confusing)**   Spanish cooking and Mexican cooking should not be confused; it is not as spicy. (What is not as spicy?)

- ◆ **(Revision)**   Spanish cooking is not as spicy as Mexican cooking.

- ◆ **(Confusing)**   The vase has been in our family for one hundred years that you dropped.

- ◆ **(Revision)**   The vase that you dropped has been in our family for one hundred years.

TIPS   ON PRONOUN REFERENCE

1. Don't shift pronouns unnecessarily from one person to another.
2. Learn the pronouns for first, second, and third person.
3. Make sure that every *that, this, which,* and *it* in your sentences has a clear antecedent.
4. Place pronouns as close as possible to their antecedents.

Exercise 6-4

Rewrite the following sentences to make clear any vague or ambiguous pronoun references. Add, omit, or change words as you deem necessary.

1. The reason that Consuela is so knowledgeable about buying and selling stocks and bonds is that she had once been one.
2. Jamal has been transferred to the hospital's night unit, which disappoints his wife and children.
3. Norm bought a baseball bat and hockey stick and then returned it.
4. Shamika's skill in solving difficult physics problems is partly due to the influence of her mother, who is one.
5. Although Kevin has never been there, he likes Chilean food.

© 2001 Addison-Wesley Educational Publishers Inc.

6. Elaine plays the piano very well, but she keeps it hidden.
7. Ray's secret ambition is to be a chef, but he has never studied it.
8. At registration time they check your record and transcript.
9. As Leo and Martin talked, his voice began to rise in anger.
10. Luciano Pavarotti is a great tenor who claims that he has practiced it every day since he was a child.
11. Many companies use lie detectors when interviewing job applicants because they believe they are helpful.
12. Mel has been taking tap-dancing lessons but still can't do it very well.
13. After having been an executive of a large bank for many years, Anne has taken a job at a small company, which created many problems.
14. My roommate doesn't wash his own dishes or clean his room, and it makes me very angry at times.
15. Although Ramon and Felipe are twins, he appears older than his brother.

AVOIDING SEXISM IN PRONOUN USAGE

One of the healthy trends taking place in our society is the recognition that American English has a masculine bias, particularly in its use of pronouns. Because English lacks a singular pronoun that refers to both sexes, *he, his,* and *him* have traditionally been used to refer to men and women when the gender of the antecedent is composed of both males and females or is unknown.

When we constantly use masculine pronouns to personify "the professor," "the lawyer," and "the supervisor," we are subtly rejecting the notion of a female professor, lawyer, or supervisor. Using *he, his,* and *him* as generic terms misleads your audience because these pronouns do not accurately represent the people behind them. Fortunately, there are several ways to make our language gender-fair to avoid exclusion of women.

a. Reword the sentence.

   ◆ **Traditional:**   A writer can often get ideas when he is listening to music.
   ◆ **Better:**   A writer can often get ideas when listening to music.

b. Change the sentence to the plural.

   ◆ Writers often get ideas when they are listening to music.

c. Substitute another pronoun for the masculine pronoun.

   ◆ A writer can often get ideas when she is listening to music.
   ◆ A writer often gets ideas when he or she is listening to music.
   ◆ When writing, one can often get ideas while listening to music.

Editing Exercise

The paragraph below describes the contributions of Frank Lloyd Wright to American architecture. The paragraph contains several errors in pronoun agreement and reference. Improve the paragraph by correcting the errors, revising the sentences when necessary.

Ask anyone who knows about architecture and they will be aware of the importance of Frank Lloyd Wright. No other architect has influenced modern American design more than he. One of Wright's best-known principles is that buildings must stand as unobtrusively as possible against its natural settings. As a child, Wright spent many summers on his mother's family farm in Wisconsin where you couldn't help but develop a keen love of the land. He decided that buildings, like plants, should emerge from the soil and be a part of them. Therefore, building materials should be natural and simple, such as wood, stone, and brick. They should be presented in their natural colors, shapes and textures; even its flaws should show. Wright simplified the components, shapes, and decor of buildings to make it more natural and less synthetic. He built low, horizontally straight ceilings so that the building would seem nestled in their setting, not tower above it. Windows became huge "light screens" rather than squares cut into walls. They looked out to dense foliage, a waterfall, or other natural features. He even omitted garages and basements from homes in warm regions, arguing that you do not need them in a warm, dry climate. Toward the end of his career Wright developed house plans that used inexpensive, prefabricated materials to help the average American afford themselves a good home.

The exclusive use of masculine pronouns (*he, his, him*) with indefinite pronouns such as *anybody, everyone, someone,* and *everybody* is another example of usage that is not gender-fair.

◆ **Traditional:**   Everyone took his seat.

© 2001 Addison-Wesley Educational Publishers Inc.

The use of *his* in this example to refer to humanity in general is still widespread. To avoid the sole use of masculine pronouns, four possibilities are available:

a. Substitute *his or her.*

    ◆ Everyone took his or her seat.

    Because this form can be awkward, many writers and readers prefer other solutions to this problem.

b. Reword the sentence.

    ◆ The members of the audience took their seats.

c. If you must use a single personal pronoun that does not refer to a specific individual, alternate between "he" and "she." Be careful not to change the gender of a particular person.

    ◆ The last runner in the marathon will receive a prize for her endurance and refusal to quit. She will also be given a trophy.

    Do not write:

    ◆ The last runner in the marathon will receive a prize for his endurance and refusal to quit. She will also be given a trophy.

d. Some writers prefer the following method to avoid only masculine pronouns:

    ◆ Everyone took their seats.

    While avoiding the exclusive use of the masculine pronoun, this sentence combines a plural pronoun (*their*) with a singular antecedent (*Everyone*). Those who prefer this version should be aware that it is not yet accepted in formal written English.

WRITING SENTENCES

Avoiding Common Errors in Pronoun Usage

As you saw in this chapter, writing can be confusing and readers can be confused if pronouns do not agree with the words to which they refer. In this exercise you will be writing sentences demonstrating the correct use of pronoun agreement and reference.

1. Write two sentences using a collective noun in each as the subject requiring a singular pronoun as its antecedent.
2. Use the collective nouns from the preceding sentences as the subjects of two sentences, each requiring a plural pronoun as its antecedent.

3. Write two sentences that contain mistaken shifts in person. Then revise each sentence correctly.

4. Write two sentences that contain unclear pronoun references. Then revise each sentence correctly.

5. Write two sentences in which you illustrate your solution to the exclusive use of masculine pronouns with indefinite pronouns.

© 2001 Addison-Wesley Educational Publishers Inc.

▶Review Test 6-A

Common Errors in Pronoun Agreement and Reference

Λ. *In the space provided, write the letter corresponding to the kind of error in pronoun usage each sentence contains. If the sentence is correct, write "d."*

a. shift in person   b. unclear pronoun reference   c. failure to agree in number   d. correct

_____ 1.   Neither of the two suspects could afford their own attorney.

_____ 2.   When the typical male watches television, they jump from one channel to another.

_____ 3.   Rollie painted his garage and installed new garage doors, which surprised his wife.

_____ 4.   Anyone who claims that they overpaid their bill may file a claim with the manager.

_____ 5.   The loggers complain that the new regulations have harmed their industry, which is controversial.

_____ 6.   Both Jay and Tim agree that he was cheated.

_____ 7.   I was surprised to discover that you have to present two forms of identification before cashing a check at my bank.

_____ 8.   Many students who watched the television series on astronomy were better able to understand the theories of Galileo and Kepler as explained by their professor.

_____ 9.   Con plays golf five days a week, which angers his wife.

_____ 10.   Anne's ability to solve difficult mathematical problems is partly due to the fact that her father had been one.

_____ 11.   The identity of the witness was concealed in order to protect her.

_____ 12.   Beginning skiers who have not taken lessons run the risk of injury if they try to ski on the expert ski runs and trails immediately.

_____ 13.   Statistics have clearly demonstrated that drivers who do not use their seatbelts are more likely to suffer an injury if you have an accident.

_____ 14.   The new sales clerk did not know how to use a cash register, but he denied it.

_____ 15.   The oboe, a member of the woodwind family, has many beautiful concertos written for it.

B. *In the space before each number write the letter corresponding to the correct pronoun.*

_____ 16. Every new drug must pass rigorous tests before (a. it   b. they) can be approved by the Food and Drug Administration.

_____ 17. (a. These   b. This) kind of rose will not bloom in cold climates.

_____ 18. Both the painter and the carpenter have submitted (a. his   b. their) estimates.

_____ 19. Many an inexperienced mountain climber has lost (a. his   b. their) life attempting to reach the top of Kilimanjaro.

_____ 20. Jangling your car keys or constantly looking at your wristwatch can be signs that (a. one is   b. you are) impatient.

_____ 21. Each magazine and book was cataloged according to (a. its   b. their) subject.

_____ 22. When you visit a foreign country for the first time, (a. Americans b. you) should prepare by studying travel books and learning a few appropriate phrases.

_____ 23. Mrs. Alvarez said that each of us was responsible for preparing (a. his or her   b. our) own meals.

_____ 24. Senator Carlson told the panel that (a. that   b. those) kind of proposed federal regulation would discourage individual savings.

_____ 25. The cast of the play was praised by the director for (a. its   b. their) performance on opening night.

© 2001 Addison-Wesley Educational Publishers Inc.

►Review Test 6-B

Common Errors in Pronoun Agreement and Reference

A. In the space provided, write the letter corresponding to the kind of error in pronoun usage each sentence contains. If the sentence is correct, write "d."

a. shift in person   b. unclear pronoun reference   c. failure to agree in number   d. correct

_____ 1. Neither of his two daughters has their own telephone.

_____ 2. The first time an American drives a car in England, they are likely to be confused by the movement of traffic.

_____ 3. Lavern worked hard and saved her money, which surprised her parents.

_____ 4. Everyone is entitled to their own opinion with respect to the best candidate.

_____ 5. Many people in this country are alcoholics, which is unfortunate.

_____ 6. Both Jerry and Rudy were upset with his semester grade.

_____ 7. Ralph was disappointed to learn that you have to take a course in calculus in order to major in engineering.

_____ 8. Many refugees from Vietnam have succeeded in maintaining their ancient traditions while adjusting to their new homes in the United States.

_____ 9. Richard has been transferred to the night shift, which pleases his wife very much.

_____ 10. The reason that Constance is such an expert at gardening is that she had once been one.

_____ 11. A beginning reporter on a newspaper is assigned important stories after they demonstrate their ability.

_____ 12. Drivers who listen to music and do not pay attention to the traffic run the risk of causing an accident.

_____ 13. People with fair skin should not stay in the sun too long, or you will risk developing skin cancer.

_____ 14. Lester was too shy to ask Marilyn for a date, and he was teased about it.

_____ 15. Norman bought a bowling ball and a baseball bat and then returned them.

B. *In the space before each number write the letter corresponding to the correct pronoun.*

_____   16.   Every airline passenger must walk through a metal detector before
             (a. he or she   b. they) may board the airplane.

_____   17.   (a. That   b. Those) kinds of puzzles drive me crazy.

_____   18.   Both Scott and Tony have completed (a. his   b. their) homework.

_____   19.   Many a speculator in the stock market has lost (a. his or her   b. their)
             entire fortune.

_____   20.   Cracking your knuckles or tapping your fingers is often a sign that
             (a. one is   b. you are) nervous.

_____   21.   Each dog and cat was classified according to (a. its   b. their) breed.

_____   22.   When studying a foreign language, one should avoid translating each
             word separately into (a. his or her   b. your) own language.

_____   23.   Each of the workers was responsible for furnishing (a. his or her
             b. their) own tools.

_____   24.   (a. That   b. Those) kind of television program tends to glamorize vio-
             lence.

_____   25.   The faculty of the engineering school was praised by the president for
             (a. its   b. their) dedication to the college.

© 2001 Addison-Wesley Educational Publishers Inc.

Writing Paragraphs

Using Transitional Words and Phrases

In the preceding chapters you learned to arrange your ideas in paragraphs in a logical order. Now you will learn that you can make your paragraphs coherent by linking one sentence to the next by using *transitional words and phrases*. They signal the curve and direction of the thought as you read through the paragraph. With them, the reader is prepared for each new idea and can relate each new statement to the last. Without them, a paragraph can sound like a list of unrelated ideas.

Notice how each sentence in the following paragraph stands isolated from the next, making it sound wooden and stiff.

◆ Speaking and writing are different in many ways. Speech depends on sounds. Writing uses written symbols. Speech developed about 500,000 years ago. Written language is a recent development. It was invented only about six thousand years ago. Speech is usually informal. The word choice of writing is often relatively formal. Pronunciation and accent often tell where the speaker is from. Pronunciation and accent are ignored in writing. A standard diction and spelling system prevails in the written language of most countries. Speech relies on gesture, loudness, and the rise and fall of the voice. Writing lacks gesture, loudness, and the rise and fall of the voice. Careful speakers and writers are aware of the differences.

Notice how much smoother this paragraph becomes when transitional words, phrases, and other linking devices are used They make the paragraph more coherent and the thought much easier to follow.

◆ Speaking and writing are different in may ways. Speech depends on sounds; writing, *on the other hand,* uses written symbols. Speech was developed about 500,000 years ago, *but* written language is a recent development, invented only about six thousand years ago. Speech is usually informal, *while* the word choice of writing, *by contrast,* is often relatively formal. *Although* pronunciation and accent often tell where the speaker is from, *they* are ignored in writing because a standard diction and spelling system prevails in most countries. Speech relies on gesture, loudness, and the rise and fall of the voice, *but* writing lacks *these* features. Careful speakers and writers are aware of the differences.

Transitional words and phrases show the relationship between sentences. In some ways they are like traffic signs. They tell the reader what is ahead, warning of a turn or curve, advising when to slow up, and so on.

Examine the following sentences for their use of transitions:

◆ The shortstop took an extra hour of batting practice. *As a result*, she hit two home runs in the game. ("*As a result*" shows how the second sentence is the effect or consequence of the first.)

◆ Many older people look forward to retirement. *However*, some want to continue to work beyond the maximum age limit. ("*However*" alerts the reader to a contrasting idea ahead.)

Here is a list of some of the most common transitional words that connect sentences, making them more coherent.

also	however	on the contrary
although	in addition	on the other hand
and	in conclusion	second
as a result	in fact	similarly
besides	later	still
but	likewise	that is
consequently	meanwhile	therefore
finally	moreover	though
for example	nevertheless	whereas
furthermore	next	yet

Another device to link sentences in the paragraph is the *pronoun*, particularly when it refers to the subject of a previous sentence.

◆ *Jogging* has been popular with people of all ages. *Its* benefits include cures for problems such as insomnia and depression.

The use of *Its* makes it clear that the benefits of jogging are being discussed.

By repeating key words, you can also connect your sentences more smoothly.

◆ The Israeli army is considered to be one of the most efficient in the world. *Israeli* citizens regard it as an honor to serve in their country's armed forces.

If *Israeli* were not repeated, the relationship between the two sentences would not be clear. The *repetition of sentence structure* is another way of establishing a connection between two sentences.

◆ In the United States, most men and women marry before the age of twenty-five. In Ireland, most men and women marry after the age of twenty-five.

© 2001 Addison-Wesley Educational Publishers Inc.

By repeating the structure of the first sentence, the writer has smoothly connected the second sentence.

Exercise A   Using Transitions

Here are ten sentences. Supply the missing transition that seems most fitting for each. Reword the sentences as necessary, but try to avoid using the same transition more than once.

1. Bruce was the most popular student on the campus; _____, his defeat in the Homecoming King election was a surprise.
2. Most employers want their job applicants to have experience; a few, _____, are willing to provide on-the-job training.
3. He vowed never to call her again; _____, he would try to forget her.
4. Venezuela produces more oil than it needs; Japan, _____, imports all of its oil.
5. Carol ignored her sister's advice; _____, she paid too much for her computer.
6. Many so-called American cars are made in other countries; the Behemoth, _____, is made in Japan.
7. Don put the steaks on the grill and then went out to the backyard to talk to his guests; _____, the steaks were burning.
8. Henry's doctor advised him to lose weight; _____, he ate several large potatoes and ice cream for dinner last night.
9. Some college graduates have a choice of jobs awaiting them; computer majors, _____, usually receive handsome offers.
10. _____ she had promised to return in an hour, she never came back; her friends began to look for her.

Exercise B   Fixing Choppy Sentences

The paragraph below is filled with choppy and disconnected sentences. Rewrite the paragraph, inserting the appropriate transitions and connecting words and phrases. Reword the paragraph as necessary.

Humanity's first walk on the moon occurred on the evening of July 16, 1969. American astronauts Neil Armstrong, Mike Collins, and Ed Aldrin lifted off in *Apollo II*. Thirty-four hours passed in flight. They began a live color broadcast of their activities. They traveled about 250,000 miles by the third day. They went into an elliptical orbit around the moon. Their landing craft gradually approached the surface of the moon. With advice from Houston headquarters, they brought the ship down toward the surface above a rocky crater. Armstrong changed his mind and decided to aim for another landing site. They touched down. The astronauts remained in their cabin for six hours. They opened the hatch and slowly went down the ladder. Armstrong reached the second rung. He let down a television camera. His foot landed on the surface. He stopped to say his now famous words: "That's one small step for man, one giant leap for mankind."

Writing Tips

Using Traffic Signs in Paragraphs

Transitions give the reader directions, just as a traffic sign gives a driver a direction. Here are some common transitions arranged according to their purpose:

Addition (developing with ideas and details): and, also, too, furthermore, in addition, then

Time (stating when): before, after, earlier, since, later, now, meanwhile, until

Space (stating where): here, there, above, below, behind, on this side, on the other side, to the right, to the left

Qualification (stating exceptions or modifying): but, however, though, nevertheless, though

Repetition (restating for emphasis and clarity): in other words, in particular, in summary

Exemplification (illustration): for example, that is

Cause and Effect (showing consequences): as a result, consequently, therefore

Comparison and Contrast (showing similarities and differences): similarly, by comparison, likewise, by contrast, on the other hand, on the contrary

Summary (restating chief ideas): in brief, in conclusion, in summary, finally

Exercise C   Using Transitions

The following paragraph describes the steps necessary when pruning roses. Note the use of transitions ("first," "Next," "Also," "This," "Finally"). Read the paragraph carefully and then respond to "a" or "b" below.

When pruning roses, first cut all dead or diseased canes flush with the bud union. Prune any broken or wounded canes or canes with cankers below the injuries. Next, cut out weak canes that are thinner than a pencil. Also remove canes growing into the center of the plant and canes that crisscross. This increases air circulation and discourages diseases. Finally, trim all but three or four of the newest and strongest canes flush with the bud union.

—Better Homes and Gardens, *New Gardening Book*, p. 237

a. In a paragraph of at least six sentences, summarize a memorable episode in a book, movie, or television program. Place transitional words or phrases where needed.

b. In a paragraph of at least six sentences, summarize the steps needed when doing your least favorite task or chore. Place transitional words or phrases where needed.

© 2001 Addison-Wesley Educational Publishers Inc.

Writing Tips

He Said, She Said . . .

Plagiarism is presenting someone's ideas or words as your own without giving proper credit. It is stealing, and many colleges and universities discuss it in their catalogs or student codes. Most of the time, students plagiarize without meaning to; they simply don't know which material requires an attribution. Here are some ways to avoid the quicksand of plagiarism:

- Enclose all quoted passages within quotation marks and state their source immediately before or after.
- Even if you paraphrase (restate or summarize) someone else's ideas, give credit to the source.
- If a fact or statistic is not generally known, provide your reader with the source where you found it.

Computer Activity

Choose a writing suggestion from "a" or "b" in Exercise C on page 132.

When you have finished your paragraph, exchange your file with a classmate who has completed the same exercise.

Use the BOLD command to emphasize the transitional words or phrases that you find in your classmate's paragraph. Ask him or her to do the same for your paragraph.

CHAPTER 7

Common Errors Involving Verbs

One reason why many mistakes are made in verb usage is that every sentence contains at least one verb, and consequently there are more chances to go wrong. Furthermore, the verbs most often used in the English language are irregular, which means that they change in a variety of ways that makes any kind of generalization about them impossible. This also means that they must be memorized. To make matters even worse, verbs change their forms and appearance more often than any other part of speech, offering a series of choices and snares that force us to pick our way through them carefully and deliberately.

Is the case hopeless, then? Is it impossible to learn to use verbs correctly and confidently? Not at all; despite the difficulties mentioned above, problems with verbs fall into a few manageable categories. A common problem, for instance, is not knowing the correct form of the verb needed to express when a particular action is taking place. Another difficulty is not knowing the correct form of an irregular verb. This chapter will present solutions to these and other common problems that many writers and speakers have in using verbs.

Before we begin, however, look at the following sentences to see whether you use the correct verb form. Each sentence contains a verb that is often used incorrectly. The incorrect verb is in brackets.

- ◆ Araceli watched in horror as the dog *dragged* [*not drug*] her new silk blouse across the floor.
- ◆ Although I *saw* [*not seen*] Madonna at the restaurant, I was too shy to ask for an autograph.
- ◆ We got lost in the museum and then discovered that the bus had *gone* [*not went*] without us.
- ◆ Marcia *sneaked* [*not snuck*] out of the play before intermission.

◆ The governor's popularity rating *sank* [*not sunk*] when she broke her promise not to raise taxes.

If you discovered that you have been using any of these verbs incorrectly, this chapter will give you some practical tips for their correct use. We will begin by examining the principal parts of regular and irregular verbs, moving next to the most common problems connected with the use of verbs, including shifts in tense and troublesome pairs like *lie* and *lay*, and *sit* and *set*.

REGULAR VERBS

All verbs have four principal parts: the *present*, the *past*, the *past participle*, and the *present participle*. By learning these four parts you can build all of the verb tenses. Incidentally, the word *tense* comes from a Latin word meaning *time*. When we talk about the **tense** of a verb, therefore, we mean the *time* expressed by a verb: the *present* tense (or time), the *past* tense, and the *future* tense.

Regular verbs form the *past* and *past participle* by adding -*ed* or -*d* to their present tense forms. The past participle is the form used with the helping verbs *have, has,* or *had* or with a form of *be* (*am, is, are, was, were*). The **present participle** is formed by adding -*ing* to the present form, and it is used with a form of *to be* to form the *progressive tenses* (I am studying, I was studying, I have been studying, and so on).

Here are the four principal parts of some common regular verbs.

Present	Past	Past Participle	Present Participle
shop	shopped	shopped	shopping
dance	danced	danced	dancing
wash	washed	washed	washing
love	loved	loved	loving
help	helped	helped	helping

Notice that the past tense form (*shopped, danced, washed,* and so on) and the past participle are identical and are formed by adding -*ed* or -*d* to the present tense form. Remember, too, that the past participle form is used with helping verbs: I *have* talked, I *had* talked, she *has* talked; I *was* helped, we *were* helped, they *had* been helped, and so on.

IRREGULAR VERBS

Irregular verbs are irregular in the way their past tense and past participle forms are made. Instead of adding -*ed* or -*d* for their past tense and past participle forms, irregular verbs change in ways that cannot be predicted. This means that you will have to memorize their past tense and past participle forms. Fortunately, irregular verbs form their present participles in the same way as regular verbs: by adding -*ing* to the present form.

© 2001 Addison-Wesley Educational Publishers Inc.

To understand why it is difficult to make any generalization about irregular verbs, let us examine the verbs *sing* and *bring*. From our familiarity with the English language we know that *sing* is present tense ("I *sing* in church every Sunday"), *sang* is the past tense ("I *sang* last Sunday"), and *sung* is the past participle ("I have *sung* every Sunday this month"). Imagine the confusion of someone learning English who, having mastered *sing*, applies the same changes by analogy to the verb *bring*. He logically concludes that the past tense of *bring* is *brang* ("I *brang* my lunch yesterday") and that the past participle is *brung* ("I have *brung* my lunch"). To native speakers of English these forms are humorous; to others who have not mastered the inconsistencies of our verbs, there is nothing within the verb *bring* to suggest that the past tense and past participle are *brought* ("I *brought* my lunch yesterday" and "I *have brought* my lunch").

The English language contains over two hundred irregular verbs, and they are the verbs most often used. Consult your dictionary if you are not sure about the past tense and past participle forms of irregular verbs. Don't trust your ear; what "sounds right" may only be the result of having repeatedly heard, said, and written the incorrect form. The "piano" you have been playing all these years may be out of tune.

Below is a list of some of the most common irregular verbs, as well as a few regular verbs that often present problems. Practice their correct forms by putting "I" in front of the present and past tense forms, "I have" in front of the past participle form, and "I am" in front of the present participle form: "I *begin*. I *began*. I have *begun*. I am *beginning*." Practice saying them correctly until they sound correct and natural.

Present Tense	Past Tense	Past Participle	Present Participle
I arise	I arose	I have arisen	I am arising
awake	awoke (or awaked)	awaked, awoken	awaking
bear	bore	born (pertaining to birthday) borne (carried)	bearing
begin	began	begun	beginning
blow	blew	blown	blowing
break	broke	broken	breaking
bring	brought	brought	bringing
burst	burst	burst	bursting
catch	caught	caught	catching
choose	chose	chosen	choosing
come	came	come	coming
dig	dug	dug	digging
dive	dived, dove	dived	diving

Present Tense	Past Tense	Past Participle	Present Participle
do	did	done	doing
drag	dragged	dragged	dragging
draw	drew	drawn	drawing
drink	drank	drunk	drinking
drive	drove	driven	driving
drown	drowned	drowned	drowning
eat	ate	eaten	eating
fly	flew	flown	flying
freeze	froze	frozen	freezing
give	gave	given	giving
go	went	gone	going
grow	grew	grown	growing
hang	hung	hung	hanging
hang (execute)	hanged	hanged	hanging
hide	hid	hidden	hiding
know	knew	known	knowing
lay	laid	laid	laying
lead	led	led	leading
leave	left	left	leaving
lie	lay	lain	lying
light	lighted, lit	lighted, lit	lighting
ride	rode	ridden	riding
ring	rang	rung	ringing
rise	rose	risen	rising
run	ran	run	running
see	saw	seen	seeing
set	set	set	setting
shake	shook	shaken	shaking
shine (glow)	shone	shone	shining
shine (polish)	shined	shined	shining
shrink	shrank, shrunk	shrunk, shrunken	shrinking
sing	sang	sung	singing

© 2001 Addison-Wesley Educational Publishers Inc.

Present Tense	Past Tense	Past Participle	Present Participle
sink	sank	sunk	sinking
sit	sat	sat	sitting
sleep	slept	slept	sleeping
sneak	sneaked	sneaked	sneaking
speed	sped	sped	speeding
spring	sprang	sprung	springing
strike	struck	struck	striking
swim	swam	swum	swimming
swing	swung	swung	swinging
take	took	taken	taking
tear	tore	torn	tearing
throw	threw	thrown	throwing
wake	woke, waked	waked, woken	waking
wear	wore	worn	wearing
write	wrote	written	writing

Suggestions for Using Irregular Verbs

1. Resist the temptation to add -ed to an irregular verb: do not write or say catch*ed*, burst*ed*, know*ed*, and so on.
2. Be sure that you use the correct form after forms of the helping verbs *have* and *be*.
   Have, *has*, and *had* are used before the *past participle* (the forms in the third column above):

   - She *has done* several music videos for her newest album.
   - We *had begun* to eat dessert before the guest of honor finally arrived.
   - I *have flown* on an airplane and *ridden* on a train.

   Am, are, is, was, were, has been, and other forms of *be* are used with the past participle forms to form all passive voice verbs:

   - She *was given* a varsity letter for managing the softball team.
   - The dogs *were caught* before they could attack anyone.
   - The sketch *had been drawn* especially for my father and was *hung* over his fireplace.

   Forms of *be* are also used before the *present participle* (the forms in the fourth column above) to form the progressive tenses:

   - Chemistry *is beginning* to make more sense to me.

◆ They *have been winning* more of their matches this season.

◆ The soda cans *were bursting* from being put in the freezer by accident.

TIPS ON FORMING THE PAST TENSE, PAST PARTICIPLE, AND PRESENT PARTICIPLE FORMS

1. To form the past tense and past participle forms of a regular verb, add -ed or -d to the present tense. To form the present participle, add -ing to the present tense.
2. Irregular verbs change their spelling and therefore have to be memorized. Study the list on pages 137–39 for the correct past tense and past participle forms of irregular verbs.

Exercise 7–1

Fill in the blank in each sentence with the past tense form of the verb in parentheses.

1. A new theory about the dinosaurs' extinction _____ recently. (*arise*)
2. Some scientists now believe that a giant comet _____ the earth some 65 million years ago. (*strike*)
3. The comet _____ twenty-five miles deep into the earth's crust. (*dive*)
4. The comet _____ a giant crater when it landed at the tip of the Yucatan Peninsula. (*dig*)
5. A giant fireball soon _____ into the air. (*burst*)
6. The fireball _____ small particles which blocked the sun's light. (*bear*)
7. Eventually, the earth _____ too dark and cold for animals or plants to survive. (*grow*)
8. As a result, dinosaurs and some other animal species _____ extinct. (*become*)
9. Scientists _____ the press some interesting evidence for their theory. (*give*)
10. However, the debate over this theory, which _____ in the early 1980s, still continues today. (*begin*)

Exercise 7–2

Fill in the blank in each sentence with the past participle form of the verb in parentheses.

1. I had not _____ how a bill becomes a law until Jorge explained the process. (*know*)
2. He had _____ to Washington, D.C., to observe Congress last year. (*fly*)
3. The Congressional committee had already _____ hearings to explore and debate the bill. (*begin*)
4. Once the members had _____ several amendments to the bill, they voted on it. (*write*)

© 2001 Addison-Wesley Educational Publishers Inc.

5. To no one's surprise, the bill was _____ an overwhelming vote of approval. (*give*)

6. After the Congressional clerk had _____ the revised bill to the Senate, a separate committee there also voted its approval. (*give*)

7. Finally, the bill had _____ to the President for his approval. (*come*)

8. He had _____ how eagerly the public and politicians supported the bill, but he still thought carefully about it. (*see*)

9. Although conflicting opinions about the bill had _____ his party apart, he soon approved it. (*tear*)

10. Finally, the bill which Jorge and many others in our state supported had _____ a law. (*become*)

USING THE CORRECT TENSE

You have noticed in your study of verbs that they can show different tenses or times by the ending *-ed* or *-d*, by a change in spelling, and by the helping verbs that go with them. The forms of the verb change according to the time expressed—when the action or state of being occurs. Each tense has a specific purpose, and careful speakers and writers select the appropriate tense according to that purpose.

Here is a list of the six common tenses in English and their uses.

- ◆ **Present**   I jog (am jogging).
- ◆ **Past**   I jogged (was jogging).
- ◆ **Future**   I will[1] jog (will be jogging).
- ◆ **Present Perfect**   I have jogged (have been jogging).
- ◆ **Past Perfect**   I had jogged (had been jogging).
- ◆ **Future Perfect**   I will[1] have jogged (will have been jogging).

The following list shows the six common tense forms of *take*. Showing all of the forms of a verb in this way is called **conjugating a verb**.

CONJUGATION OF TAKE

Present Tense

Singular	Plural
I take	we take
you take	you take
he, she, or it takes	they take

---

[1]*Shall* is often substituted for *will* in the future and future perfect tenses.

Past Tense

Singular	Plural
I took	we took
you took	you took
he, she, or it took	they took

Future Tense

Singular	Plural
I will (shall) take	we will (shall) take
you will take	you will take
he, she, or it will take	they will take

Present Perfect Tense

Singular	Plural
I have taken	we have taken
you have taken	you have taken
he, she, or it has taken	they have taken

Past Perfect Tense

Singular	Plural
I had taken	we had taken
you had taken	you had taken
he, she, or it had taken	they had taken

Future Perfect Tense

Singular	Plural
I will (shall) have taken	we will (shall) have taken
you will have taken	you will have taken
he, she, or it will have taken	they will have taken

Each of the six tenses has an additional form called the **progressive form,** which expresses continuing action. The progressive is not a separate tense but an additional form of each of the six tenses in the conjugation. It consists of a form of the verb *be* plus the present participle of the verb.

© 2001 Addison-Wesley Educational Publishers Inc.

Progressive Forms

Present Progressive:	am, are, is taking
Past Progressive:	was, were taking
Future Progressive:	will (shall) be taking
Present Perfect Progressive:	has, have been taking
Past Perfect Progressive:	had been taking
Future Perfect Progressive:	will (shall) have been taking

The present tense is used in the following situations:

a. To express a condition or an action that exists or is going on now.

- Her car *is* fast.
- But she *is driving* under the speed limit.

b. To express an action that is habitual.

- He *competes* in calf-roping events every summer.
- He always *beats* his opponents.

c. To express a truth or an idea that is always true.

- There *is* no game like baseball.
- Cincinnati *is* the home of the Reds baseball team.

The past tense expresses an action or a condition completed in the past.

- The Coalition forces *bombed* Iraq on January 17, 1991.
- Sheldon *visited* his mother last night.

The future tense expresses an action that will take place in the future.

- Javier *will race* his bicycle in the next Olympics.
- Uncle Jim *will be* fifty years old next August.

The present perfect tense is used for an action that began in the past and continues into the present:

- *I have gone* to many freshwater fishing tournaments. [*And I still go.*]
- *I have lived* in Atlanta since 1997. [*And I still live in Atlanta.*]
- Our neighbor's dog *has barked* for two days now. [*And he's still barking.*]

The present perfect tense can also be used for an action that started in the past and has been completed at some indefinite time:

- The fire in the warehouse *has been extinguished.*
- My grandfather *has been* to a doctor only once in his lifetime.

The past perfect tense is used for an action that began and ended in the past. In other words, it describes an action that was completed before something else happened.

- *I had lived* in Mobile before I moved to Atlanta. [NOT: I lived in Mobile before I moved to Atlanta.]
- Everyone knew that Clark's father *had been* a member of President Clinton's cabinet. [NOT: Everyone knew that Clark's father was a member of President Clinton's cabinet.]
- Muriel asked us if we *had watched* the Rose Bowl Parade on television. [NOT: Muriel asked us if we watched the Rose Bowl Parade on television.]

The future perfect tense is used for an action that begins and will end in the future before a particular time.

- Her parents *will have been married* 40 years next Thanksgiving.
- *I will have used up* all of my vacation time by the time your visit ends next week.

A Few Suggestions for Using the Correct Tense

1. Do not use the past tense of a verb when it should be in the present tense.

   - Margie took a course in anthropology last year. She said that it was an interesting subject that studied cultures and societies throughout the world. (Incorrect. "Was" and "studied" imply that anthropology no longer is interesting and does not study other societies and cultures. The correct verbs are "is" and "studies.")

2. Use the present infinitive (*to write, to invent, to leap,* and so on) unless the action referred to was completed before the time expressed in the governing verb.

   - Helen and Rita planned *to stay* [not *to have stayed*] awake for "Saturday Night Live."
   - I am fortunate *to have had* [not *to have*] my life jacket during the stormy boat trip.

3. When a narrative in the past tense is interrupted by a reference to a preceding event, use the past perfect tense.

   - No one could believe that I *had known* him before he became a movie star.
   - The film's ending made no sense to me because I *had missed* the beginning.

© 2001 Addison-Wesley Educational Publishers Inc.

REMINDERS ABOUT TENSES

1. Use the past tense only if the action referred to took place at a specific time in the past.
2. Use the past perfect tense ("had" plus the past participle) only when you want to place a completed action before another action in the past.

Exercise 7-3

In the space before each sentence, identify the tense of the italicized verb by writing past, present, future, present perfect, past perfect, or future perfect.

1. Many people *have criticized* rap music.
2. They *believe* that the themes and languages featured in rap music are too vulgar, violent, or sexist.
3. Perhaps such critics *will be relieved* to know that a growing number of performers are producing a more optimistic breed of rap.
4. Sean "Puff Daddy" Combs, for example, *has won* new fans with his wholesome lyrics and upbeat themes.
5. Puff Daddy *had burst* onto the rap scene as a producer for superstars Mary J. Blige and Jodeci before starting his own singing career.
6. Puff *sold* more than five million copies of his debut album, "No Way Out."
7. Many of his fans especially like his videos, in which he *incorporates* samples of older songs into his own tunes.
8. Missy Elliott *is* another rap artist who is trying to make rap music more acceptable to the listening public.
9. As a child, Elliott *had listened* to wholesome rappers Sugarhill Gang and Run-DMC.
10. She *liked* the way they employed lighthearted lyrics and rhythms into their music.
11. Other rap artists, such as Lauryn Hill and Salt-N-Pepa, *have mixed* elements of pop or rhythm-and-blues into their rap music.
12. Such artists can gather new "crossover" fans who *had enjoyed* pop or rhythm-and-blues but had never liked rap.
13. The Fugees, Timbaland and Magoo, and singer Will Smith *are* among other entertainers who are taking advantage of the public's welcome to playful, uplifting rap music.
14. It's no surprise, then, that rap *has seen* a larger increase in record sales than any other category of music.
15. Music industry analysts now wonder if one day rap music *will have grown* even more popular and profitable than rock and roll.

In the space before each sentence, write the verb shown in parentheses in the tense indicated.

_____ 1. There (*be*—present) some simple steps you can take to prepare your mind and body for an exam.

_____ 2. First, you should (*sleep*—present perfect) at least eight hours the night before the test.

_____ 3. The best students always (*eat*—past) a healthy breakfast before taking their exams.

_____ 4. I (*drink*—present perfect) orange juice for an energy boost before tests this semester.

_____ 5. Some students said their concentration (*grow*—past) stronger after they had drunk a cup of coffee.

_____ 6. Once you (*sit*—present perfect) down at your desk, relax your body and mind.

_____ 7. (*Draw*—present) in a deep breath, hold it for a few seconds, and then release it.

_____ 8. My brother reported that his tension (*leave*—past) his body when he tried this breathing technique.

_____ 9. Make sure you (*lay*—present perfect) your pencils, calculators, and other needed supplies on the desk ahead of time.

_____ 10. Most important, read all of the instructions that the instructor (*give*—present perfect) you before the exam begins.

SHIFTS IN TENSE

Having learned the use of the six common tenses, you should use them consistently, avoiding unnecessary shifts from one tense to another. If, for example, you begin an essay using the past tense to describe events in the past, do not suddenly leap to the present tense to describe those same events. Similarly, don't abruptly shift to the past tense if you are narrating an incident in the present tense. This does not mean that you can't use more than one tense in a piece of writing. It does mean, however, that you must use the same tense when referring to the same period of time.

In the paragraph below, the writer uses past tense verbs to describe events that occurred in the past, and then shifts correctly to the present tense to describe events occurring in the present.

◆ I learned to respect fine craftsmen when I was a young girl helping my father build the house that I lived in until I married. My father had an exact, precise air about him that could make sloppy people like me somewhat nervous. When he

© 2001 Addison-Wesley Educational Publishers Inc.

laid out the dimensions of the house or the opening of a door he did it with an exactness and precision that would not allow for the careless kind of measurements that I would settle for. When he measured a board and told me to cut it, I knew that it would have to be cut in an unwavering line and that it would fit exactly in the place assigned to it. Doors that he installed still fit tightly, drawers slide snugly, and joints in cabinets and mortices can scarcely be detected. Today, when I measure a piece of new screenwire to replace the old or a fence to put around the rosebushes, I can still hear the efficient clicking of his 6-foot rule as he checks my calculations.

This passage is correct in its use of tenses. The events of the past are recalled by the author and narrated in the past tense ("I learned," "My father had," "he laid out," and so on). When she shifts to the present she changes her tense accordingly ("Today, when I measure," "I can still hear," and so on). The paragraph below, on the other hand, is confusing because of its inconsistent use of tenses, shifting from the past to the present tense to refer to the same time.

◆ America's journey to the moon began on the morning of July 16, 1969, when three American astronauts lifted off in Apollo II. Neil Armstrong, Mike Collins, and Buzz Aldrin were on their way to the moon. They will travel at a speed of 24,300 miles per hour. When they were thirty-four hours into the flight, the astronauts begin a live broadcast in color of their activities. Over 500 million people throughout the world have watched. The astronauts report they were impressed by the sight of the earth as they pull away from it. Aldrin said, "This view was out of this world." As they neared the moon's surface, the propulsion system was fired and the spacecraft's velocity goes from 6,500 mph to 3,700 mph as it went into elliptical orbit around the moon. After undocking Eagle, the Lunar Module, they brought it closer to the moon's surface until they are close enough to see a sheet of moon dirt blow by the rocket exhaust. Armstrong shut off the engine and reports, "Tranquillity Base here. The Eagle has landed."

You probably noticed that the first sentence is in the past tense ("America's journey to the moon *began* . . . " and "three American astronauts *lifted* off . . . "), signaling the reader that the paragraph will be related in the past tense. Therefore, we are not prepared for the shift to the present tense in the third sentence ("They *will travel* . . . "), the return to the past tense and subsequent jump to the present tense in the fourth sentence, and so on, through a series of scrambled tenses that continue to jerk the reader from past to present to future without warning. The writer of this paragraph could not decide (or perhaps forgot) when the events he or she was writing about took place. To avoid such confusion, keep in mind the tense forms you are using.

Exercise 7-5

Some of the following sentences contain confusing tense shifts. Rewrite them so that the tenses are consistent. If a sentence is correct, mark "C" in front of it.

1. Most people know that cigarettes were bad for their health, but many don't know exactly how cigarettes affect their bodies.
2. First, the nicotine speeds up the heartbeat and the blood pressure rose.
3. The tar found in cigarettes is even more harmful because it bore ingredients that cause cancer.
4. Tar also brings breathing problems such as shortness of breath and a chronic cough.
5. Your lungs also took in carbon monoxide when you smoke.
6. It then became more difficult for your blood to bring oxygen to vital tissues.
7. People who hang onto their smoking habits took chances with their health.
8. But they enjoy sitting down and lighted up a cigarette.
9. People now began their smoking habits at a younger age than ever before.
   . Most smokers know they should quit, but this is easier said than did.

T Pairs of Irregular Verbs: "Lie" and "Lay"; "Sit" and "Set"

Fo   regular verbs cause more trouble than most of the others: *lie* and *lay*, and *sit* and *set*. U   ry speakers and writers can easily confuse them, but careful speakers and writers observ   eir differences.

Lie a ay

"To li   eans "to remain in position or be at rest." (We are ignoring the other meaning—"to   falsehood"; when *lie* carries this meaning, it is a regular verb.) *Lie* never takes an object— it is, you never *lie* anything down. *Lie* is usually followed by a word or phrase that tells w   (*lie* down, *lie* on the grass, and so on).

The principal parts of *lie* are *lie* (the present tense form), *lay* (the past tense), and *lain* (the past participle). The present participle is *lying*. Because our ear tells us that a "d" sound is usually the sign of the past tense, we are tempted to say or write *laid* for the past tense, instead of the correct form *lay*.

- ◆ **Present:**   Our dog often *lies* by the fire on cold nights.
- ◆ **Past:**   Roberta *lay* [*not laid*] by the pool for hours yesterday.
- ◆ **Present Perfect:** The dishes have *lain* [*not laid*] in the sink all day.

The present participle *lying* is used with helping verbs; it should not be confused with *laying*.

© 2001 Addison-Wesley Educational Publishers Inc.

◆ The children have been *lying* [*not laying*] on the porch and telling ghost stories.
◆ Your soccer ball is *lying* [*not laying*] in the middle of the street.

"To lay" means to place or put something somewhere, and it is a **transitive verb**—that is, it requires an object to complete its meaning: lay the *package* down, lay your *head* down, and so on. The principal parts of *lay* are *lay* (present tense), *laid* (past tense), *laid* (past participle), and *laying* (present participle).

◆ **Present:**   Please *lay* your essay on my desk.
◆ **Past:**   Paul *laid* his Rangers cap on the floor under his chair.
◆ **Present Perfect:** We have *laid* over two hundred bricks in the new driveway.

The present participle *laying* is used with helping verbs; it is followed by an object.

◆ We were *laying* bricks in uneven lines and had to remove them.
◆ As planes flew overhead, the President was *laying* a wreath at the Vietnam War Memorial yesterday.

The most effective way of mastering *lie* and *lay* is to memorize their forms: *lie, lay, lain, lying; lay, laid, laid, laying.*

Sit and Set

"To sit," meaning "to occupy a seat," is an **intransitive verb**—it never takes an object. This means that you never "sit" anything down, for example. The principal parts are *sit* (the present tense), *sat* (the past tense), and *sat* (the past participle). The present participle is *sitting*. Study the following sentences carefully:

◆ Jack Nicholson *sits* in the front row at many Lakers games. (present tense)
◆ We always *sat* in the back row at movies. (past tense)
◆ My sister *has sat* next to us in Spanish class all year. (past participle)
◆ Have you been *sitting* in the balcony for all of the performances this season? (present participle)

"To set" resembles "to lay" in meaning. "To set" means "to put in place," and, like *lay*, it is a *transitive* verb and is followed by another word (a direct object) to complete its meaning.* Its principal parts remain the same in all forms: *set* (present tense,) *set* (past tense),

---

*In a few idioms such as "The hen *sets* on her nest" and "The sun is *setting*," *set* does not require a direct object. In most other cases, however, it is followed by a direct object.

and *set* (past participle). The present participle is *setting*. Study the following sentences carefully.

◆ Jin-Sun always *sets* the compact disc player for "Continuous Play." (present tense)

◆ Last night I *set* the volume control too high and almost blew the speakers. (past tense)

◆ I have *set* your Carly Simon disc back on the shelf. (past participle)

◆ *Setting* his old records near the heater was careless. (present participle)

As in the case of *lie* and *lay*, the most effective way of mastering *sit* and *set* is to memorize their forms: *sit, sat, sat, sitting; set, set, set, setting.*

TIPS **FOR USING "LIE" AND "LAY" AND "SIT" AND "SET"**

1. "To lie" means "to be at rest"; you don't *lie* anything down. The forms are *lie, lay, lain,* and *lying.*

2. "To lay" means "to place or put somewhere"; an object must always follow this verb. The forms are *lay, laid, laid,* and *laying.*

3. "To sit" means "to occupy a seat"; you don't *sit* anything down. The forms are *sit, sat, sat,* and *sitting.*

4. "To set" means "to put in place," and except for idioms like "The hen sets" and "The sun sets," it is always followed by an object. The forms do not change in the present and past tenses or the past participle: *set, set,* and *set.* The present participle is *setting.*

Exercise 7-6

Use the correct form of "lie" and "lay" in the following sentences.

1. Yesterday afternoon I _____ at the beach.
2. It is my favorite stretch of sand, and I have _____ there every summer since childhood.
3. Because the sky was overcast, not many people were _____ on the beach.
4. My radio _____ by my head, playing my favorite tunes.
5. I had _____ my pink volleyball in the sand beside me.
6. After _____ in the sun for a few minutes, I fell asleep.
7. When I woke up, the ball was not where I had _____ it.
8. This was no time to _____ around in the sand; I decided to find it.
9. After _____ the radio and towel next to my ice cooler, I began searching for the ball.

© 2001 Addison-Wesley Educational Publishers Inc.

10. I asked everyone who _____ on the beach if they had seen the ball.
11. After looking everywhere on the beach, I _____ down by the pier and became very despondent.
12. It was all my fault because I had _____ the ball near me, but I had not kept my eye on it.
13. Soon a big but friendly dog _____ down next to me.
14. I caught a glimpse of something pink _____ in the sand by his head.
15. There _____ my prized volleyball—with a few teeth marks but still good as new.

Exercise 7-7

Use the correct form of "sit" and "set" in the following sentences.

1. Everything was finally _____ for our Super Bowl party.
2. Trenton and I had _____ in the kitchen for hours last night, deciding which refreshments to serve.
3. We worried whether there would be room for all of our friends to _____ on the couch in front of the television set.
4. We _____ out some extra folding chairs to make certain that everyone had a seat.
5. "Some of them will _____ on the floor," Trenton said.
6. I had already _____ a tray of cups and plates on the coffee table.
7. I asked him to _____ our new flower vase in the other room so that it would not be broken.
8. Everyone _____ down as soon as they arrived.
9. The children were _____ in front so that they could see the television.
10. Trenton _____ down and soon the ball game began.
11. We didn't notice that our cat had _____ down by my cousin Rita.
12. Rita began sneezing violently and overturned a bowl of popcorn which _____ nearby.
13. I _____ a box of tissues near her and she recovered from her attack.
14. The cat, meanwhile, was now _____ on the television and had somehow become entangled in the antenna.
15. Although several people had _____ by the television set trying to repair the antenna, the picture disappeared, and so did our party.

WRITING SENTENCES

The Correct Form of the Verb

Two common problems when using verbs are dealt with in this chapter: not knowing the correct form of the verb needed to express when a particular action is taking place, and not

Editing Exercise

The paragraph below describes the custom of sending flowers to express various feelings or emotions. As you read, you will notice several errors in verb usage. Improve the paragraph by correcting the errors, revising the sentences when necessary.

The use of sending flowers to express deep feelings begun in early Roman times. One of the most famous were the white lily, which frequently laid in the hands of the Virgin Mary in numerous paintings; it symbolizes purity and chastity. Many other early artists use flowers not only for their beauty but for the subtle meanings they add. The Elizabethans and Victorians had gave meanings to nearly every flower which growed in Britain. By the end of the nineteenth century, however, the language of flowers was largely forgot. Today, most people do not know the meanings that had been associated with many common flowers. Although nearly everyone knows that a red rose means true love, for example, many people do not know that other flowers can convey similar feelings. The red tulip and little blue forget-me-not are declarations of love, and the sturdy ivy, whether growing on a wall or in a porcelain vase setting on a table, promises fidelity. Honeysuckle, which can be growed in most parts of this country, shows love for friends and relatives. While many people send a bouquet to someone in mourning, few choose flowers specifically for meaning, such as marigolds for grief or red poppies for consolation. After you have chose a flower for its specific meaning, you should attach a note which explains that meaning to its recipient.

knowing the correct form of an irregular verb. This writing exercise will give you an opportunity to show that you do not suffer from either problem.

1. Using two of the verbs listed on pages 137–39, write two sentences showing the correct use of the present perfect tense.
2. Using two additional verbs listed on pages 137–39, write two sentences showing the correct use of the past perfect tense.

© 2001 Addison-Wesley Educational Publishers Inc.

3. Using two other verbs on pages 137–39, write two sentences showing the correct use of the future perfect tense.
4. Write a sentence correctly using *sit* in the past tense.
5. Write a sentence correctly using *set* in the past tense.
6. Write a sentence correctly using *lie* in the present perfect tense.
7. Write a sentence correctly using *lay* in the present perfect tense.

© 2001 Addison-Wesley Educational Publishers Inc.

▶Review Test 7-A

Common Errors Involving Verbs

A. *Identify the tense of the italicized verb in each sentence by using the appropriate letter.*

    a. present perfect tense   b. past tense   c. past perfect tense   d. present tense

_____   1.   I *have drawn* the conclusion that most people would rather inherit money than earn it.

_____   2.   Matt usually *drags* his girlfriend along to help him shop for clothes.

_____   3.   Germany *began* its economic recovery immediately after 1945.

_____   4.   We *had begun* to eat when the cook left angrily.

_____   5.   My cousins *have come* from Illinois to visit San Diego.

_____   6.   If we *had known* it was your birthday, we would have taken you to a movie.

_____   7.   The birds *flew* in all directions when they saw Kip's German shepherd dog.

_____   8.   Frank *bears* quite a burden as a single father.

_____   9.   My dog *hides* under the bed when she realizes it's time for her bath.

_____   10.   Beth *has come* to my birthday parties since our college days.

B. *Using the appropriate letter, select the correct form of the verb in the following sentences.*

_____   11.   The news of the rock star's death has (a. shaken   b. shook) the music world.

_____   12.   Angela had (a. taken   b. took) the driver's exam twice before she finally passed it.

_____   13.   The blast of the horn (a. waken   b. woke) Lyle from his nap.

_____   14.   Chris has (a. began   b. begun) to design clothes for fashion shows and plays.

_____   15.   Buck (a. sings   b. sung) beautifully in the shower, but nowhere else.

_____   16.   Within a few years the small sprout had (a. grew   b. grown) into an imposing tree.

_____   17.   Let's hope that George (a. seen   b. sees) the error of his ways.

_____   18.   You (a. have swam   b. have swum) much faster in your recent races.

_____   19.   We fled before the fire had (a. ran   b. run) its course down the valley.

_____   20.   I know where my husband (a. has had   b. has hidden) my Chanukah presents.

_____ 21. The hunter (a. lay   b. laid) a tarp over his tent when the rain began.

_____ 22. Sacramento (a. lies   b. lays) north of San Francisco.

_____ 23. The telephone had (a. rang   b. rung) a dozen times before the message machine clicked on.

_____ 24. Sandor (a. hanged   b. hung) the mistletoe over every door in the house.

_____ 25. Have you (a. ridden   b. rode) in Tom's new Pontiac yet?

© 2001 Addison-Wesley Educational Publishers Inc.

▶Review Test 7-B

Common Errors Involving Verbs

A. Identify the tense of the italicized verb in each sentence by using the appropriate letter. Use the space provided.

a. *present perfect tense*   b. *past tense*   c. *past perfect tense*   d. *present tense*

_____   1.   Herb's driver's license *had expired* before he bought his new car.
_____   2.   The tunnel connecting France and England *began* operating in 1994.
_____   3.   The dog Virgil *lies* at my feet while I watch television.
_____   4.   Many swimmers *have tried* to swim from Santa Monica to Catalina Island.
_____   5.   Before the cement *sets*, I will carefully set a tile in place.
_____   6.   The mood of the voters *depends* on how their own lives are affected.
_____   7.   The stock market *has plummeted* each Friday for the last month.
_____   8.   Too much exposure to sunlight *causes* skin cancer, according to my doctor.
_____   9.   Paul's dirty laundry *lay* in a heap next to his bed.
_____ 10.   Ten writers *had participated* in the preparation of the movie script.

B. Using the correct letter, select the correct form of the verb in the following sentences. Use the space provided.

_____ 11.   Because Sharon was driving too fast, she did not notice the box that was (a. laying   b. lying) in the road ahead of her.
_____ 12.   The mob stormed the police station and (a. dragged   b. drug) the murderer away.
_____ 13.   The tomatoes had (a. laid   b. lain) in the field for a week before they could be gathered.
_____ 14.   Each side claimed that the other had (a. broke   b. broken) the treaty.
_____ 15.   After the clock in the tower had (a. rang   b. rung) three times, the troops rushed to the city square.
_____ 16.   None of the guests at the dude ranch had (a. ridden   b. rode) a horse before.
_____ 17.   During the time-out the players (a. drank   b. drunk) a few sips of water.
_____ 18.   After he had (a. began   b. begun) to play his piano solo, Richard started to feel nauseous.

_____ 19. The salesman claimed that the car had been (a. driven   b. drove) only three thousand miles.

_____ 20. Although Marcus lost the match, he knew that he had (a. did   b. done) his best.

_____ 21. In her senior year at college, Loretta realized that she had (a. chose   b. chosen) the wrong major.

_____ 22. When Charles was still living at home, he (a. gave   b. give) his parents a trip to Europe for their wedding anniversary.

_____ 23. Three paintings by Picasso that (a. hanged   b. hung) in the museum were stolen over the weekend.

_____ 24. In the Wild West days, cattle thieves were often (a. hanged   b. hung).

_____ 25. After my sister had (a. sat   b. set) in the dentist's waiting room for forty-five minutes, she decided to leave.

© 2001 Addison-Wesley Educational Publishers Inc.

Writing Paragraphs

Developing Paragraphs

One of the most common weaknesses in college writing is thin and underdeveloped paragraphs. While there is no exact rule about the minimum number of sentences required in a paragraph, a short paragraph is often a sign that the writer did not follow through in his or her thinking about the topic. As a result, many weak paragraphs consist of little more than a topic sentence and one or two generalities, as if the writer hoped that the reader would complete the thought for the writer.

You will often encounter brief paragraphs in newspaper writing, where the narrow column of the page requires shorter paragraphs for the readers' convenience. Brief paragraphs are also used to show a division or shift in the section of an essay or to draw attention to a startling fact or an important statement. In general, however, it is a good rule to examine carefully any paragraphs that you have written which contain only one, two, or three sentences. The chances are good that they are too thin and skimpy.

The length of a paragraph depends on the topic. The best measuring stick is your topic sentence: what promise did you make in it to your reader? As a result of your topic sentence, are a series of examples expected? Is a definition of a term used in the topic sentence promised? Or do you imply that you will present a comparison or contrast between two objects or people? The expectations raised by your topic sentence determine, to a great degree, the length and the kind of development of your paragraph.

Here is a student-written paragraph describing the last few minutes in a grocery store before it closes for the weekend. The paragraph is underdeveloped because the writer makes a few vague observations, but nothing that we can see or hear—nothing that makes the topic sentence come alive.

◆ The last few minutes before closing time are chaotic at the Vons market where I work. There is confusion everywhere, and everyone is trying to leave on time. Customers and clerks are frantic, and there is always a problem at the last minute.

Notice how vague the paragraph is: "There is confusion everywhere," "Customers and clerks are frantic," and "there is always a problem." But what kind of confusion? Why are the customers and clerks frantic? And what kinds of problems erupt at the last minute? We do not know the answers to these questions, and as a result, the paragraph is blurred and indistinct.

The student was asked to revise his paragraph, and here is his revision. Notice how he has developed the topic sentence with details that make the scene more vivid.

◆ The last few minutes before closing time are chaotic at the Vons market where I work. As the checkout clerks begin to total their registers, the store is invaded by last-minute shoppers desperate for cigarettes, milk, or bread. A few customers are still in the vegetable section squeezing each tomato or cantaloupe as the manager paces by nervously. The butcher and his assistants are removing the meat from the display case and putting it in the freezer, slamming the doors like guards at Fort Knox. A little boy is running up and down the aisles calling out for his mother who returns to the store hysterically looking for him. My friend Manuel, who restocks the shelves, waits impatiently for all of us to leave so that he can bring out his carts full of boxes of canned goods. Finally, the last customer is escorted to the door, and I sit down on an upturned soda case to rest for a few minutes before changing my clothes. In the stockroom a transistor radio begins to blare out rock lyrics. Suddenly there is a tap on the front door of the store. A customer says he didn't get his deposit back on the soda bottle he had returned.

As you can easily see, the revised paragraph is fully developed. It offers the sights and sounds of closing time, helping us to see and hear the chaos mentioned in the topic sentence. By comparing the two versions you can appreciate the difference between an undeveloped and a developed paragraph.

Developing a Paragraph by Examples

One of the most common ways to develop a paragraph is by using *examples*. A paragraph developed in this manner begins with a generalization, which it then supports with specific cases or examples. The examples should be typical, to the point, and supportive of the generalization.

In the following paragraph Maya Angelou, the Nobel Prize poet, uses examples to help you to see and hear the children as well as to smell the evening's refreshments.

The weeks until graduation were filled with heady activities. A group of small children were to be presented in a play about buttercups and daisies and bunny rabbits. They could be heard throughout the building practicing their hops and their little songs that sounded like silver bells. The older girls (nongraduates, of course) were assigned the task of making refreshments for the night's festivities. A tangy scent of ginger, cinnamon, nutmeg and chocolate wafted around the home economics building as the budding cooks made samples for themselves and their teachers.

—Maya Angelou, *I Know Why the Caged Bird Sings*, p. 146.

The next paragraph, written by a student, develops its topic sentence by a series of examples of the ways in which the immune system is being studied.

© 2001 Addison-Wesley Educational Publishers Inc.

◆ The immune system is being studied intensely today, primarily because of its importance to medical research and treatment. The AIDS virus, for example, destroys white blood cells that regulate the immune system, which then loses its ability to respond to new diseases or eliminate cancer. In organ transplants, the immune system may attack the new organ as "foreign" unless physicians can find ways to suppress the response. And many scientists believe that regulating and stimulating immune system molecules like interferon provides the best hope for developing cures for cancer.

Exercise A Developing with Examples

Write a paragraph of at least six sentences on one of the topics below, using examples to develop your paragraph. Begin by writing your topic sentence and then listing specific examples to make the topic sentence clear. Then write your paragraph.

- the benefits of coming from a large family
- athletes who do not fit the image
- immigrants who have overcome handicaps
- corruption in public office
- outstanding local attractions to visit
- a friend with many accomplishments
- people to avoid at a party
- advice to a kid brother or sister
- some stereotypes that are true
- commercials that are actually enjoyable

Writing Tips

For Example . . .

A paragraph developed by example may be based on one example, or it may be developed by a series of examples that support the topic sentence. In either case, you should follow certain guidelines:

- Don't cite exceptions or rare instances as examples to prove your point.
- The best examples are often taken from your own experience. Personal examples aren't always available, of course, but when they are, they have an impact.
- Don't present your examples in a haphazard, random order. Follow a plan.

WRITING PARAGRAPHS

The first paragraph below describes various sounds and the pleasures they give. The second paragraph maintains that ours is a pleasure-oriented society, and it supplies examples to support that idea. Read both paragraphs carefully and then respond to the directions that follow.

a.   When it comes to food, sounds, too, can be aphrodisiac. I myself have a tin ear; I can't even hum "Happy Birthday," but I can unhesitatingly evoke the hissing sound of an onion browning in oil, the syncopated rhythm of a knife mincing vegetables, the burble of the boiling pot into which unfortunate shellfish will fall in an instant, the *crack* of nuts being shelled, the patient song of the mortar grinding seeds; the liquid notes of wine being decanted into goblets, the chink of silver, crystal, and china on the table, the melodious murmur of after-dinner conversation, the satisfied sighs and the nearly imperceptible guttering of candles lighting the dining room.

—Isabel Allende, *Aphrodite*, pp. 109–10.

b.   That we are living in a pleasure-oriented society is difficult to deny. Implicit in TV commercials is a general concern over what one is "getting out of life," and surely what people mean is pleasure. Hair must be shampooed to a silky sheen for the pleasurable touch. Both sexes must wear delicate fragrances to gratify the olfactory sense. Even the quasiserious, somewhat intellectual magazines, directed toward "thinking" people, run page after page of liquor advertisements. In addition, nearly every popular song celebrates the glory of physical lovemaking. The casual talk of celebrities on interview programs often focuses on the high-class lifestyle their fame makes possible.

—Thelma Altshuler and Richard Janaro, *The Art of Being Human*, p. 462

Exercise B   Developing with Examples

Write a paragraph of at least six sentences on one of the topics below, using examples to develop your paragraph. Begin by writing your topic sentence and listing at least three examples to support the topic sentence.

- materialism in America
- everyday heroes
- common fears
- the benefits of writing well
- types of ethnic foods
- the worst pets to have

© 2001 Addison-Wesley Educational Publishers Inc.

Writing Tips

Tougher Than Mount Everest . . .

Do you have a case of writer's block that you can't seem to conquer? The best way to resume writing is to *forget* about writing—that is, for a while. Exercise can help, so take a short jog, walk briskly, or lift some weights. Watch a funny television show to relax your mind. Take a nap: maybe your block is the result of fatigue. If all of these tricks fail, your instructor will have some ideas about how to move your paper along.

Computer Activity

Follow the directions for writing about one of the topics listed in Exercise B on page 162.

When you are finished, transfer your file to another student whom you have selected as a writing partner.

Ask your classmate to list the three examples found in your paragraph. Do the same for his or her paragraph.

CHAPTER 8

Compound and Complex Sentences

One of the marks of a good writer is the ability to use a variety of sentence types. The *simple* sentence is an important weapon to have in your writing arsenal, but it is limited in the ways it can be used and in the jobs it can perform. *Compound* and *complex* sentences give you additional alternatives for expressing your ideas, usually in more precise ways.

In Chapter 3 you were given a brief introduction to compound and complex sentences. In this chapter you will learn more about them, including how they are formed and punctuated and how they can make your writing more exact and interesting.

COMPOUND SENTENCES

You will recall from Chapter 3 that a simple sentence has a single subject-verb combination:

- ◆ The Beatles performed dozens of songs.
- ◆ The Beatles performed and recorded dozens of songs.
- ◆ The Beatles and the Rolling Stones performed dozens of songs.
- ◆ The Beatles and the Rolling Stones performed and recorded dozens of songs.

A **compound sentence** consists of two or more simple sentences (or *independent clauses*) containing closely related ideas and usually connected by a comma and a coordinating conjunction (*and, but, so, for, nor, or, yet*). Below are some examples of compound sentences. Notice how each sentence consists of two independent clauses with related ideas joined with a comma and a coordinating conjunction:

◆ The average income of American young couples has increased, *but* many of them cannot afford to buy a home.

◆ Robin Williams is my favorite actor, *and* "The Bird Cage" is my favorite movie.

◆ Vince offered to help cook dinner, *so* Janet asked him to make the salad.

If these sentences were divided into halves, each half could stand as an independent clause or simple sentence:

◆ The average income of American young couples has increased. Many of them cannot afford to buy a home.

◆ Robin Williams is my favorite actor. "The Bird Cage" is my favorite movie.

◆ Vince offered to help cook dinner. Janet asked him to make the salad.

By combining these simple sentences with commas and coordinating conjunctions, the results are longer, smoother compound sentences. But remember: the independent clauses in a compound sentence must contain a closely related idea, and they are usually joined with a coordinating conjunction. Never try to combine two independent clauses with *only* a comma. The result will be a *comma-splice,* a serious sentence fault. (See Chapter 9 for ways to avoid and to correct comma-splices.)

Exercise 8-1

Below is a series of independent clauses, each followed by a comma. Change each clause into a compound sentence by adding a second independent clause containing a related idea and combining the two clauses with a coordinating conjunction (and, but, so, for, nor, or, and yet). Try to use each of the coordinating conjunctions at least once.

1. Elvis Presley's grave site at his former home, Graceland, is visited by more than 700,000 tourists each year, _____.

2. The Women's National Basketball Association completed its first season in 1997, _____.

3. The senator resigned after being convicted of fraud, _____ _____.

4. Everyone has trouble spelling certain words, _____.

5. Many people are willing to pay high prices to eat greasy snails in French restaurants, _____.

6. A growing number of drivers are forsaking traditional sedans and wagons for large all-terrain vehicles, _____.

7. Theresa gave up her habit of eating a huge bag of potato chips every day, _____.

8. Most people do not pay the entire balance on their credit-card account every month, _____.

© 2001 Addison-Wesley Educational Publishers Inc.

9. Climax, Colorado, is the highest settlement in the United States, _____
    _____.

10. Tony has not seen a movie since *Titanic*, _____.

11. We have heard many clever ways to mark the Millennium, _____
    _____.

12. Our supervisor said our paychecks will be one week late because of a computer
    error, _____.

13. Most colleges require SAT or ACT scores from applicants, _____
    _____.

14. Today's canyon hike was strenuous, _____.

15. We waited more than an hour, _____.

Most independent clauses are connected by coordinating conjunctions. You may, however, use a *semicolon* (;) to connect the clauses if the relationship between the ideas expressed in the independent clauses is very close and obvious without a conjunction. In such cases the semicolon takes the place of both the conjunction and the comma preceding it. For example:

◆ Robert Penn Warren was this country's first official Poet Laureate; he was named on February 26, 1986.

◆ I love enchiladas and chile rellenos; they are my favorite kinds of Mexican food.

When using a semicolon, be certain that a coordinating conjunction would not be more appropriate. Using a semicolon in the following sentence would be confusing because the relationship between the two clauses would not be clear:

◆ **(Confusing)**   I have never played hockey; I like to watch hockey games on television.

By substituting a coordinating conjunction for the semicolon, you can make clear the relationship between the clauses:

◆ **(Revised)**   I have never played hockey, *but* I like to watch hockey games on television.

Tips for Punctuating Compound Sentences

1. If the clauses in a compound sentence are connected by a coordinating conjunction, place a comma in front of the conjunction. Do not try to combine independent clauses with only a comma—the result would be a *comma-splice*, a serious sentence error. Notice the following:

    ◆ **(Comma-splice)**   Calcium is important in one's diet, it is particularly important for pregnant women.

◆ **(Correct)**   Calcium is important in one's diet, and it is particularly important for pregnant women.

2. Do *not* place a comma before a coordinating conjunction if it does not connect independent clauses.

◆ **(Incorrect)**   Herbs add flavor to salads, and are easy to grow.

◆ **(Correct)**   Herbs add flavor to salads and are easy to grow.

◆ **(Incorrect)**   My cousin Phil was born in Syracuse, but later moved to Buffalo.

◆ **(Correct)**   My cousin Phil was born in Syracuse but later moved to Buffalo.

In both sentences above, the conjunctions do not connect independent clauses, and therefore they should not be preceded by commas. In Chapter 11 you will learn the rules for using the comma, including its use before *and* when it connects items in a series.

Exercise 8-2

Place a comma before any conjunction connecting independent clauses in the following sentences. Some sentences do not need commas.

1. There are approximately 2,500 radio stations in the United States which play country music but only about fifty which play jazz.
2. Foreign-language stations are becoming more prevalent and they have increased about thirty-three percent in the past decade.
3. No comedy stations currently exist on radio but comedy programs are among the most popular on television.
4. The Rolling Stones, the Eagles, and Pink Floyd musical groups are comprised of middle-aged or senior citizen performers yet they gross more revenue in ticket sales to their concerts than any other band.
5. Sales of compact discs of gospel, rock, and rap have grown in the last decade but sales of country, pop, and classical CDs have declined.
6. Approximately forty-four million compact discs are sold in the United States annually and sometimes I believe they're scattered on my son's bedroom floor.
7. Sales of cassette tapes are declining so consumers apparently prefer CDs.
8. Some music fans now prefer CDs to live concerts for the recordings are usually clearer.
9. To earn platinum status, an album must sell at least one million LPs, cassettes, or compact discs and must make at least $2 million.
10. Multi-platinum status indicates sales of two million units and at least $4 million in sales.

© 2001 Addison-Wesley Educational Publishers Inc.

11. New albums by Metallica, Toni Braxton, and Hootie and the Blowfish have already attained multi-platinum and their fans continue to buy more copies.
12. Michael Jackson and a trio of opera tenors share the honor of having multi-platinum CDs and some observers find this fact amusing.
13. Reggae legend Bob Marley has been dead for more than a decade yet a recent release of his music managed to sell over a million copies.
14. It is now possible to create one's own CD consisting of songs taken from other CDs and recording companies are uncertain about the effect of this innovation on their sales.
15. Further breakthroughs in the recording industry are inevitable and will undoubtedly increase our listening pleasure.

REMINDERS FOR COMPOUND SENTENCES

1. A compound sentence consists of two or more independent clauses connected by a semicolon or a coordinating conjunction (a word like *and, but,* and *or*).
2. If the clauses in a compound sentence are connected by a coordinating conjunction, place a comma in front of the conjunction.
3. Independent clauses must never be combined with a comma *only.* You must use a comma *and* a coordinating conjunction.

COMPLEX SENTENCES

Because their ideas can be shifted around to produce different emphases or rhythms, **complex sentences** offer the writer more variety than do simple sentences. Complex sentences are often more precise than compound sentences because a compound sentence must treat two ideas equally. Complex sentences, on the other hand, can establish more exact relationships. In Chapter 3 you learned that there are two kinds of clauses: *independent* and *dependent.* An *independent clause* can stand alone and form a complete sentence. A *dependent clause,* however, cannot stand alone. Even though it has a subject and a verb, it fails to express a complete thought. It must be attached to an independent clause in order to form a grammatically complete sentence.

You can recognize dependent clauses by the kinds of words that introduce them, making them dependent. The technical terms for these introducing words are *subordinating conjunctions* and *relative pronouns.* Notice that each of the following dependent clauses begins with such a word:

- ◆ *after* we reached our motel that night
- ◆ *if* you speak a foreign language
- ◆ *because* baldness is inherited
- ◆ *which* shocked everyone

Although these clauses contain subjects and verbs, they do not express complete ideas; therefore, they are dependent clauses. By adding an independent clause to each, however, you can change them into complete, grammatically correct *complex* sentences:

- ◆ After we reached our motel that night, we called our children.
- ◆ If you speak a foreign language, you have an advantage when applying for many jobs.
- ◆ Because baldness is inherited, Steve and his brothers lost their hair while in their late twenties.
- ◆ Our guide in Moscow was a young man who collected heavy metal music cassettes.
- ◆ The graduation speaker made a vulgar gesture which shocked everyone.

Note: A dependent clause is usually followed by a comma when it begins a sentence. If an independent clause comes first, no comma is needed.

The following list contains the most common dependent clause introducing words. Whenever a clause begins with one of them (unless it is a question), it is a dependent clause in a complex sentence.

after	than
although	that
as, as if	though
as though	unless
because	what, whatever
before	when, whenever
how	where, wherever
if	whether
in order that	which, whichever
once	while
since	who, whose, whoever
so that	whom

Exercise 8-3

If the italicized clause in each sentence is a dependent clause, write "dep" in the blank; if it is an independent clause, write "ind."

_____   1.   Several Soviet women are among the heroic pilots *who flew missions in World War Two*.

© 2001 Addison-Wesley Educational Publishers Inc.

_____ 2. *Russians still talk* about how Lily Litvak shot down a dozen German planes during her brief career.

_____ 3. While pursued by enemy planes, Litvak would quickly maneuver *until she was behind her foes and able to attack freely.*

_____ 4. Many German pilots kept an eye out for the white rose painted on Litvak's plane *because they wanted the honor of downing the famous Russian ace.*

_____ 5. *Litvak's final skirmish came* when she was surrounded by a squadron of German planes and shot down by eight of them.

_____ 6. During another famous air battle, *two Soviet women pilots faced 42 German planes* who they knew were planning an attack on a town.

_____ 7. *After the two aces destroyed some German planes,* the other German pilots turned back for home.

_____ 8. After that encounter one of the Soviets parachuted from her exploding plane, and *the other pilot landed safely.*

_____ 9. Perhaps the most stunning story is that which features Irs Kasherina, *who had to stand up and fly through enemy fire while holding her co-pilot's lifeless body off the controls.*

_____ 10. *The Soviet women pilots were respected and feared by their German enemies,* who renamed them the "night witches of the skies."

Exercise 8-4

Add an independent clause to each of the following dependent clauses, thereby creating a complex sentence.

1. After I complete my college education, _____.
2. _____ before I realized it.
3. If I could have any career in the world, _____.
4. Whenever I have a few extra dollars in my pocket, _____
   _____.
5. Because I am older than most students, _____.
6. _____ as though it were all my fault.
7. _____ wherever you are.
8. Once my studies are done for the day, _____.
9. Unless you're willing to pay the price, _____.
10. _____ after I have done my homework.
11. Though the odds were against me, _____.
12. _____ because I was too late.
13. As I drove home from school, _____.
14. _____ since I was tired of cooking my own meals.
15. _____ where my friends and I go for a relaxing evening.

Three Kinds of Dependent Clauses

Now that you can recognize dependent clauses in complex sentences, it is time to take a closer look at them so that you will know how to use them correctly and make your own sentences more interesting and mature.

All dependent clauses share three traits: they all have a subject and a verb, they begin with a dependent clause introducing word, and they must be combined with independent clauses to form a complete sentence. So much for the similarities; let us now consider the differences among them.

Dependent clauses can be used in sentences in three different ways: as adverbs, as adjectives, and as nouns. Consequently, we label them *adverb clauses*, *adjective clauses*, and *noun clauses*.

REMINDERS FOR COMPLEX SENTENCES

1. Dependent clauses begin with words like "after," "if," although," and other words on the list on page 170. A dependent clause cannot stand alone—it must be combined with an independent clause in order to be complete.
2. When a dependent clause begins a sentence, it is followed by a comma. If the independent clause comes first, no comma is needed.
3. A complex sentence is one that contains a dependent clause.

Adverb Clauses   **Adverb clauses** act as adverbs in a sentence—they modify verbs, adjectives, and adverbs. Like single-word adverbs, they can be recognized by the questions they answer. They tell *when, where, why, how,* or *under what conditions something happens.* They can also be recognized because they begin with subordinating conjunctions. In the following sentences the adverb clauses are italicized.

- *When I was a senior in high school*, I broke my arm playing basketball. (The adverb clause tells *when.*)
- Jack's dog follows him *wherever he goes.* (The adverb clause tells *where.*)
- *Because she could speak Spanish fluently*, Edith was hired as an interpreter at the courthouse. (The adverb clause tells *why.*)
- She threw the shot put *as if it were a tennis ball.* (The adverb clause tells *how.*)
- I would help you *if I could.* (the adverb clause tells *under what conditions.*)

Adverb clauses can usually be moved around in a sentence. In the first sentence above, for example, the adverb clause can be placed at the end of the sentence without affecting its

© 2001 Addison-Wesley Educational Publishers Inc.

basic meaning: I broke my arm playing basketball *when I was a senior in high school*. Notice that an adverb clause is followed by a comma when it comes at the beginning of a sentence; when it comes at the end of a sentence, it is not preceded by a comma.

Exercise 8-5

Underline all of the adverb clauses in the following sentences and supply any missing commas.

1. Although interest rates on credit cards are high many cardholders do not mind paying hundreds of dollars a year in interest.
2. Because credit cards are a profitable business for banks the competition for new customers is heating up.
3. More than ten million consumers applied for cards when AT&T introduced its Universal card.
4. Because more than six thousand financial institutions issue cards many issuers of cards are trying to stand out from the competition.
5. They offer such benefits as travel discounts, contributions to charities, and other features when cardholders use their cards to charge anything from meals to vacations.
6. Studies have shown that the use of charge cards stimulates spending because it is not necessary to have cash at hand.
7. Fast-food customers, for example, spend twice as much on average when they use a credit card.
8. Although most U.S. consumer spending is by cash and checks the use of plastic cards is increasing.
9. Though economists talk about the cashless society it will be a few years before such a phenomenon occurs.
10. If the card companies have their way the cashless society will come about sooner rather than later.

Adjective Clauses **Adjective clauses** modify nouns and pronouns in a complex sentence. Like all clauses, they have subjects and verbs. But as dependent clauses, they must be attached to independent clauses to express complete ideas and to form grammatically complete sentences.

Most adjective clauses begin with the relative pronouns *which, whom, that, who,* and *whose,* but a few are introduced by *when, where, why,* and *how.* Adjective clauses usually follow immediately the noun or pronoun they modify. In the following sentences the adjective clauses are italicized:

◆ Anne Frank's diary, *which she began in 1942,* was terminated by her capture and death in 1945. (The adjective clause modifies *diary.*)

◆ Angela's father, *whom you met last night,* is from Baltimore. (The adjective clause modifies *father.*)

◆ Many of the monuments *that have survived in ancient Egypt through thousands of years* were built at a terrible cost in human suffering and death. (The adjective clause modifies *monuments*.)

◆ Any pitcher *who deliberately hits a batter* will be ejected. (The adjective clause modifies *pitcher*.)

◆ Drivers *whose cars are left unattended* will receive citations. (The adjective clause modifies *Drivers*.)

Exercise 8–6

Underline the adjective clauses in the following sentences. In the space before each sentence, write the noun or pronoun modified by the clause.

_____ 1. The Great Smoky Mountains, which are in the Appalachian Highlands of Tennessee and North Carolina, received their name from the smoke-like haze enveloping them.

_____ 2. I spent last weekend visiting the Smoky Mountains with my uncle Joe, who is a trained naturalist.

_____ 3. We saw many of the 230 species of birds that live in the Smoky Mountains, including rarely seen eagles and falcons.

_____ 4. We hiked up to some craggy mountain heights where majestic ravens and hawks make their nests.

_____ 5. I was not used to waking an hour before sunrise, which is the best time of day for bird activity and viewing.

_____ 6. Uncle Joe took photographs of deer, bats, woodchucks, and skunks, which are numerous and easy to spot.

_____ 7. We caught no glimpses of the shy coyote and bobcat that inhabit the Smokies, however.

_____ 8. While walking along the Roaring Fork Nature Trail, we encountered one of the wily black bears that are so prevalent in the Smoky Mountains.

_____ 9. Though frightened and shaky, Uncle Joe and I recalled some tricks which usually keep bears from attacking.

_____ 10. We whistled, clapped, shouted, and made other loud noises which bears hate.

_____ 11. Joe, who is familiar with animals and their customs, told me not to "play dead" to fool the bear.

_____ 12. Because bears are superb climbers, he also told me that scurrying up one of the trees that were behind us should not be attempted.

_____ 13. After several minutes, the bear turned and crossed over to a stream that trickled nearby.

© 2001 Addison-Wesley Educational Publishers Inc.

_____ 14. That night, we camped beside the Cataloochee Creek, which runs through lush meadows and softly sloping dales.

_____ 15. I will never forget the scent of violets and azaleas which sweeten those gentle Smoky Mountain breezes.

Punctuating Adjective Clauses   Perhaps you noticed that the adjective clause in sentences 1 and 11 in Exercise 8-6 and those in the first two examples on page 173 (*which she began in 1942* and *whom you met last night*) were set off by commas. That is because they are *nonessential* (or *nonrestrictive*) adjective clauses. Nonessential clauses merely give additional information about the nouns or pronouns they modify. If we were to omit the adjective clauses in the two examples on page 173 cited above, they would still convey their central idea:

- Anne Frank's diary, *which she began in 1942,* was terminated by her capture and death in 1945. (The adjective clause provides nonessential information.)
- Anne Frank's diary was terminated by her capture and death in 1945. (Although the adjective clause has been removed, we still can identify the subject.)
- Angela's father, *whom you met last night,* is from Baltimore. (The fact that you met her father last night is nonessential.)
- Angela's father is from Baltimore. (By identifying the subject as *Angela's father,* the writer is able to delete the nonessential clause without destroying the sentence.)

The punctuation rule for *nonessential* adjective clauses is easy: they should be set off by commas. Essential clauses—those needed to identify the subject—should not be set off by commas. In the first example on page 174, the omission of the adjective clause would be confusing:

- Many of the monuments were built at a terrible cost in human suffering and death.

This is a complete sentence, but the adjective clause is essential because it tells the reader *which* monuments the writer is referring to. Therefore, it is needed to identify the subject and is not set off with commas:

- Many of the monuments *that have survived in ancient Egypt through thousands of years* were built at a terrible cost in human suffering and death.

The punctuation rule for essential adjective clauses, therefore, is simple: They should *not* be set off by commas. Chapter 11 gives additional examples concerning the punctuation of essential and nonessential clauses.

REMINDERS FOR PUNCTUATING ADJECTIVE CLAUSES

1. If the adjective clause is essential to the meaning of the sentence, do *not* set it off with commas.
2. If the adjective clause is *not* essential to the meaning of the sentence, set it off with commas.

Exercise 8-7

Underline all adjective clauses in the following sentences and supply any missing commas.

1. Woody Harrelson who is familiar to most people as an actor is also an active environmentalist.
2. Anyone who has fair skin should avoid prolonged exposure to the sun.
3. The bus driver whom I recalled knowing in high school apologized for arriving ten minutes late.
4. A couple of orange crates that served as shelves for our stereo and speakers when we were students also held our books.
5. The letter which did not bear a return address or postmark aroused great curiosity and a little fear.
6. Mary Robinson who was the first woman president of the Republic of Ireland now serves the United Nations.
7. The chemistry lab which had inadequate ventilation was closed by health inspectors.
8. The volcano that erupted in the Philippines did millions of dollars of damage.
9. Oil paintings which are worthless during a painter's lifetime are sometimes valuable many years later.
10. Sunspots that are observed only by astronomers can affect weather patterns throughout the year.
11. The Chicago Cubs baseball fans who are well known for their long-suffering hopes for their team continue to hope for a pennant win.
12. Heart attack victims who wish to embark on a vigorous exercise program should first consult with their physicians.
13. Leonard Bernstein who conducted the New York Philharmonic Orchestra was a composer and pianist as well.
14. A clause in the insurance policy which I bought twenty years ago voided my recent claim for auto-body repairs.
15. Television programs that are criticized by the critics are sometimes very popular with the viewers.

Noun Clauses   **Noun clauses** do the same things in sentences that single nouns do: they function as subjects, objects, or subject complements. Unlike adjective clauses and

© 2001 Addison-Wesley Educational Publishers Inc.

adverb clauses, noun clauses do not join independent clauses to form complete sentences. Instead, they replace one of the nouns in independent clauses. As a result, they function as subjects, objects, or subject **complements** of independent clauses. They are usually introduced by such words as *that, who, what, where, how,* and *why.*

◆ As a subject: *Why a particular material reacts with light in a particular way* requires a complicated explanation.

◆ As a direct object: I have just finished reading a book that promises *that the reader can improve his or her I.Q. by following its suggestions.*

◆ As the object of a preposition: When selecting courses, you should be guided by *what your counselor recommends.*

◆ As a subject complement: The sticker price of the car was *more than I expected.*

Exercise 8-8

Underline the noun clauses in the following sentences. Some sentences may have more than one noun clause.

1. I will always remember when I heard that Princess Diana had died.
2. Where we spend New Year's Eve will be decided by a family vote.
3. I was surprised to hear that *Cats* was Broadway's longest-running show.
4. Why Salt Lake City leads the world in the consumption of Jell-O is a mystery.
5. We could not understand how he injured his knee while watching television.
6. The crowd was pleased by what the speaker said.
7. Can you believe that Reno is farther west than San Diego?
8. What Lincoln said that afternoon at Gettysburg will always be remembered.
9. Most people learn ethics by how others act, rather than by what they are told.
10. My grandmother taught me how to make Irish soda bread.
11. Professor Menjee said that Mozart liked to play billiards.
12. How relieved we were to learn that the chemistry test had been canceled.
13. The congressman said that eliminating poverty requires the cooperation of all segments of society.
14. Whatever he does is overlooked by those who work for him.
15. There will always be controversy about who was responsible for the Great Depression of the 1930s.

Exercise 8-9

In the space before each sentence, identify the italicized noun clause according to the way it is used in the sentence, using the following letters:

    a. subject   b. direct object   c. object of preposition   d. subject complement

_____   1.   Even the veteran detectives were shocked by *what they found.*

_____ 2. Roy's cheerful smile was *what we missed* most about him.

_____ 3. *How Donny can eat a quart of ice cream every night and not gain weight* amazes me.

_____ 4. Because of his deafness, Beethoven could not hear *how many of his compositions sounded.*

_____ 5. With her attorney's help, the defendant remembered *where she was on the night of the crime.*

_____ 6. Sales of real estate in our city are affected by *what happens to interest rates.*

_____ 7. *That I would not be selected for the team* had not even occurred to me.

_____ 8. By the look on his face we could tell *what had happened to Glenn.*

_____ 9. Most chefs sample *what they are preparing* as they work in the kitchen.

_____ 10. *How gender affects the workplace* was the topic of Ms. Wallace's speech.

WRITING SENTENCES

Using a Variety of Sentence Types

As you saw in this chapter, one of the marks of a good writer is the ability to use a variety of sentence types. This exercise asks you to try your hand at writing exact and interesting sentences.

1. Write a compound sentence in which the independent clauses are combined with a comma and a coordinating conjunction.
2. Write a compound sentence in which the independent clauses are combined with a semicolon.
3. Write two complex sentences each containing an independent and an adverb clause. Underline the adverb clause in each.
4. Write two complex sentences containing an independent and a noun clause in each. Underline the noun clause in each.
5. Write two complex sentences containing essential (restrictive) adjective clauses. Underline the adjective clause in each.
6. Write two complex sentences containing nonessential (nonrestrictive) adjective clauses. Underline the adjective clause in each, and be sure to punctuate them correctly.

© 2001 Addison-Wesley Educational Publishers Inc.

Editing Exercise

The paragraph below compares and contrasts two types of people: "morning peo-ple" and "night people." You will notice that the sentences in the paragraph lack variety and the use of transitions. As a result, the paragraph seems to be a series of unrelated sentences. Revise the paragraph by combining ideas where appropriate through the use of compound and complex sentences, as well as transitions. Revise the sentences as necessary.

Morning people and night people often clash. Morning people function best in the early hours of the day while night people work better during the evening hours. Morning people are up at dawn to start their day. Night people see the sunset at the beginning of their day. Morning people are cheerful at early hours when night people are still not awake or ready to speak to other humans. Morning people have some advantages over night people. Most work shifts start in the morning. They end in the early evening. This arrangement is perfect for morning people. Night people, however, may find it hard to adjust to rising early. They may suffer low productivity in the mornings. That problem may make them seem lazy or apathetic. Night people, however, have some advantages over morning people. They can use the quiet, late hours of the evening to get work done. They can also enjoy amusements such as nightclubs and parties without tiring. It would be ideal to maintain an energetic pace from the start of a day to its close. Yet most people can only manage enthusiasm during one or the other.

© 2001 Addison-Wesley Educational Publishers Inc.

▶Review Test 8-A

Compound and Complex Sentences

A. *If the italicized group of words in each of the following sentences is an independent clause, write "a" on the line in front of the sentence; if it is a dependent clause, write "b"; if it is not a clause, write "c."*

_____ 1. *After visiting the Grand Canyon,* we plan to visit the Dollhouse Museum in Dallas.

_____ 2. *The right bait makes all the difference in fishing,* the guide told me.

_____ 3. Once you've finished eating, *please wash your dishes and put them away.*

_____ 4. Chip saw a strange orange streak in the sky last night, and he believes *that it was a UFO.*

_____ 5. Haiti has suffered political turmoil *in recent years.*

B. *Using the appropriate letter, identify the structure of the following sentences.*

        a. simple sentence   b. compound sentence   c. complex sentence

_____ 6. Oh, I see a bug!

_____ 7. If you are not careful, the dog will eat your pork chop.

_____ 8. President William McKinley was welcoming guests to the Pan-American Exposition in 1901 when he was assassinated.

_____ 9. Various cultures have different gestures to indicate contempt or anger, a fact that can confuse the foreign visitor.

_____ 10. The opera singer Leontyne Price has retired, but she continues to teach voice.

C. *Each of the following sentences contains one or two blanks. If a comma should be inserted in one or both blanks, write "a" on the line in front of the sentence. If no commas are needed, write "b."*

_____ 11. The Mach _____ which is a unit used to measure sound _____ is named for Austrian physicist Ernst Mach.

_____ 12. Mercury is one of the planets _____ that can be seen without the aid of a telescope.

_____   13.   Dan Vogel _____ who was my neighbor in Des Moines _____ taught me how to dance the tango.

_____   14.   Shopping for clothes bores my husband _____ so I select his new suits.

_____   15.   Her eldest daughter _____ whom you met last night _____ will attend Smith College next fall.

_____   16.   Many commercials for food feature cats _____ and dogs.

_____   17.   Before returning the videotape to the video store _____ be sure to rewind the tape.

_____   18.   The jury ruled that Dominic was responsible for the damage to the car _____ that he struck.

_____   19.   Many women _____ who marry today _____ retain their maiden names.

_____   20.   Can you name an American President and Vice-President _____ who served together but were not elected?

_____   21.   The process of impeachment is such a serious act _____ that it has rarely been attempted in our history.

_____   22.   When the summer was over _____ few traces of the vacation crowd were visible.

_____   23.   Her parents prepared their wills _____ and placed their assets in a trust.

_____   24.   We wanted to thank our guide _____ but we didn't know how to say it.

_____   25.   Anyone _____ who wants to lose weight _____ must exercise as well as diet.

© 2001 Addison-Wesley Educational Publishers Inc.

▶Review Test 8-B

Compound and Complex Sentences

A. *If the italicized group of words in each of the following sentences is an independent clause, write "a" on the line in front of the sentence; if it is a dependent clause, write "b"; if it is not a clause, write "c."*

_____ 1. *Overcoming the disadvantage* of not learning English until he was an adult, Vladimir Nabokov wrote several novels in the English language.

_____ 2. *David Letterman relies on his writers,* but Jay Leno depends on his quick wit.

_____ 3. Cricket is a game *that I have never understood.*

_____ 4. Last week I received a telephone call from a friend *who has been living in England for the past two years.*

_____ 5. *To everyone's surprise, including the owner's,* the horse came in first.

B. *Using the appropriate letter, identify the structure of the following sentences.*

a. simple sentence   b. compound sentence   c. complex sentence

_____ 6. Janice carefully packed up her camera and film, but she forgot them while leaving for the airport the next morning.

_____ 7. Ms. Sheehy claims that it is unwise to cram at the last minute for an examination.

_____ 8. Boasting of his ability to hit the ball out of the park, Chris strode to the plate and promptly struck out.

_____ 9. Mr. Wiggins watered the cabbage while Mrs. Wiggins slept.

_____ 10. Interviewed on television last night, the ambassador announced the date for the opening of the conference.

C. *Each of the following sentences contains one or two blanks. If a comma should be inserted in one or both blanks, write "a" on the line in front of the sentence. If no commas are needed, write "b."*

_____ 11. When George Washington was elected president _____ some of his supporters wanted to make him king of the United States.

_____   12. Many Americans _____ who spend their waking hours watching television _____ have difficulty in separating the programs from reality.

_____   13. Last week the Pulitzer committee announced the recipients of the prizes for outstanding editorial writer _____ and the outstanding cartoonist.

_____   14. Babe Ruth was an outstanding pitcher _____ before he became an outfielder.

_____   15. One of my favorites memories _____ of my trip to Italy last summer was a gondola trip in Venice.

_____   16. A group of senior citizens _____ who had pedaled across the state _____ showed slides of their trip to our club.

_____   17. The old hotel _____ which had been slated for razing next summer _____ burned down last weekend.

_____   18. Despite the popular myth to the contrary _____ snakes can be found in Ireland.

_____   19. Although Jerry has lived in Florida for several years _____ he still misses the changing of the seasons in the Ozarks of Missouri.

_____   20. Photographs of Mars and Saturn have added to our knowledge of the universe _____ and to the formation of our own planet system.

_____   21. The pianist suddenly stopped playing and swatted a fly _____ that had been buzzing about his head.

_____   22. Tamara was brought to this country _____ when she was only an infant.

_____   23. The dog growled menacingly _____ but he remained under the porch.

_____   24. Your offer of help is appreciated_____ but I have solved the problem.

_____   25. Jacqueline complained _____ that I spend too much time at the computer.

© 2001 Addison-Wesley Educational Publishers Inc.

WRITING PARAGRAPHS

DEVELOPING A PARAGRAPH BY COMPARISON AND CONTRAST

In many of your college classes you will be asked to write a paragraph in which you are to point out the similarities and differences between two subjects. Technically speaking, comparisons reveal similarities and differences, and contrasts are concerned only with differences. In practice, however, comparisons suggest likenesses, and contrasts point out differences.

When organized and developed carefully, a paragraph of *comparison and contrast* has a unity and logic that helps the reader understand our ideas. If your paragraph, however, is only a series of scrambled likenesses or differences that leads nowhere, the result will be chaos.

Your first job in organizing your comparison and contrast paragraph is to decide what you want to emphasize: the differences or the similarities between the two objects. This can best be done by making two lists, one for the differences, and the other for the similarities. The next step is to list the differences or similarities in their order of importance, beginning with the least significant and building up to the most dramatic and important.

To be certain that your paragraph has clarity and coherence, you should organize it in one of the following ways: *point-by-point,* or *the block method.*

Point-by-Point

When you compare or contrast each subject point by point, you move back and forth between the two subjects, as in the following paragraph:

◆ College freshmen are often surprised by the differences between their high school days and their experiences in college. In high school, attendance was taken daily and a school secretary often called the student's home to verify that a missing student was not truant. In college, many instructors never take attendance, nor do they make any effort to contact parents concerning absences or failing work. In high school, counselors and teachers gave individual help and attention to students who needed it, and after-school sessions were available for extra tutoring. In college, the student is responsible for his or her own academic performance, and it is up to the student to seek help. In most high schools the students are approximately the same age, but in a typical college class the students range in age from teenagers to grandmothers. Social life is important in high school, but in college it is squeezed in only when possible. Finally, students in high school are often treated as children, but they are assumed to be responsible adults in college.

The Block Method

The second way to organize a comparison or contrast paragraph is to use the block method, first presenting all of the relevant details or aspects of one object, and then all of the corresponding qualities of the other.

The following paragraph follows this pattern, describing first the skills needed for the piano, and then those required for the typewriter or computer keyboard.

◆ Students of the piano often find that their dexterity at the keyboard aids them when learning to use the typewriter or computer. Playing the piano requires the ability to coordinate the movements of the eyes and hands, as the pianist reads the musical score and places her fingers on the appropriate keys. And if the pianist hopes to play with any measure of success, she also needs a sense of rhythm. Using the keyboard of the typewriter or computer requires these same skills. An accurate typist must read carefully the material she is typing, scarcely glancing at her hands on the keyboard. If she wishes to type rapidly, she must develop a rhythmic pattern in the movements of her fingers. It is not surprising, then, that many pianists are excellent typists.

The point-by-point pattern is particularly helpful for complex comparisons and for longer paragraphs. The block pattern (or object-by-object) should be used only when there are few points to be cited. Regardless of the method of organization you use, transitions will help your reader follow your ideas. Words like *however, too, alike, in common, moreover, on the other hand, but, similarly, instead, both,* and so on show relationships between ideas.

Exercise A   Using Comparison and Contrast

Write a paragraph of at least six sentences using either the block or the point-by-point arrangement. The following pairs may serve as topics, or you may choose your own. In either case, write a topic sentence for your paragraph and underline it.

- two popular comedians or entertainers
- two friends or relatives
- two instructors
- two different sports
- two religions
- two political parties
- two views of a controversial subject such as capital punishment

© 2001 Addison-Wesley Educational Publishers Inc.

> ## Writing Tips
>
> ### On the other hand . . .
>
> Paragraphs that compare and contrast objects should have transitions that show the relationship they establish. If you are showing how two things are similar, use words like *similarly, likewise, in like manner.* If you are showing the differences, use words like *but, yet, or, and yet, however, still, nevertheless, on the other hand, on the contrary, in contrast,* and *nonetheless.*

WRITING PARAGRAPHS

The paragraph below describes the two categories of fertilizers. It is developed by presenting contrasting details. Read the paragraph carefully and then respond to the assignment that follows it.

Fertilizers fall into two general categories: organic and inorganic. Organic fertilizers are those formed naturally, including such things as compost, mulch, and manure. Inorganic fertilizers are man-made or mined, often referred to as chemical fertilizers. Organic fertilizers break down slowly and give small amounts of essential nutrients to plants. Inorganic fertilizers act quickly, giving large amounts of these same essential nutrients to plants. The amount of nutrients provided varies with the composition of each fertilizer. Both organic and inorganic fertilizers contain three essential or primary nutrients vital to good plant growth: nitrogen, phosphorus, and potassium (or potash).

—Better Homes and Gardens, *New Gardening Book,* p. 12

Exercise B   Using Comparison and Contrast

Select one of the following pairs and write a paragraph developed by comparison and contrast using either block or point-by-point arrangement.

- street smarts and school smarts
- cities and small towns
- two competing brands of cars
- winners and losers
- e-mail and phone calls
- a novel and its movie version
- two siblings
- two friends
- two politicians

Writing Tips

Could You Eat Pizza at Every Meal?

Your sentences need variety for the same reason your daily diet does: repetition breeds boredom. You should use a variety of sentence types: mix shorter with longer sentences, use compound and complex sentences as well as simple sentences, vary the length of your sentences, don't begin every sentence with the subject, and make sure your vocabulary doesn't become stale. Use a thesaurus or dictionary to find alternatives for words you tend to overuse.

Computer Activity

Using the block arrangement, write a paragraph of comparison and contrast for one of the topics listed in Exercise A on page 186 or B on page 187.

When you have completed your paragraph, exchange files with your writing partner.

Ask you classmate to rewrite your paragraph by using the point-by-point statements in an ascending or descending order of importance. For example, comparing automobiles involves model, price, comfort size of engine, etc. Which of these is most important? What is next in importance?

Be sure to do the same kind of rewriting for your classmate's paragraph.

© 2001 Addison-Wesley Educational Publishers Inc.

9

Correcting Sentence Fragments, Run-on Sentences, and Comma-Splices

The purpose of writing is to communicate facts, ideas, and feelings in a clear and effective manner. If we make serious mistakes in sentence structure or grammar, our readers are confused and irritated, and communication fails. This chapter deals with ways to remedy three serious kinds of errors a writer can make: *sentence fragments*, *run-on sentences*, and *comma-splices*.

SENTENCE FRAGMENTS

A **sentence** is a group of words containing at least one independent clause. It has a subject and a verb, and it conveys a certain sense of completeness. A **sentence fragment,** on the other hand, is a group of words lacking an independent clause. Although it looks like a sentence because it begins with a capital letter and ends with a period or other end punctuation, it leaves the reader "hanging," waiting for more to follow.

Sentence fragments are common in conversation, particularly in responses to what someone else has said or as additions to something we have just said. Their meanings and missing parts are usually clear because of the context of the conversation and the speaker's gestures. In writing, however, it is best to avoid sentence fragments. Although professional writers occasionally use them for special effects, fragments usually suggest that the writer is careless and unable to formulate a complete thought.

189

One of the best ways to avoid sentence fragments is to read your written work *aloud*. Your voice will often detect an incomplete sentence. Another tip: Don't be fooled by the length of a so-called sentence. A long string of words without an independent clause is still a sentence fragment, despite its length. Here is an example of such a fragment:

◆ The election of Nelson Mandela, an end to news censorship, abolition of executions, and powersharing with former white leaders, among other dramatic changes for South Africa.

At first glance this "sentence" is complete—after all, it begins with a capitalized word and concludes with a period. Despite its length, however, it is a sentence fragment because it does not contain an independent clause and therefore cannot convey a complete thought.

The following list contains the most common types of fragments that people write:

1. Prepositional phrase fragments
2. Infinitive fragments
3. Participle fragments
4. Noun fragments
5. Dependent clause fragments

By understanding each type of fragment, you can eliminate them from your writing. Now we will look at the various types of sentence fragments and the ways to correct them.

Phrases as Fragments

One of the most common kinds of sentence fragments is the *phrase*. (A **phrase,** you recall, is a group of words lacking a subject and a verb and acting as a single part of speech within a sentence.) *Prepositional phrases*, *infinitive phrases*, and *participle phrases* are often confused with complete sentences.

The Prepositional Phrase as a Fragment   A prepositional phrase never contains a subject and a verb. Therefore, it can never stand alone as a sentence. The following sentences are followed by prepositional phrases masquerading as sentences:

◆ **(Fragment)**   Some of the world's fastest boats raced for the cherished America's Cup. *Off the coast of southern California.*

◆ **(Fragment)**   Whitey Ford won a record ten World Series games. *During his career as a pitcher for the New York Yankees.*

◆ **(Fragment)**   After delaying it several weeks, Jeff finally began his term paper. *On the subject of religious cults in America.*

© 2001 Addison-Wesley Educational Publishers Inc.

Because prepositional phrases are parts of sentences, the best way to correct this kind of fragment is to join it with the sentence to which it belongs. Notice how the fragments above are eliminated when they are joined to the preceding sentences:

- ◆ **(Sentence)**   Some of the world's fastest boats raced for the cherished America's Cup off the coast of southern California.
- ◆ **(Sentence)**   Whitey Ford won a record ten World Series games during his career as a pitcher for the New York Yankees.
- ◆ **(Sentence)**   After delaying it for several weeks, Jeff finally began his term paper on the subject of religious cults in America.

The Infinitive Phrase as a Fragment   An infinitive is the "to" form of the verb : *to help, to see, to start,* and so on. Many fragments are the result of the writer trying to use an infinitive as the verb in a sentence:

- ◆ **(Fragment)**   *To save money for a new car.* Hyo-Min works an extra shift every week.
- ◆ **(Fragment)**   After final exams, we're going camping at Yosemite. *To relax, catch some fish, and breathe fresh air.*
- ◆ **(Fragment)**   Scientists have repeatedly warned us. *To stop polluting our water before it is unsafe for human use.*

Most fragments consisting of infinitives can be corrected by combining them with the sentence they belong to.

- ◆ **(Sentence)**   To save money for a new car, Hyo-Min works an extra shift every week.
- ◆ **(Sentence)**   After final exams, we're going camping at Yosemite to relax, catch some fish, and breathe fresh air.
- ◆ **(Sentence)**   Scientists have repeatedly warned us to stop polluting our water before it is unsafe for human use.

The Participle Phrase as a Fragment   The present participle is the "-ing" form of the verb: *helping, seeing, starting, walking.* Present participles can never serve as verbs in a sentence unless they have helping verbs with them (see Chapters 2, 3, 4, and 7). Like the infinitive, the participle phrase is often confused with the main verb in a sentence, and the result is a fragment:

- ◆ **(Fragment)**   *Growing up in a large, poor family in the Appalachian Mountains.* He feared that a college education would be an impossibility.
- ◆ **(Fragment)**   Madame Tussaud's Wax Museum is a popular tourist attraction in London. *Featuring likenesses of historical personages reproduced in lifelike poses.*

◆ **(Fragment)**   *Exercising every day, cutting down on calories, and avoiding ice cream and other desserts.* I was able to lose twenty pounds last summer.

Fragments like these can be corrected by attaching them to the independent clauses preceding or following them:

◆ **(Sentence)**   Growing up in a large, poor family in the Appalachian Mountains, he feared that a college education would be an impossibility.

◆ **(Sentence)**   Madame Tussaud's Wax Museum is a popular tourist attraction in London, featuring likenesses of historical personages reproduced in lifelike poses.

◆ **(Sentence)**   Exercising every day, cutting down on calories, and avoiding ice cream and other desserts, I was able to lose twenty pounds last summer.

Another way to correct fragments like these is to supply them with their missing subjects or verbs (or both):

◆ **(Sentence)**   He grew up in a large, poor family in the Appalachian Mountains, and he feared that a college education would be an impossibility. (*Supplying the missing subject and verb and combining the fragment with another sentence*)

◆ **(Sentence)**   Madame Tussaud's Wax Museum is a popular tourist attraction in London. It features likenesses of historical personages reproduced in lifelike poses. (*Supplying the missing subject and verb and creating two separate sentences*)

◆ **(Sentence)**   Because I exercised every day, cut down on calories, and avoided ice cream and other desserts, I was able to lose twenty pounds last summer. (*Changing the fragment into a dependent clause and changing the sentence into a complex sentence*)

Exercise 9-1

Some of the following word groups contain sentence fragments. Underline the fragment, writing on the line the kind of fragment it is. Then correct the fragment by one of the methods explained above. If the group does not contain a fragment, write "C."

_____   1.   Kite-flying has been a popular pastime. Throughout much of human history.

_____   2.   Kites were invented in China about three thousand years ago.

_____   3.   The earliest kites must have been very lightweight and elegant. Consisting of silk sails stretched across bamboo frames.

© 2001 Addison-Wesley Educational Publishers Inc.

_____ 4. Simple and convenient, kites were often used. To perform a variety of tasks.

_____ 5. Measuring weather, delivering love notes, and carrying signals. Kites proved to be accurate, multi-purpose tools.

_____ 6. In fact, one of the Wright brothers' earliest flights was conducted in a sort of motorized kite.

_____ 7. Modern kite-builders are able to make kites that have a special ability. To fly in stunt formations or even hover.

_____ 8. Instead of silk, most kites are now made of rip-stop nylon which was originally used. To make parachutes for American soldiers in World War II.

_____ 9. It is called "rip-stop" because holes and tears will not spread. Throughout the fabric after the kite is accidentally punctured.

_____ 10. Coming in a variety of complex styles and costing as much as a hundred dollars or more. Kites aren't just child's play anymore.

Noun Fragments

Another type of fragment is a noun followed by a modifier with no main verb:

◆ **(Fragment)**   The planet Venus, known to have a rough surface scarred by volcanoes and quakes.

◆ **(Fragment)**   A newly invented crib, comforting babies by imitating movements of the womb.

◆ **(Fragment)**   The annual Candace Awards, given for leadership and achievement by the National Coalition of 100 Black Women.

Most noun fragments can be corrected by supplying the missing verbs:

◆ **(Sentence)**   The planet Venus is known to have a rough surface scarred by volcanoes and quakes.

◆ **(Sentence)**   A newly invented crib comforts babies by imitating movements of the womb.

◆ **(Sentence)**   The annual Candace Awards are given for leadership and achievement by the National Coalition of 100 Black Women.

Dependent Clauses as Fragments

Dependent clauses cannot stand alone as complex sentences. But because they contain subjects and verbs, they often end up as fragments. Dependent clauses can be spotted by the kinds of words that introduce them: subordinating conjunctions like *after, although, as, because,* and *if* or relative pronouns like *who, which,* and *that* (see page 170 for a list of words that introduce dependent clauses).

A dependent clause set off as a complete sentence can be corrected by combining it with the independent clause preceding or following it. Another method is to delete the subordinating conjunction or relative pronoun, thereby converting it to an independent clause.

- ◆ **(Fragment)**   The world's oldest living trees are the bristlecone pines. *Which grow in California.*

- ◆ **(Revised)**   The world's oldest living trees are the bristlecone pines which grow in California.

- ◆ **(Fragment)**   Slave importation was outlawed in 1808. *Although 250,000 more were imported illegally in the next fifty years.*

- ◆ **(Revised)**   Slave importation was outlawed in 1808, although 250,000 more were imported illegally in the next fifty years.

TIPS FOR AVOIDING SENTENCE FRAGMENTS

1. Read your paper aloud. You will usually be able to hear whether or not you have written a fragment.
2. Be sure that every word group has a subject and a verb.
3. Look for the most common types of fragments:
   - Phrase fragments (prepositional phrases, *to* and *-ing* phrases)
   - Noun fragments (a noun followed by modifiers but without a verb)
   - Dependent–clause fragments

Exercise 9-2

Correct any sentence fragments in the following word groups, using any of the methods explained above. If the sentence is correct, write "C" in front of it.

1. Believe it or not, there is a set of rules about how to display the American flag. Which the War Department wrote in 1923.
2. Citizens may display their flags any time they want to. Although it is traditional to fly them only from sunrise to sunset.
3. The White House, unusual because its flag flies both day and night.
4. The awesome sight of the flag above Baltimore's Fort McHenry inspired Francis Scott Key to write "The Star Spangled Banner."
5. No other flag may be flown above or to the right of the U.S. flag. Except at the United Nations headquarters in New York City.

© 2001 Addison-Wesley Educational Publishers Inc.

6. A rule that most Americans are familiar with, that the flag should never touch the ground or floor.
7. A flag may cover the casket of military personnel or other public officials. If it is not permitted to touch the ground or be lowered into the grave.
8. Disposal of a worn or damaged flag in a dignified way, preferably by burning.
9. The U.S. Supreme Court's decision to allow destruction of the flag as a means of political protest was a disappointment to many Americans.
10. Politicians still debate whether American schoolchildren should be required to pledge their allegiance to the flag. Although reciting that oath is not mandatory now.

RUN-ON SENTENCES

A **run-on sentence** is just the opposite of a sentence fragment. It is a group of words that *looks* like one sentence but is actually two sentences run together without punctuation. Normally, of course, two or more independent clauses are separated by a coordinating conjunction or a semicolon. But if the conjunction or the semicolon is omitted, the result is a run-on sentence.

Run-on sentences can be corrected in four ways:

1. By inserting a comma and a conjunction (*and, but, for, or, yet, nor, so*) between the independent clauses.

    ◆ **(Run-on)**   Years ago I took calculus I have forgotten practically all I once knew about the subject.

    ◆ **(Revised)**   Years ago I took calculus, but I have forgotten practically all I once knew about the subject.

2. By changing one of the independent clauses into a dependent clause.

    ◆ **(Run-on)**   In the first inning the Rockies were losing six to two three innings later they were winning twelve to eight.

    ◆ **(Revised)**   Although the Rockies were losing six to two in the first inning, three innings later they were winning twelve to eight.

3. By inserting a semicolon between the two independent clauses.

    ◆ **(Run-on)**   St. Augustine, Florida, is America's oldest city it was settled by Spain in 1565.

    ◆ **(Revised)**   St. Augustine, Florida, is America's oldest city; it was settled by Spain in 1565.

4. By using a period or other end punctuation between the independent clauses, making them two separate sentences.

- ◆ **(Run-on)**   The Gideon decision is one of the landmark cases of the U.S. Supreme Court it grants all poor defendants the right to free counsel.

- ◆ **(Revised)**   The Gideon decision is one of the landmark cases of the U.S. Supreme Court. It grants all poor defendants the right to free counsel.

TIPS FOR AVOIDING RUN-ON SENTENCES

1. Read your paper aloud. Listen for a break marking the end of each thought.
2. Be sure that every independent clause is followed by a period or other end punctuation, a semicolon, or a comma and a coordinating conjunction.

Exercise 9-3

Using any of the methods explained above, correct any run-on sentences in the following word groups. If a sentence is correct, mark "C" in front of it.

1. Wolfgang Amadeus Mozart was a child prodigy of extraordinary musical talent.
2. In Vienna, Munich, Rome, and London, he played, improvised, and composed his audiences cheered wildly.
3. Despite such a promising beginning, Mozart's adult life was often miserable it was filled with tumult and disappointment.
4. He withdrew from friends and companions, becoming increasingly absorbed in his world of music.
5. The Emperor Joseph II was a great fan of Mozart he was hired as the official court composer for Joseph.
6. Despite his father's protests, Mozart married Constanze Weber evidence shows that they were deeply in love.
7. Mozart had not only a passion for the writing of music he was also interested in the mechanical aspects and design of the piano.
8. He wrote several operas which are still performed one of his most popular is *The Marriage of Figaro*.
9. Mozart's operas and concert tours were successful, yet he became financially desperate.
10. While writing his *Requiem Mass* he became seriously ill his fans throughout Europe grieved his death in 1791.

© 2001 Addison-Wesley Educational Publishers Inc.

COMMA-SPLICES

A **comma-splice** consists of two independent clauses connected ("spliced") by only a comma instead of being joined with a comma *and* a coordinating conjunction or with a semicolon. A comma-splice is only slightly less irritating to a reader than the run-on sentence: the writer made some attempt (although mistakenly) to separate two independent clauses. Nevertheless, a comma-splice is a serious error in sentence construction because it is difficult to read. Furthermore, it suggests, like the fragment and run-on sentence, that the writer cannot formulate or recognize a single, complete thought.

Comma-splices can be corrected in the same ways as run-on sentences:

1. By using a period or other end punctuation between the independent clauses, making them two sentences.

   ◆ **(Comma-splice)**   For many years sociologists referred to the United States as a "melting pot," that term has been replaced by the term "pluralistic society."

   ◆ **(Revised)**   For many years sociologists referred to the United States as a "melting pot." That term has been replaced by the term "pluralistic society."

2. By inserting a comma and a coordinating conjunction between the independent clauses.

   ◆ **(Comma-splice)**   Dennis enrolled in a course in hip-hop dancing, now all of the women want to dance with him.

   ◆ **(Revised)**   Dennis enrolled in a course in hip-hop dancing, and now all of the women want to dance with him.

3. By inserting a semicolon between the two independent clauses.

   ◆ **(Comma-splice)**   Sue told me I'd like the new Shania Twain album, she was right.

   ◆ **(Revised)**   Sue told me I'd like the new Shania Twain album; she was right.

4. By changing one of the independent clauses into a dependent clause.

   ◆ **(Comma-splice)**   Miguel studied classical music at a conservatory in New York, he plays drums in a rock group.

   ◆ **(Revised)**   Although Miguel studied classical music at a conservatory in New York, he plays drums in a rock group.

TIPS FOR AVOIDING COMMA-SPLICES

1. Do not use a comma alone to separate your sentences.
2. Read your sentence aloud. When you signal a new thought, use a period or other end punctuation, a semicolon, or a comma *and* a coordinating conjunction.

Exercise 9-4

Using any of the methods explained above, correct any comma-splices in the following word groups. If a sentence is correct, mark "C" in front of it.

1. "Iceman" is the nickname for Similaun Man, his body was recently found in the Similaun Glacier near the border between Italy and Austria.
2. Iceman is a major archeological discovery, Austria and Italy fought over the right to claim and examine him, Austria won custody but must allow Italy access for research.
3. The man is thought to be about 5,300 years old, but he is remarkably well preserved, even his eyeballs are complete.
4. He was about forty years old, scientists could determine his age by measuring tooth wear and certain traits of his bones.
5. Some of Iceman's ribs were apparently broken just before his death, other ribs had been broken much earlier in his life but had healed.
6. Tattoos on the trunk and legs of Iceman may indicate acupuncture or another ancient form of medical treatment.
7. The clothing and equipment found with Iceman are the earliest of their kind found in Europe, they represent the Neolithic period.
8. Iceman was wearing seven or eight pieces of clothing on the day of his death, they were well crafted from eight different animal species.
9. His clothes include a deerskin coat and calfskin shoes, a cape made of woven grass shows that Iceman was probably a farmer or shepherd.
10. About twenty items were scattered near Iceman's body, a copper axe, a quiver with fourteen arrows, and a flint knife are among them.
11. One of the objects is mysterious, it is a small marble disc suspended from a leather strap.
12. As for his last meal, food evidence in his stomach consists of a sloe berry, some cereal grain, and bits of meal bone.
13. Iceman was found when passersby noticed his head partially protruding above the surface of the ice, it is easy to imagine the discoverers' initial horror at their discovery.
14. The cause of Iceman's death was probably a fall, indicated by the ribs which had been broken just before his death.

© 2001 Addison-Wesley Educational Publishers Inc.

15.   Among the questions that remain are the purpose of his trek into the glacier and the reason for his traveling alone.

Comma-Splices and Conjunctive Adverbs

Some comma-splices are the result of the writer's confusing a **conjunctive adverb** with a coordinating conjunction. A conjunctive adverb is a kind of connecting word that looks like a conjunction but is actually an adverb. Conjunctive adverbs are words such as:

◆   accordingly, also, besides, consequently, furthermore, hence, however, moreover, nevertheless, nonetheless, otherwise, therefore

When one of these words appears *within* an independent clause, it is usually set off by commas:

◆   **(Correct)**   It was obvious from her face, *however,* that she was disappointed.

◆   **(Correct)**   I believe, *nevertheless,* that Maxim will continue to play.

◆   **(Correct)**   Iran and Iraq, *moreover,* also plan to sign the treaty.

When a conjunctive adverb appears *between* main clauses, it must be preceded by a semicolon (and often followed by a comma) or a period. If the semicolon or period is omitted, the result is a comma-splice:

◆   **(Comma-splice)**   Hershey is famous for its chocolate, however, the company also makes pasta.

◆   **(Correct)**   Hershey is famous for its chocolate; *however,* the company also makes pasta.

◆   **(Correct)**   Hershey is famous for its chocolate. *However,* the company also makes pasta.

◆   **(Comma-splice)**   The Internal Revenue Service has been warned by Congress to treat citizens more fairly, consequently, it has audited fewer income-tax returns in recent years.

◆   **(Correct)**   The Internal Revenue Service has been warned by Congress to treat citizens more fairly; *consequently,* it has audited fewer income-tax returns in recent years.

◆   **(Correct)**   The Internal Revenue Service has been warned by Congress to treat citizens more fairly. *Consequently,* it has audited fewer income-tax returns in recent years.

Remember: Conjunctive adverbs are not conjunctions and can never by used by themselves to link clauses or sentences.

Exercise 9-5

Correct any comma-splices in the following groups of words. Use any of the methods presented above. If a sentence is correct, mark "C" in front of it.

1. The easiest way to become an American citizen is to have been born here, however, natives of other countries may become citizens through the process of naturalization.

2. To begin this process, aliens must first obtain application forms from a local office of the Immigration and Naturalization Service, or from the clerk of a court which handles naturalization cases.

3. There are several requirements for those who seek citizenship, nevertheless, it is not altogether impossible.

4. Applicants must be at least eighteen years old, moreover, they must be able to prove at least five years of lawful residence in the United States.

5. For spouses of U.S. citizens, on the other hand, the required residence period is usually only three years.

6. Applicants must also show an understanding of the English language, therefore, many aspiring citizens take night classes in English.

7. Knowledge of America's history and government is also required, in fact, the applicants will take a test on these subjects.

8. A fee must be paid by the applicants when they turn in their citizenship application, consequently, they receive an appointment for a hearing.

9. Applicants may bring attorneys with them to the hearing, however, it is optional.

10. There is a thirty-day waiting period after the hearing, eventually the court may approve the applicant's application and finally administer the official oath of citizenship.

WRITING SENTENCES

Avoiding Fragments, Run-on Sentences, and Comma-Splices

This writing exercise requires that you can recognize and correct three of the most serious kinds of errors a writer can make: sentence fragments, run-on sentences, and comma-splices.

1. Write a prepositional phrase fragment. Next, correct it by using one of the methods recommended in this chapter.

2. Write an infinitive fragment. Next, correct it by following the suggestions in this chapter.

3. Write a participle fragment. Next, correct it by one of the methods explained in this chapter.

4. Write a dependent clause fragment. Next, correct it by following one of the suggestions in this chapter.

5. Write a run-on sentence. Correct it by inserting a comma and a conjunction between the independent clauses.

© 2001 Addison-Wesley Educational Publishers Inc.

6. Write a run-on sentence. Correct it by changing one of the independent clauses into a dependent clause.
7. Write a run-on sentence. Correct it by inserting a semicolon between the two independent clauses.
8. Write a comma-splice. Correct it by using a period or other end punctuation between the independent clauses, making them two sentences.
9. Write a comma-splice. Correct it by inserting a comma and a conjunction between the independent clauses.
10. Write a comma-splice. Correct it by changing one of the independent clauses into a dependent clause.

Editing Exercise

The paragraph below describes the various types of cactus throughout the Southwest, and it is developed by using classification as an organizing device. Rewrite the paragraph, eliminating the sentence fragments, comma-splices, and run-on sentences. Revise the sentences as necessary.

No symbol of the Great American Desert is more recognizable than the cactus. Thriving in dryness and heat that would kill most other plants. Cactuses can live for long stretches without water, precious rainwater is stored in their stems. Although a bane to humans, the narrow needles on most kinds of cactus shield the plants from attack by animals. Several types of cactus common throughout the Southwest. Opuntias, usually called prickly pears, the oldest known cactus. They grow broad pads which are flavorful they are used in many Southwestern and Latin American recipes. The graceful organ pipe species, also prized for its tasty fruit. Chollas are common hikers and campers hate them because their long and painful thorns break off easily and are difficult to remove from flesh. The giant saguaro is often likened to a human standing with arms raised and bent at the elbow. The saguaro can grow as high as fifty feet, it may live for more than two hundred years. All of these common types of cactus are endangered as human settlements inch ever closer, bringing pollution and clearing entire groves. Disease, worms, and a growing rodent population, all additional threats to the silent strength and defiant beauty of desert cactus.

© 2001 Addison-Wesley Educational Publishers Inc.

◢Review Test 9-A

Correcting Sentence Fragments, Run-on Sentences, and Comma-Splices

On the line in front of each number write the letter corresponding to the kind of error each sentence contains. If a sentence is correct, write "d" in front of it.

      a. sentence fragment   b. run-on sentence   c. comma-splice   d. correct

_____   1.   Pets that are cute in the pet store often become unmanageable at home.

_____   2.   Twice a year clocks are adjusted this causes confusion for some people.

_____   3.   By studying the nutrition labels on food and calculating the amount of calories and grams consumed daily.

_____   4.   Alex explained that because of the cost of postage, he will no longer send Christmas cards.

_____   5.   Walter was determined to paint his kitchen, his wife complained, however, about the mess he had created.

_____   6.   Laws protecting whales from becoming endangered have been passed by many nations in recent years, some nations, however, are reluctant to enforce the laws.

_____   7.   Our city library furnishes computers for their patrons to use.

_____   8.   Most community college students have part-time jobs and are raising families.

_____   9.   Luis demonstrated the art of making tortillas, he prefers them to bread or rolls.

_____ 10.   Montreal, the largest city in Quebec, where French can be heard in both business and social settings.

_____ 11.   Many libraries are taking steps to preserve their old and valuable books.

_____ 12.   Ralph joked that Galena's typing skills attracted him at first she met him when they were working at an insurance office.

_____ 13.   Many physicians are discouraging their children from becoming physicians, nevertheless, applications for medical school are increasing.

_____ 14.   Being very tall is an advantage when playing volleyball.

_____ 15.   Although the Olympics committee vetoed the idea of recognizing billiards as an Olympic sport.

_____ 16.   Many baseball fans complain that the game is run as a business nevertheless, attendance continues to increase every year.

_____ 17. Arturo was embarrassed to discover that he had forgotten his wallet, his girlfriend paid for the meal.

_____ 18. Swimming is supposed to be the best all-around exercise Marco prefers jogging, however.

_____ 19. Young children expend huge amounts of energy in their daily activities.

_____ 20. The maintenance and expenses related to owning rental property, while considering the benefits and income involved.

_____ 21. Educators used to worry about the amount of time children spent watching television, now they worry about the influence of the Internet.

_____ 22. Hal paid as much for his stereo speakers as I paid for my complete stereo set.

_____ 23. Many people who claim that it is more economical to lease a car than to buy one, as well as to drive a new car every three years.

_____ 24. Terrorism has emerged as one of the serious challenges facing our nation, but our political leaders seem unable to remove it as a threat.

_____ 25. Boys and their games seem to follow a different set of behavioral rules from those observed by girls this phenomenon was discussed in a recent magazine article.

© 2001 Addison-Wesley Educational Publishers Inc.

▶Review Test 9-B

Correcting Sentence Fragments, Run-on Sentences, and Comma-Splices

On the line in front of each number write the letter corresponding to the kind of error each sentence contains. If a sentence is correct, write "d" in front of it.

a. sentence fragment   b. run-on sentence   c. comma-splice   d. correct

_____ 1. A position was advertised for someone who could use a computer and speak Spanish, over two-hundred people applied.

_____ 2. Because the current was swift and the girl could not swim.

_____ 3. The state of Virginia, which boasts of its rich history.

_____ 4. The Chinese and Japanese smoke more cigarettes per capita than Americans do, according to recent studies.

_____ 5. Francisco goes hunting however, he carries a camera instead of a gun.

_____ 6. The motor boat sank in the lake its propeller had become entangled on a submerged cable.

_____ 7. The storm continued throughout the night, in the morning we discovered that all of our food was soaked with water.

_____ 8. Roy's grandmother is ninety-four, and she continues to mow her own lawn.

_____ 9. Spending hours at a time surfing the Internet, like someone casually flipping the pages of an encyclopedia.

_____ 10. Our town has an airport, however, it is too small to accommodate passenger planes and commercial flights.

_____ 11. A large pizza with anchovies, onions, sausage, and mushrooms.

_____ 12. Believing that the threat of flooding has passed, the villagers returned to their homes.

_____ 13. To seek a cure for depression and to determine its causes.

_____ 14. The closing ceremonies of the Olympics were impressive music and fireworks were everywhere.

_____ 15. Jacqueline apparently does not have a "green thumb," none of the flowers that she planted have lived.

_____ 16. Thanksgiving is not a national holiday in Mexico.

_____ 17. Financial advisors recommend that credit card balances be paid as soon as possible, some even urge that credit cards be destroyed.

_____ 18. Many words have interesting histories "anecdote," for example, comes from a Greek word meaning "unpublished."

_____ 19. Phil's career goals are a good-paying job, a beautiful wife, and a vacation home in Miami Beach.

_____ 20. Soccer continues to be the most popular sport in Europe, where it is called "football."

_____ 21. The sale of carbon paper, having declined in recent years because of the advent of photocopying and the computer.

_____ 22. Sheldon finally completed painting his garage he painted it the same color as his house.

_____ 23. Many American Presidents did not have a college degree, said Freddie, citing this fact as his reason for dropping out of college.

_____ 24. Keep an eye on the mainsail, meanwhile, we will repair the tiller.

_____ 25. Realizing that he was uncoordinated and possessing no sense of rhythm, Ralph gave up his dream of being a dancer.

© 2001 Addison-Wesley Educational Publishers Inc.

WRITING PARAGRAPHS

DEVELOPING A PARAGRAPH BY CLASSIFICATION

College instructors often ask their students to sort things or ideas according to their individual characteristics. You might be asked by your literature or drama teacher to show how Shakespeare's plays have traditionally been divided into three large groupings. Your biology instructor may ask you to explain the various types of pollution. Or your political science instructor may want you to contrast the powers granted to the three branches of the Federal government. In all of these assignments, you will be showing how parts of a whole are different. The method of development used is *classification*.

The following paragraph uses classification as a developmental device to show the various types of personality disorders according to the particular characteristic most prominent in each.

◆ Several types of personality disorders have been identified by psychologists and psychiatrists. It must be kept in mind that in given cases the dividing lines are often unclear and that an individual will have some characteristics of more than one type. Nevertheless, three clusters of personality disorders have been devised. Paranoid, schizoid, and schizotypal personality disorders are associated with individuals who often seem odd or eccentric. Histrionic, narcissistic, antisocial, and borderline personality disorders cause their sufferers to be dramatic, emotional, and erratic. Their behavior is more colorful, more forceful, and more likely to get them into contact with mental health or legal authorities than is true of disorders in the first cluster. The final classification includes those who have avoidant, dependent, compulsive, and passive-aggressive personality disorders. In this cluster of disorders, unlike the others, there is often anxiety and fearfulness, and individuals suffering from them are more likely than the others to seek help.

In the next paragraph the author classifies the five basic types of sacrifice as they are presented in the book of Leviticus in the Bible.

◆ The book of Leviticus describes five basic types of sacrifice among the ancient Hebrews. The first was the burnt offering, in which the entire carcass of an animal was sacrificed by fire. The second type was the cereal offering, an offering of a product of the field and obviously not of such serious character as a burnt offering. Third was the peace offering, apparently the form of animal sacrifice for ordinary occasions. Fourth was the sin offering, made for sins committed unwittingly. Fifth was the sacrifice required when one committed a breach against God or against his neighbor through deception, perjury, or robbery.

Words and Phrases Used in Classification Paragraphs

When writing a paragraph based on classification, you will probably need to use words and phrases like the following:

- There are *several types of* reactions to . . .
- There are *numerous kinds of* . . .
- Skin cancers *can be classified as* . . .
- The judicial system *is composed of* . . .
- Facial muscles *comprise* . . .
- *One type of* engine . . .
- *Another type of* engine . . .
- *Finally*, there is . . .

Exercise A   Using Classification

Select one of the following topics and develop it into a paragraph based on classification. Underline your topic sentence.

- campus types
- bores
- part-time jobs
- daytime television
- commercials
- gifts
- bosses

Writing Tips

Writing with Class . . .

When you develop a paragraph by classification, you are sorting things or ideas according to similar characteristics. It is one way of answering the question, "What (or who) is it and where does it belong?" To classify, therefore, is to group things in categories. In this kind of paragraph, be certain that your categories are logical and do not overlap. To divide your student body into "men, women, and athletes," for instance, would be inaccurate because "athletes" obviously includes individuals from the first two groups. Be certain that your parts account for all elements of the object. To divide the federal government into the judicial and legislative branches would be incomplete because the executive branch is omitted. Finally, when classifying, make certain that every item fits into a category and that there are no items left over.

© 2001 Addison-Wesley Educational Publishers Inc.

WRITING PARAGRAPHS

The two paragraphs below are developed by classification. Notice that each begins with a topic sentence that signals the reader how the paragraph will be organized: "Burns are classified as first, second, or third degree . . ." and "There are different shapes of teeth that are analogous to the function they perform." Read both paragraphs carefully and then respond to the assignment that follows.

a.   Burns are classified as first, second, or third degree depending on their depth, not on the amount of pain nor the extent of the burn. A first degree burn involves just the outer surface of the skin. The skin is dry, painful, and sensitive to the touch. A mild sunburn is an example. A second degree burn involves the tissue beneath the skin in addition to the outer skin. The symptoms are swollen, puffy, weepy, or blistered skin. A third degree burn involves the outer skin, tissue beneath the skin, and any underlying tissue or organs. The skin is dry, pale white or charred black, swollen, and sometimes broken open.

—Health Net, *Healthwise Handbook*, p. 167

b.   There are different shapes of teeth that are analogous to the function they perform. On each jaw, in front, there are four teeth with edges adapted for biting— the incisors. On each side of these is a canine tooth that is pointed for tearing food. In back of each canine are two premolar teeth. These are sometimes referred to as the bicuspid teeth because of the presence of two points, or cusps. Since the cusps of the upper and lower premolar teeth mesh in chewing, they act to cut or shear food. Behind the premolars there are three molar teeth on each side of the jaw. These teeth are characterized by relatively flat surfaces that permit the food to be ground between them.

—Frederick Cornett and Pauline Gratz, *Modern Human Physiology*, pp. 231–32

Exercise B   Using Classification

Select one of the following subjects and develop it into a paragraph based on classification. Be sure that your topic sentence lets your reader know how your paragraph is developed.

- clubs on your campus
- flowers in your garden
- neighborhoods in your city
- favorite foods
- types of popular music
- methods of relaxation
- computer games

Writing Tips

What's another word for . . . ?

Consider investing in a thesaurus to keep your word choice fresh, exact, and colorful. A thesaurus is a book that lists the various synonyms of words in various arrangements. Thesauruses do not define words; they give words of similar meaning. Consequently, you have to be careful about selecting a synonym from the list they supply. *Roget's International Thesaurus,* with 256,000 words and phrases, is the most popular thesaurus and is available at most libraries and booksellers. Most word-processing programs include a thesaurus feature which can replace designated words instantly.

Computer Activity

Using the words and phrases that are suggested on page 208, select a topic from Exercise A or B.

Be sure to explain your basis for classification in your paragraph. When you have finished your paragraph, divide your computer screen and list the categories into which the general subject of your paragraph has been divided.

Are the categories sufficient to include all items within your general subject, or do they overlap? If they do, rewrite your paragraph to make clear distinctions.

© 2001 Addison-Wesley Educational Publishers Inc.

CHAPTER 10

Confused Sentences

To write sentences that are not confusing, we have to make certain that they are grammatically correct. This means, for example, that their subjects and verbs agree and that their pronouns and antecedents are linked without confusion. But clarity and correctness depend on other considerations as well. In this chapter we will look at some of the other ways to avoid illogical, inexact, or confused sentences.

MISPLACED AND DANGLING MODIFIERS

Modifiers are words that describe other words in sentences. They may be single words, phrases, or clauses; they may come before the word they modify, or they may follow it. In either case, a modifier should appear near the word it modifies, and the reader should not be confused about which word it modifies.

A **misplaced modifier** is one that is not close to the word it modifies, and as a result it modifies the wrong word. Sentences with misplaced modifiers are usually confusing and often humorous because of the unintended meaning. But by placing the modifier next to the word it modifies or by rewording the sentence, we can make the meaning of such sentences clear.

Notice the unintended meanings in the following sentences; in each sentence, the modifier has been misplaced.

- Yoko Ono will talk about her husband John Lennon who was killed in an interview with Barbara Walters.
- Two cars were reported stolen by the Riverside police yesterday.
- For sale: Mixing bowl set designed to please a cook with round bottom for efficient beating.
- An event that appears every seventy-six years, Professor Silver showed us slides of Halley's Comet.

You probably had little difficulty in trying to unscramble the intended meaning in these sentences. As we will see in this chapter, however, not all sentences can be revised as easily.

Exercise 10-1

Rewrite any of the following sentences that contain misplaced modifiers. If a sentence is correct, write "C" in front of it.

1. Lorri Horn went to dinner with her new husband in a green dress.
2. Carmela gave a Rolex wristwatch to her mother with a diamond-studded face.
3. We talked for several hours about Veronica's trip to Yosemite on her couch.
4. Tom and Solace saw two horror films at the Cinplex which haunted them for weeks.
5. Mr. Thais tried out his new skis on the Alps that he received for Chanukah.
6. Miss Milwe ate a pretzel at the circus which she dipped in cheese.
7. The Health Department charged that hamburgers were served at a restaurant filled with grease and mouse hairs.
8. Ricardo complained that his neighbors yelled at each other while he tried to study in a loud voice.
9. Nancy read a novel which was written by Danielle Steele while she waited for her appointment with the dentist.
10. Last night we heard about the earthquake on television.
11. A long line of tourists waited in front of the hotel for the bus that was to take them to the airport.
12. Diana Garcia discussed the high cost of living with her neighbor.
13. Most colleges in the United States are increasing their efforts to recruit minority students.
14. Miss Kovaric served strawberries to her guests covered in whipped cream.
15. Mark Berger bought a motorcycle for his wife with five speeds.

A variation of the misplaced modifier is the **squinting modifier,** a modifier that usually appears in the middle of a sentence so that it can modify either the word that precedes it or the one that follows it. As a result, the squinting modifier makes the sentence ambiguous. The following sentences contain squinting modifiers:

◆ Applicants who can already dance normally are placed in an advanced class. (Who are placed in the advanced class? Applicants who dance normally? More probably, they are normally placed in an advanced class.)

◆ Senator Olivares decided during the Christmas holiday to announce her opposition to the bill. (While she was on her Christmas holiday, did Senator Olivares decide to announce her opposition to the bill? Or did she decide to announce her opposition as soon as the holiday began?)

© 2001 Addison-Wesley Educational Publishers Inc.

As you can see, sentences with squinting modifiers have two possible meanings. Therefore they can be revised in two ways, depending on the meaning:

◆ Applicants who can dance are normally placed in an advanced class.

◆ Applicants who dance normally are usually placed in an advanced class.

◆ During the Christmas holiday Senator Olivares decided that she would announce her opposition to the bill.

◆ Senator Olivares decided that during the Christmas holiday she would announce her opposition to the bill.

Exercise 10–2

Rewrite any of the following sentences that contain squinting modifiers. If a sentence is correct, write "C" in front of it.

1. Students who study carefully pass the state examination.
2. Jogging remarkably shed my extra pounds.
3. Going to the movies often is expensive.
4. Paddling through the Everglades lazily relaxed us.
5. Hong Kong is under the control of China after more than a century of British rule.
6. Those who gamble secretly take chances with their finances.
7. Elena's story about her vacation in Hawaii that she told slowly put us to sleep.
8. Anyone who sings occasionally hits a wrong note.
9. The tax lawyer advised his clients early in the year to establish a trust fund.
10. Donna reminded her husband regularly to get a physical examination.
11. Tameka's brother promised every week to call her.
12. As he approached the cashier, Ivan realized he had forgotten his wallet.
13. The nurse who was assisting quietly removed the sponge from the open wound.
14. The building that had been painted last week burned down.
15. During the intermission the master of ceremonies announced a change in the cast.

A **dangling modifier** is a modifier that has no word in the sentence for it to modify. It is left "dangling," and as a result it ends up accidentally modifying an unintended word, as in the following example:

◆ After reviewing my lecture notes and rereading the summaries of each chapter, the geology examination was easier than I had thought.

According to this sentence, the geology examination reviewed the lecture notes and reread the summaries of each chapter. But this is obviously not the meaning intended. To correct this sentence, we must first determine *who* was doing the action. By supplying the missing subject, we can then improve the sentence:

- After reviewing my lecture notes and rereading the summaries of each chapter, I found that the geology examination was easier than I had thought.
- **or:** After I reviewed my lecture notes and reread the summaries of each chapter, the geology examination was easier than I had thought.

Here are some more sentences with dangling modifiers:

- Sound asleep, the alarm clock was not heard by Frank.
- Arriving home after midnight, the house was dark.
- Frightened by the noise, the barks of the dog woke us up.

By supplying subjects and rewording these sentences, we can make their meanings clear:

- Sound asleep, Frank did not hear the alarm clock.
- When we arrived home after midnight, the house was dark.
- Frightened by the noise, the dog woke us up by its barking.

TIPS FOR CORRECTING MISPLACED AND DANGLING MODIFIERS

1. Place every modifier close to the word it modifies.
2. If the word meant to be modified is not in the sentence, insert it close to its modifier.
3. Reword or punctuate the sentence so that the intended meaning is clear.

Exercise 10–3

Rewrite any of the following sentences containing dangling modifiers. If a sentence is correct, write "C" in front of it.

1. Barking at passing cars and inspecting the shrubbery of the neighborhood, we found the dog that had escaped from its kennel.
2. Featuring dual airbags and antilock brakes, the Saturn salesman said that the new model was the safest car on the road.
3. Snorting and pawing at the ground, the crowd cheered for the bull.
4. Because of its emphasis on the environment, Professor Sandusky's speech was received favorably by the students.
5. Having forgotten to water the garden, my basil and gardenias died.
6. Waving and smiling to her friends, the television camera slowly panned across the crowd.
7. Having been to Chicago three times, the city is still full of surprises and unexplored pleasures.

© 2001 Addison-Wesley Educational Publishers Inc.

8. Despite its small size the spaniel barked viciously at the mail carrier.
9. Having missed the subway, my essay was turned in late and received a lower grade than I had expected.
10. After removing what seemed to be tons of trash, the room was finally neat and tidy.
11. As a young boy my mother told me stories of her childhood in Armenia.
12. Having painted over the graffiti, the fence regained its former beauty.
13. Stirring the soup constantly, the aroma filled the room.
14. Having never read any science fiction, Isaac Asimov's name was unfamiliar to me.
15. To avoid cavities, you must floss daily.

ILLOGICAL COMPARISONS

A **comparison** is a statement about the relation between two or more things:

◆ Wal-Mart is larger than any other retailer in the United States.
◆ My father's 1990 Chevrolet runs as well as my new Honda.
◆ Tiger Woods won the Masters golf tournament with a lower score than any other golfer in the annual event's history.

When making a comparison, be certain that the things being compared are similar and that your comparison is complete. Omitted words often make the comparison unclear, illogical, or awkward.

◆ **(Unclear)**   Tulsa is closer to Oklahoma City than Dallas.

This sentence is not clear because the comparison is not stated fully enough. Be sure that the comparisons are full enough to be clear.

◆ **(Revised)**   Tulsa is closer to Oklahoma City than it is to Dallas.
◆ **(Illogical)**   The population of Mexico City is growing at a faster rate than that of any major city in the world.

This sentence is illogical because it compares its subject with itself. When comparing members of the same class, use *other* or *any other*.

◆ **(Revised)**   The population of Mexico City is growing at a faster rate than that of any other major city in the world.
◆ **(Unclear)**   The average hourly wage for a woman is lower than a man.

This sentence is unclear because it compares an hourly wage with a man. Be sure that items being compared are comparable.

◆ **(Revised)** The average hourly wage for a woman is lower than a man's.

Exercise 10–4

Revise any of the following sentences that contain illogical comparisons. If a sentence is correct, write "C" in front of the number.

1. Many dry cleaners charge more for cleaning women's garments than men.
2. Mr. Mills-Coyne is in a better mood than yesterday.
3. Life in Manhattan is faster than small towns.
4. Schoolwork at UCLA is much more demanding than many other universities.
5. Juan is a faster runner than his brother Leo.
6. Tara Lipinski was younger than any other world figure skating champion when she won the Olympic Gold Medal.
7. Jupiter is larger than all of the planets in our solar system.
8. Public school teachers in Connecticut are paid a higher wage than the teachers of any state in the nation.
9. Sasha paid less for her Mustang convertible than Clarissa.
10. Tea has been grown, drunk, and traded by the Chinese longer than any country.
11. Prices at the Blue Shoe restaurant are cheaper than the Albatross Cafe.
12. Magic Johnson had more assists than any basketball player when he retired.
13. The average woman has more body fat than a man.
14. Ragweed causes reactions more powerful than any other pollen.
15. Stephen King's novels are more frightening than Kingsley Amis.

CONFUSING ADJECTIVES AND ADVERBS

Adjectives and adverbs are modifiers; they limit or describe other words.

◆ **(Adjective:)** *Moderate* exercise suppresses the appetite.
◆ **(Adverb:)** The surgeon *carefully* examined the sutures.

Many adverbs end in *-ly* (*hurriedly, graciously, angrily*); some of the most common, however, do not (*here, there, now, when, then, often*). Furthermore, some words that end in *-ly* are not adverbs (*silly, manly, hilly*).

Using Adjectives after Linking Verbs

You will recall from Chapter 2 that the most common linking verbs are *be, appear, become, grow, remain, seem,* and the "sense" verbs (*feel, look, smell, sound,* and *taste*). Words that follow such verbs and refer to the subject are *adjectives*—never adverbs. In the follow-

© 2001 Addison-Wesley Educational Publishers Inc.

ing sentences, the adjective (called a *predicate adjective* because it follows the verb and modifies the subject) comes after a linking verb:

◆ Patrick's ideas are *exciting*. (*Exciting* modifies *ideas*.)
◆ Their wedding reception was *expensive*. (*Expensive* modifies *wedding reception*.)
◆ That detergent makes my hands feel *rough*. (*Rough* modifies *hands*.)

The rule for deciding whether to use an adjective or an adverb after a verb, therefore, is simple: if the verb shows a condition or a state of being, use an adjective after it. Here are some additional examples that illustrate the rule:

◆ The hamburger smells *tantalizing*.
◆ Mike's girlfriend appeared *nervous*.
◆ The math final seemed *easy*.
◆ Rimsky looked *handsome* in his new suit.

Most of us would not write or say, "This soup is warmly," or "She is beautifully." In both cases we would instinctively use an adjective rather than an adverb. The choice is not so obvious with "bad" and "well," however. Study carefully the use of these words in the sentences below.

◆ **(Incorrect):**   Ibrahim had some of my homemade soup and now he feels *badly*. (*Badly* is an adverb following a linking verb; it cannot modify the pronoun he.)

◆ **(Correct):**   Ibrahim had some of my homemade soup and now he feels *bad*. (*Bad* is an adjective modifying he.)

◆ **(Incorrect):**   I feel badly about that. (As in the first example above, *badly* is an adverb and therefore cannot modify the pronoun I.)

◆ **(Correct):**   I feel *bad* about that. (*Bad* is an adjective modifying I.)

◆ **(Incorrect):**   That hat looks very *well* on Barbara. (*Looks* is a linking verb, and therefore we need an adjective after the verb to modify the noun *hat*. *Well* is an adverb except when it means "to be in good health.")

◆ **(Correct):**   That hat looks very good on Barbara. (*Good* is an adjective modifying the noun *hat*.)

◆ **(Correct):**   Although Kate has been sick, she looks *well* now. (*Well*, as noted above, is an adjective when it means "to be in good health." In this sentence it follows the linking verb *looks* and modifies *she*.)

Using Adverbs to Modify Verbs

When a verb expresses an *action* by the subject, use an *adverb* after it—not an adjective. Study the following sentences:

- ◆ **(Incorrect):**   Because Jack was unfamiliar with the city, he drove *careful*.
- ◆ **(Correct):**   Because Jack was unfamiliar with the city, he drove *carefully*.

- ◆ **(Incorrect):**   Lorraine spoke very *quiet* of her many accomplishments.
- ◆ **(Correct):**   Lorraine spoke very *quietly* of her many accomplishments.

- ◆ **(Incorrect):**   Teesha picked up the expensive glass *delicate*.
- ◆ **(Correct):**   Teesha picked up the expensive glass *delicately*.

Verbs that sometimes show condition or state of being in one sentence but an action by the subject in another sentence can be troublesome:

- ◆ The dog smelled the meat *carefully*. (*Smelled* is an *action* verb.)
- ◆ The meat smelled *rotten*. (*Smelled* is a *linking* verb.)
- ◆ The alarm sounded *suddenly*. (*Sounded* is an *action* verb.)
- ◆ His cries sounded *pitiful*. (*Sounded* is a *linking* verb.)
- ◆ Claire appeared *tired*. (*Appeared* is a *linking* verb.)
- ◆ Claire appeared *abruptly*. (*Appeared* is an *action* verb.)

TIPS FOR CHOOSING ADVERBS OR ADJECTIVES

The choice of an adverb or an adjective depends on the kind of verb in the sentence:
1. If the verb is *linking* and you want to describe the subject, an *adjective* is correct.
2. If you want to modify a verb that shows *action*, an *adverb* is correct.

Exercise 10-5

Write the letter of the correct word on the line preceding the sentence.

_____   1.   Screw on the lid (a. tight   b. tightly) or the applesauce will not stay fresh.
_____   2.   Please make your dog stop staring so (a. strange   b. strangely) at me.
_____   3.   I wish the group chatting behind us at the theater had been more (a. quiet   b. quietly).
_____   4.   Because of her unreliable car, she rarely arrives (a. punctual   b. punctually) at work.

© 2001 Addison-Wesley Educational Publishers Inc.

_____ 5. Because Sheila has never studied physics, she believes that these experiments are (a. awful   b. awfully) difficult.

_____ 6. Because of his wrenched knee, Sam cannot walk as (a. quick   b. quickly) as his buddies.

_____ 7. Franco felt (a. bad   b. badly) about smashing up his girlfriend's new car.

_____ 8. Bridget was (a. bad   b. badly) hurt in the rugby scrum.

_____ 9. Although Louis's jambalaya tasted (a. delicious   b. deliciously), it contained many calories and grams of fat.

_____ 10. Jerry thought he would pass the driving test (a. easy   b. easily), but he failed it twice.

_____ 11. Horace claimed that he was not treated (a. fair   b. fairly) by his employer.

_____ 12. The music and the costumes matched the play (a. perfect   b. perfectly).

_____ 13. We encountered a herd of cows moving (a. slow   b. slowly) across the road.

_____ 14. Despite her inexperience, Irena played the cymbals (a. loud   b. loudly) and confidently in the concert.

_____ 15. Jeff tied his tie too (a. tight   b. tightly) and became uncomfortable during his job interview.

PARALLEL STRUCTURE

When writing about items in a series, be sure that you present each item in the same grammatical form. In other words, each item should be an adjective or a prepositional phrase or an infinitive, and so on. When all items in a series are in the same grammatical form, the sentence or passage is said to have **parallel structure.**

Notice the use of parallel structure in the following sentences:

◆ Mike _approached_ the plate, _tugged_ at his belt, _adjusted_ his grip, then _swung_ the bat. (parallel verbs)

◆ Tanya sang _softly, confidently,_ and _seductively._ (parallel adverbs)

◆ _To lose weight, to study conscientiously,_ and _to spend less time on the telephone_—these were Ken's New Year's resolutions. (parallel infinitive phrases)

◆ Ahmad quit smoking _because it was an expensive habit, because his wife had quit,_ and _because his doctor had urged him._ (parallel dependent clauses)

Parallel structure is a writing technique worth acquiring because it makes sentences smoother and shows the connection between ideas. For these reasons, professional writers and public speakers often make use of parallel structure. It helps to "bind up" a sentence, making its parts and meaning much easier to grasp.

Study carefully the following excerpt from Abraham Lincoln's second inaugural address. It has been arranged so that the parallelism can easily be seen.

With malice toward none,
  with charity for all,
  with firmness in the right, as God gives us to see the right,
    let us strive on
      to finish the work we are in;
      to bind up the nation's wounds,
      to care for him who shall have borne the battle,
        and for his widow and his orphan,
      to do all which may achieve and cherish
        a just and lasting peace
          among ourselves,
            and
          with all nations.

Contrast the rhythm and clarity of the following pairs of sentences:

- **(Faulty)**   The President claimed that he wanted to clean up the environment, improve the public schools, and reducing crime in the streets. (infinitive, infinitive, and participle)

- **(Parallel)**   The President claimed that he wanted to clean up the environment, improve the public schools, and reduce crime in the streets. (three infinitives)

- **(Faulty)**   Our new fax machine is efficient, inexpensive, and it is easily operated. (two adjectives and a clause)

- **(Parallel)**   Our new fax machine is efficient, inexpensive, and easily operated. (three adjectives)

- **(Faulty)**   Her baby has already started walking and to talk. (participle and infinitive)

- **(Parallel)**   Her baby has already started walking and talking. (two participles)

Correlative Conjunctions

You can also achieve effective parallel construction by using **correlative conjunctions.** As mentioned in Chapter 2 correlatives are connectives used in pairs, and therefore they are handy tools for linking similar grammatical patterns with ideas of similar importance. The most common correlatives are *either/or, neither/nor, not only/but also,* and *both/and.*

Here are some examples of correlative conjunctions used to achieve parallel structure:

- Sheila is proficient not only on the clarinet but also on the saxophone.

© 2001 Addison-Wesley Educational Publishers Inc.

◆ Neither the musicians nor the producers could have predicted the success of rock music on television.

◆ The President's remarks were addressed both to Congress and to the American people.

When using correlative conjunctions, be sure to place them as closely as possible to the words they join.

◆ **(Incorrect)**   She *neither* wanted our advice *nor* our help.
◆ **(Correct)**   She wanted *neither* our advice *nor* our help.

◆ **(Incorrect)**   Ellen will be flying *both* to Minneapolis *and* Chicago.
◆ **(Correct)**   Ellen will be flying to *both* Minneapolis *and* Chicago.

◆ **(Incorrect)**   Richard would *neither* apologize *nor* would he admit that he was wrong.
◆ **(Correct)**   Richard would *neither* apologize *nor* admit that he was wrong.

Exercise 10-6

Rewrite any of the following sentences that contain faulty parallelism. If the sentence is correct, write "C" before it.

1. The governor said that his hobbies were fly-fishing and to play computer games with his grandchildren.
2. Lucretia was advised to follow a diet of reduced fat, low sodium, and she was encouraged to exercise daily.
3. Jesse Jackson is admired for his leadership qualities, his personal courage, and he is a gifted speaker.
4. Many people join health clubs for exercise, for relaxation, and sometimes to find romance.
5. Paula's fears include big dogs, overpriced chocolate, and to ride in elevators.
6. We're meeting at noon for lunch and to chat.
7. Caesar wants to date someone with brains, a good sense of humor, and who likes skydiving.
8. Colorful tube-like flowers can attract hummingbirds and butterflies, and they can enhance your backyard.
9. Rob's goals in life were to wear the latest clothes, drive an expensive car, and also he wanted to have a lot of money.
10. Today's buyer wants a car that is safer to drive, cheaper to maintain, and uses less gas.
11. Many people watch soap operas because they offer bizarre characters, unexpected plot twists, and memorable scenes.
12. Nicolas Cage is admired as an actor because he is not only a dramatic actor but also he is good in comedy roles.

Editing Exercise

The paragraph below contains dangling modifiers, illogical comparisons, incorrectly used adjectives or adverbs, and other weaknesses. Rewrite the paragraph, eliminating any confusing constructions or unclear sentences.

Removing an insect from a child's ear can be real frightening. Sometimes it is difficult to know if an insect is in the ear or something else. Although tempting, the insect should not be killed by poking something in its ear because you may damage the child's ear or make the bug more difficult to remove. Because insects love light, use it to coax the bug out. Pull the child's earlobe real gentle so the light can reach the ear canal easy. You can also shine a flashlight into the ear and tugging its lobe, the insect may emerge from the child's ear. Pouring a few drops of mineral oil into the ear carefully makes the insect float out. You must be sure that it is a bug before trying this method; if it is a piece of popcorn or other expanding item, you may have caused the object to swell and become more difficult to remove. If the insect does not emerge still, or if you are no longer sure that the object is an insect, call a health care professional before anyone else.

13. The ambassador from Iraq would neither apologize nor would he promise to accept the demands of the United Nations.
14. Winston Churchill said that victory would require blood and sweat and toil and tears.
15. Professor Gorra is brilliant, exact, eloquent, and he is helpful as well.

WRITING SENTENCES

Avoiding Confused Sentences

Illogical, inexact, or confused sentences not only irritate your reader: they also fail to make your meaning clear. This writing exercise will help you avoid such sentences.

1. Write two sentences, each containing a misplaced or dangling modifier. Using the suggestions in this chapter, revise each sentence.

© 2001 Addison-Wesley Educational Publishers Inc.

2. Write two sentences, each containing an illogical comparison. Using the suggestions in this chapter, revise each sentence.
3. Write two sentences, each illustrating the correct use of adjectives after linking verbs.
4. Write two sentences, each illustrating the correct use of adverbs modifying verbs.
5. Write two sentences, each using faulty parallel structure. Using the suggestions in this chapter, revise each sentence so that it has parallel structure.

© 2001 Addison-Wesley Educational Publishers Inc.

▶Review Test 10-A

Confused Sentences

A. *Write the letter of the correct word in the space provided.*

_____   1.   After a few golf lessons Bob could hit the ball (a. real   b. really) far.

_____   2.   Consuela felt (a. bad   b. badly) because she thought she was responsible for her team's loss.

_____   3.   If Congress takes the committee's views (a. serious   b. seriously), the law will be revised.

_____   4.   As the limousine turned the corner slowly, the police tried very (a. desperate   b. desperately) to keep back the crowd.

_____   5.   Because Rodney was not wearing his eyeglasses, he read the article (a. slow   b. slowly).

B. *In the space before each sentence, write the letter corresponding to the kind of error each sentence contains.*

       a. misplaced or dangling modifier   b. illogical or incomplete comparison
         c. adjective or adverb used incorrectly   d. faulty parallel structure

_____   6.   The governor said that his hobbies were fly-fishing and to work on old cars.

_____   7.   Having been to Chicago three times, the city is still full of surprises and unexpected pleasures.

_____   8.   To make certain that illegal substances were not applied, the umpires examined all of the baseballs real careful.

_____   9.   The cost of a word processor is more than an electric typewriter.

_____   10.   Having forgotten to water the flowers, my petunias died.

_____   11.   She appeared real embarrassed when she could not recognize the melody.

_____   12.   The police came quick when the shooting began.

_____   13.   To be eligible for early registration, the enrollment forms must be received by September 1.

_____   14.   Despite her small size, Tina can swim faster than any girl in her class.

_____   15.   Featuring antilock brakes and an airbag, the salesman said that the new automobile was the safest car on the road.

_____   16.   Melba was advised to follow a diet of reduced fat, low sodium, and she was encouraged to exercise daily.

_____   17.   Although he was shy as a young boy, Rick can now sing and perform in public real confident.

_____   18.   In order to avoid bee stings, a long coat or jacket is advised.

_____   19.   Winston Churchill was admired for his leadership qualities, his personal courage, and he was an eloquent speaker.

_____   20.   Snorting and pawing at the ground, the crowd anxiously cheered for the bull.

_____   21.   Mister Coleman had to walk somewhat slow because of his injured leg.

_____   22.   Having never read any science fiction, Isaac Asimov's name was unfamiliar to me.

_____   23.   Many dry cleaners charge more for cleaning women's jackets than men.

_____   24.   Mr. Liebowitz complained that his name was often spelled incorrect.

_____   25.   Because of its emphasis on the environment, Professor Markley's speech was received very favorable by the students.

© 2001 Addison-Wesley Educational Publishers Inc.

▶Review Test 10-B

Confused Sentences

A. *Write the letter of the correct word in the space provided.*

_____ 1. Nanette looked (a. sad   b. sadly) at the departing train.

_____ 2. Because the refrigerator was disconnected, the meat smelled (a. bad   b. badly).

_____ 3. Last Friday night we saw a (a. real   b. really) exciting movie about World War II.

_____ 4. Despite her inexperience, Helen did quite (a. good   b. well) in the semifinals.

_____ 5. Because I did not have time to reread my essay, I didn't notice that two words in its title were spelled (a. incorrect   b. incorrectly).

B. *In the space before each sentence, write the letter corresponding to the kind of error each sentence contains.*

a. *misplaced or dangling modifier*   b. *illogical or incomplete comparison*
c. *adjective or adverb used incorrectly*   d. *faulty parallel structure*

_____ 6. The attorney was tall, slender, and seemed to be middle-aged.

_____ 7. Barking at passing cars and inspecting the shrubbery of the neighborhood, we found the dog that had escaped from its kennel.

_____ 8. Selling shoes during the summer and waiting on tables during the school year, my tuition was paid without the help of my parents.

_____ 9. Mr. Conley claimed that students of his generation worked harder than the schools today.

_____ 10. Having missed the assignment, my term paper received a low grade.

_____ 11. The supermarket manager felt happily about the sales campaign.

_____ 12. Ernie has a good sense of humor and can tell a joke really good.

_____ 13. In my opinion, staying up all night to review before an examination is more of a handicap than useful.

_____ 14. The advertisements for the computer claimed that it is real easy to operate.

_____ 15. Trying to think of a way to begin my speech, a funny story came to mind.

_____ 16. To her surprise, Madeline made higher grades in chemistry class than her brother.

_____ 17. Life in Las Vegas is not much different from any city its size.

_____ 18. Prices at a military commissary are usually lower than other retail establishments.

_____ 19. Many people join health clubs for exercise, for relaxation, and so that they can meet others of the opposite sex.

_____ 20. Featuring an electric starter and a four-stroke engine, the salesperson claimed that the lawn mower was the best on the market.

_____ 21. Waving and smiling to their friends, the television camera panned slowly across the crowd.

_____ 22. The natives of the small Pacific island are taller than any of the inhabitants of the area.

_____ 23. Despite its small size, the dog barked very ferocious at the mail carrier.

_____ 24. To receive the discount, the advertisement states that we must purchase the lamp before next Monday.

_____ 25. The firefighters responded very quick when the alarm sounded at the old fireworks factory.

© 2001 Addison-Wesley Educational Publishers Inc.

Writing Paragraphs

Developing a Paragraph by Process and Analysis

"How is it done?" "How did it happen?" These are the questions answered by paragraphs developed by *process and analysis*. Some process paragraphs tell the reader how to change a tire, train a puppy, mix concrete, or plant a tree. Others explain how something happened or how it takes place: how the pyramids of Egypt were built, how the blood circulates through the body, or how the Roman Catholic Church elects a Pope. In all cases the purpose is to provide information to the reader as clearly and directly as possible.

Because all process and analysis paragraphs essentially explain how an act is done or a process happens, their ideas are presented chronologically. Every idea follows the previous one in a *time sequence*. If the ideas are presented out of order, the results will be chaotic. Imagine trying to put together a transistor radio from a kit whose instructions began, "After receiving a radio signal, adjust the aerial to improve reception." The first requirement, then, is to make certain that all the steps are presented in a clear sequence.

When writing the process paragraph, you should make it more than a list of steps. Such a paper would be technically correct but would have all the excitement of a set of directions for assembling a bicycle. Give your paragraph direction by giving it a topic sentence. For instance, instead of just listing in order the steps in taking a blood sample, write a topic statement that lets the reader see an overall pattern. "Taking a blood sample is more painful for the nurse than the patient" is more inviting than "There are three steps to follow in taking a blood sample." In this way your paragraph has a point of view; it is leading somewhere.

The following paragraph explains how the four-stroke engine works. Notice that it is arranged in time order.

◆ The four-stroke engine employs four distinct operations spread over four full strokes of each of its pistons. The first, the intake stroke, begins with the intake valve open and the piston at the top of its cylinder. As the rotating crankshaft drives the piston down, the resulting suction draws a mixture of air and fuel into the cylinder. Near the bottom of the stroke the intake valve closes, and the piston is forced upward by the crankshaft. The air-fuel mixture is compressed, and near the top of the piston's stroke a spark plug ignites the compressed charge of air and fuel. The temperature and pressure in the cylinder increase dramatically, forcing the piston down and transferring power to the crankshaft. Just before the piston reaches the bottom of the power stroke, the exhaust valve opens, releasing most of the burned mixture. After the high pressure blows down, the low-pressure exhaust gas remaining in the cylinder is driven out when the crankshaft forces the piston up again. The exhaust valve then closes, the intake valve opens, and the entire cycle begins again.

Writing Tips

Vocabulary–Building Books Under $10

If you possess and use an extensive vocabulary, your writing will be more interesting and exciting, as well as precise. The best way to increase your vocabulary is by reading widely. Another way is to refer to one of the many vocabulary-building books available at most college bookstores and libraries. Here are five of them, each costing less than ten dollars:

Merriam Webster's Vocabulary Builder, by Mary Wood Cornog

21st Century Guide to Building Your Vocabulary, by Elizabeth Read

Basic Word List, by Samuel Brownstein, Mitchel Weiner, and Sharon Weiner Green

601 Words You Need to Know to Pass Your Exam, by Murray Bromberg and Julius Liebb

How to Build a Better Vocabulary, by M. and M. Rosenblum Nurnberg and Morris Rosenblum

The next paragraph explains how something happens in nature—in this case, how coal is formed in the earth. Notice that the steps are presented chronologically.

◆ The story of the creation of coal goes back about 345 million years to the time when vast swampy areas of the earth were covered by dense, sun-drenched plant forests. As the plants died in the marshes, crustal disturbances occurred. Shallow seas and layers of sediments inundated the forests, and later new swamps grew in their place. In some areas this alternation of swamp and sea occurred hundreds of times. Slowly, great pressures and ample time worked chemical changes, hardening and fossilizing the layers of decayed vegetation. The result was seams of coal.

Exercise A   Using Process and Analysis

Select one of the subjects below and write a paragraph explaining how to do something, or how something happened or came about. Write at least 125 words and underline your topic sentence.

- the signs of spring's arrival
- how to tune a motorcycle or car
- how to organize a musical group
- the formation of the solar system
- how a particular discovery was made
- how to give a speech
- how to write a term paper
- how the referendum system works
- how the Spanish-American War came about
- the establishment of the Republican party

© 2001 Addison-Wesley Educational Publishers Inc.

Exercise B   Using Process and Analysis

The paragraph below gives directions for hiking to the summit of a peak. Read the paragraph carefully and then respond to the directions that follow it.

Hiking along the road, you undertake a moderate climb up the backside of Sandstone Peak. Just beyond the end of the second switchback at the crest of the climb, you'll notice an obvious and steep trail worn by use which takes off on the right. Follow it a brief if slippery distance to the top of the peak 1½ miles from the Circle X as you enjoy the splendor of the summit. Be on the lookout for soaring hawks and eagles. At one time even condors had been sighted riding the thermal currents of this wild and infrequently visited place on the lookout for prey.

—Dennis Gagnon, *Hike Los Angeles*, p. 19

Choose one of the following topics and write a paragraph explaining how to do something or how something happened.

- how to produce a "fade" haircut
- how to impress a mate's parents
- how a medical discovery occurred
- how the legend of Santa Claus began
- how to organize a class reunion
- how to choose the right college
- how to tune a guitar
- how to survive a breakup

Writing Tips

Yikes!

Have you ever opened a book, seen a sea of unending print, and felt a wave of dread? The appearance of your paragraphs can affect your readers' responses in a similar way. Extremely long paragraphs can intimidate or discourage readers. On the other hand, short paragraphs can make a reader feel that no single idea has been developed sufficiently. While there is no exact rule about the minimum number of sentences required in a paragraph, a short paragraph is often a sign that the writer did not follow through in his or her thinking about the topic. As a result, many weak paragraphs consist of little more than a topic sentence and one or two generalities, as if the writer hoped the reader would complete the thought for him or her. Newspapers often employ brief paragraphs, and they are also used to show a division or shift in the section of an essay or to draw attention to a startling fact or an important statement. In general, however, paragraphs that have only one, two, or three sentences are probably too thin and underdeveloped.

Computer Activity

Choose one of the subjects from the lists on pages 230–231 and follow the directions. When you finish your paragraph, exchange it with a classmate. Some word-processing programs permit written or voice annotations for peer-evaluation while keeping the original text unmarked.

If your computer does not have this program, use SAVE, COPY, and PASTE commands to make a second copy and transfer the file to a classmate.

Ask him or her to rearrange sentences that violate the sequential order of your paragraph.

Peer-edit your classmate's paragraph in the same manner.

When your paragraph is returned to you, compare your original with the peer-edited copy.

© 2001 Addison-Wesley Educational Publishers Inc.

11

Punctuation

When we speak, we make our meaning clear with more than just words. We pause at certain times, raise our voices for emphasis, and use various body movements. When we write, we use punctuation marks for the same purpose: to make our meaning intelligible to the reader. Every mark of punctuation carries some meaning and gives hints about how to read written English.

Careless punctuation can change meaning and confuse or even mislead the reader. Occasionally, the cost may be dramatic, as in a recently publicized Florida case in which non-profit organizations lost $2 million because a comma changed the meaning of a sentence and thereby rendered them ineligible for sales tax exemptions. Learning to punctuate correctly is not hard. It does, however, require a little patience. In this chapter we will look at the most common situations in written English that require punctuation.

END MARKS

End marks—periods, question marks, and exclamation points—are used to indicate the purpose of a sentence.

The Period

Use the period to end a statement (or **declarative sentence**), an indirect question, or a mild command (or imperative sentence).

- ◆ **Declarative sentence:** In 1831, Nat Turner led a short but bloody slave revolt in Virginia.
- ◆ **Indirect question:** Ms. Hipolito asked me whether I wanted to make an oral report on Turner's revolt.
- ◆ **Mild command:** Please make a poster for my presentation.

Use a period after most abbreviations.

◆ Ms., Dr., A.D., a.m., oz., Nov., Conn., Assn., ft.

Periods do not usually follow acronyms and abbreviations of well-known colleges, organizations, governmental agencies, and certain other abbreviations, including two-letter state abbreviations when the ZIP code is included.

◆ UCLA, NATO, IBM, UN, UFO, TV, IL, CA,

The Question Mark

Use a question mark after a direct question (or an interrogative sentence).

◆ Why did the chicken cross the street?

Do not use a question mark after an indirect question.

◆ Miss Tangum asked me why the chicken crossed the street.

Use a question mark to indicate uncertainty about the accuracy of a word, phrase, or date:

◆ The Greek philosopher Plato (427?–347 B.C.) was a disciple of Socrates.

The Exclamation Point

Use an exclamation point to end an exclamation—that is, a statement that shows strong emotion—or after a strong interjection, a word that shows strong feeling.

◆ Wow! You must be kidding!
◆ Hurry! We'll be late!

Use an exclamation point after **imperative sentences** that show strong feelings or express strong commands or requests.

◆ Please help me!
◆ Don't run!

Be careful not to overdo the exclamation point. When overused, it creates an almost hysterical tone in writing. Use a comma or a period instead of an exclamation point after a mild interjection.

◆ No, I don't think I want to.
◆ Yes, I need your help.

© 2001 Addison-Wesley Educational Publishers Inc.

If an abbreviation comes at the end of a statement, do not use an additional period as an end mark. However, use an exclamation point or question mark if one is needed.

◆ The Smithsonian Institution is in Washington, D.C.

◆ Have you ever visited Washington, D.C.?

Exercise 11-1

Supply a question mark, period, or exclamation point where needed. If there is no room in the sentence, insert a caret (^) below the line and write the appropriate punctuation above the line.

1. Your application should be mailed to D A Coleman, 19 W Bond Street, Richmond, VA 23219
2. Dr Lehane and Ms Garcia will sing duets today at 2:30 pm at the concert hall on Seventh St in Des Moines
3. Did you hear someone yell "Fire"
4. My little sister asked me whether there is a Santa Claus
5. "Do you believe in Santa Claus" I asked her
6. The newspaper columnist told our class that he types on an IBM Selectric typewriter that he purchased when he worked at the UN
7. My daughter earned her degree from UCLA but also took classes at USC and the U of Arizona
8. My alarm rings promptly at 7:00 am every day, but this morning I overslept and missed by favorite TV program and my appointment with Dr. McAndrews
9. Holy cow I've just won the state lottery
10. The world's first alphabet was developed by the Sumerians around 3000 BC
11. The Rev Martin Luther King, Jr., gave a rousing speech at the Lincoln Memorial in Washington, DC
12. No I can't believe it
13. Did you remember to wind the clock and put out the cat
14. I wonder whether forces from NATO should be sent to enforce the cease-fire
15. Please take your shoes off when entering the mosque

INTERNAL PUNCTUATION

The Comma

The comma is the punctuation mark most frequently used inside the sentence. It also offers the widest range of individual choice. As a result, many writers are uncertain concerning its proper use, and they sprinkle commas indiscriminately through their sentences. Do not use a comma unless you have a definite reason for doing so. The rules below will help you avoid cluttering your sentences with unnecessary commas while at the same time making certain you use commas to make your meaning clear.

Use a comma to separate independent clauses joined by a coordinating conjunction (*and, but, for, nor, or, so, yet*).

◆ Leo has a car, yet he prefers to ride his bicycle to work.

◆ Marcia and Hugo have been divorced for three years, but they continue to see each other frequently.

◆ Rhode Island is the smallest state, and Alaska is the largest.

When one or both independent clauses in a compound sentence are short, you may omit the commas before the conjunction.

◆ I heard the song and I liked it.

◆ I'm exhausted but I'm ready.

Note: Do not use a comma between two independent clauses that are not joined by a coordinating conjunction. This error creates a comma-splice (see Chapter 9). Use a semicolon, add a coordinating conjunction, or start a new sentence.

◆ **(Comma-splice)**   The chief mechanic examined the engine, his assistant checked the tires.

◆ **(Correct)**   The chief mechanic examined the engine, and his assistant checked the tires. (or The chief mechanic examined the engine. His assistant checked the tires. A semicolon could also be used after *engine*).

Do not use a comma before a coordinating conjunction linking two words, phrases, or dependent clauses.

◆ **(Incorrect)**   Many sailors become proficient in navigation, but neglect the problem of anchoring. (The conjunction *but* does not join two independent clauses.)

◆ **(Correct)**   Many sailors become proficient in navigating but neglect the problem of anchoring.

◆ **(Incorrect)**   Shakespeare wrote plays, and acted in the London theater.

◆ **(Correct)**   Shakespeare wrote plays and acted in the London theater.

Exercise 11–2

Add commas in the following sentences wherever needed. If no comma is needed in a sentence, place a "C" in front of it.

© 2001 Addison-Wesley Educational Publishers Inc.

1. My summer job was to stock the shelves and to take weekly inventory.
2. Mark wanted a pizza with anchovies but Gracie preferred mushrooms.
3. I read and Joe slept.
4. My sister Lois is a talented pianist but she hates to practice.
5. The U.S. women's volleyball team was relatively inexperienced yet it won the silver medal at the Olympics.
6. Four cities competed for the right to host the World's Fair, but only one would be selected.
7. The committee had met in private and refused to divulge its choice.
8. The home-improvement business has become very successful in our town and many craftsmen are now extremely busy.
9. The trash collectors have been on strike for three weeks and are demanding a meeting with the mayor.
10. The plans for the new convention center were approved by the city council; construction will begin next July.

Use a comma to separate an introductory dependent clause from the main part of the sentence.

- *Although Marshall was afraid of the water*, he learned to swim.
- *When we visited Houston last summer*, we went to a baseball game at the Astrodome.

Use a comma after a long introductory prepositional phrase.

- *After an arduous trek over snowcapped mountains and scorched desert floors*, the Mormons finally reached Utah.
- *In preparing your annual report to the board of directors*, be sure to include predictions for next year's sales.

Use a comma to set off an introductory participial phrase.

- *Pleased by the initial reaction from the voters*, the Democratic candidate stepped up his attack on his opponent.
- *Remembering the promise made to his parents*, Jeff carefully kept a record of his purchases and entered each payment in his checkbook.

Do not put a comma after participial phrases that are actually the subject of the sentence.

- **(Incorrect)**   Watering his lawn, was Mr. Dawson's only exercise.
- **(Correct)**   Watering his lawn was Mr. Dawson's only exercise.

◆ **(Incorrect)**   Reading about Oliver Cromwell's treatment of the Irish, made me more aware of the background behind the troubles in Ulster today.

◆ **(Correct)**   Reading about Oliver Cromwell's treatment of the Irish made me more aware of the background behind the troubles in Ulster today.

Use a comma to set off an introductory infinitive phrase unless the phrase is the subject of the sentence.

◆ To win the jackpot in Las Vegas, you must overcome tremendous odds.

But: To win the jackpot in Las Vegas was his dream.

◆ To impress his future in-laws, Bill wore a suit and tie.

But: To impress his future in-laws was Bill's goal.

Exercise 11-3

Insert commas in the following sentence where needed. If no comma is needed in a sentence, place a "C" in front of it.

1. Numbering nearly two million American Indians live and preserve their tribal cultures in every part of the United States.
2. Dozens of tribes across the country host pow-wows every year.
3. A huge gathering open to the public a typical pow-wow features parades, dancing, singing, crafts, and other Native American customs.
4. After a pageant in which young tribal women's beauty and achievements are admired by all one contestant is crowned as princess for the year.
5. Remembering old tribal ways and customs and passing them on to younger members are the main aims of tribal pow-wows.
6. Reflective of the influence of the surrounding Anglo culture some pow-wows feature golf tournaments and games of softball or volleyball.
7. Employing a variety of dance styles and costumes the dance contests which are crucial parts of any pow-wow draw huge crowds.
8. Circling the drummers and bobbing in a slow, smooth rhythm the female dancers sway gracefully.
9. Lids of snuff cans decorated and hung from women's dresses for the Jingle Dance produce tinny tones that are surprisingly light and musical.
10. Performers of the men's Traditional Dance are said to be reenacting the stealth of a warrior seeking his foe.
11. Unless you are a Native American you must remember that you are visiting a different culture with its own etiquette when you attend a pow-wow.
12. It is important to bring your own seating avoid sitting on benches reserved for dancers and ask permission before taking photographs.
13. When the Blanket Dance is done you will be expected to join the custom of placing at least a dollar on the blanket.

© 2001 Addison-Wesley Educational Publishers Inc.

14. Perhaps most important is the practice of standing respectfully during solemn songs such as Prayer Songs Memorial Songs and Flag Songs.
15. From the Oneida of New York to the Chumash of California a tribe planning a pow-wow is within a day's drive from virtually everywhere.

Use a comma after an introductory request or command.

◆ *Look*, we've been through all of this before.

◆ *Remember*, tomorrow is the deadline for filing your tax return.

Use a comma to separate three or more items in a series unless all of the items are joined by *and* or *or*.

◆ The gymnasium was small, crowded, and stuffy.

    But: The gymnasium was small and crowded and stuffy.

◆ Rich made some sandwiches, Jo Ann brought her guitar, and I furnished the soft drinks.

◆ John looked for the receipt in the drawer, under the bed, behind the sofa, and in his wallet.

Use a comma to separate interrupting elements (words, phrases, and clauses) when they break the flow of a sentence.

◆ It is a fact, *isn't it*, that the spleen filters the blood?

◆ I will hold your mail for you or, *if you prefer*, forward it to your hotel.

◆ We could use, *if possible*, six more cartons of eggs.

Other interrupting elements (also called *parenthetical elements* or *transitional expressions*) include the following: *as a matter of fact, at any rate, for instance, nevertheless, of course, therefore, in my opinion*, and *on the other hand*. These and similar phrases are usually set off by commas when they appear in a sentence.

◆ There are three good reasons, I believe, for changing my major.

◆ The Rams and the Jets, for example, have acquired new quarterbacks.

◆ Newark, on the other hand, is an industrial city.

Use a comma to set off direct address and words like *please, yes*, and *no*.

◆ Will you help me, *please?*

◆ *Yes*, I've seen all of Meg Ryan's films.

◆ You should wear a helmet, *Sarah*, when you ride your motorcycle.

Exercise 11-4

Add commas in the following sentences wherever needed. If no comma is needed in a sentence, place a "C" in front of it.

1. Yes I'd love to own a convertible wouldn't you?
2. My wife on the other hand remains unconvinced of the wisdom of my plans.
3. Salsa is made with tomatoes peppers onions garlic and spices.
4. The state of Oregon for example has experimented with various forms of health insurance.
5. Her part in the play includes dancing and singing and crying hysterically.
6. Yes we have decided to stay home for the holidays.
7. Tell me please why you insist on using your good china for the dog's meal.
8. Gerald scratched his head rubbed his nose and cracked his knuckles while filling out the application for his driver's license.
9. That speech in fact was written by his wife.
10. I would like to watch television with you Greta but I must finish my math problems.

Additional Uses of the Comma

Use a comma to set off modifiers that are not essential to the sense of the sentence. **Nonessential** (or **nonrestrictive**) **modifiers** are those that add information to the sentence, but they modify things or persons already clearly identified in the sentence.

Nonessential clauses are set off by commas (see Chapter 8).

♦ My mother, *who was born in St. Louis,* is the oldest of five children. (The adjective clause *who was born in St. Louis* is not essential to the identity of the subject *mother*, nor is it required for the central meaning of the sentence. Therefore, it is nonessential and is set off by commas.)

But: Anyone who was born in St. Louis is eligible to apply for the scholarship. (The adjective clause *who was born in St. Louis* is essential to the meaning of the sentence. Not everyone is eligible to apply for the scholarship—just those born in St. Louis. The clause is therefore essential and is not set off by commas.)

Nonessential appositives are set off by commas. An **appositive** is a word or phrase following a noun or pronoun which renames or explains it. Most appositives are nonessential and require commas.

♦ Alexander Hamilton, the first Secretary of the Treasury of the United States, was killed in a duel. (The fact that Alexander Hamilton was the first Secretary of the Treasury gives further information about the subject, but it is not essential to the meaning of the sentence. Therefore, the appositive is set off with commas.)

© 2001 Addison-Wesley Educational Publishers Inc.

◆ Mr. Murphy, my physics instructor, has won several national body-building titles. (Like the preceding appositive, *my physics teacher* gives additional but nonessential information about the subject and is therefore set off with commas.)

Some appositives are restrictive or serve as **essential modifiers**—that is, they are needed in the sentence to identify the element they rename. In such cases they are not set off with commas.

◆ The rapper Hammer once worked for the Oakland A's baseball team. (Which rapper worked for the Oakland A's baseball team? We would not know unless the appositive *Hammer* were included. Therefore, the appositive is essential and commas are not used.)

Use a comma to set off **coordinate adjectives.** Adjectives are coordinate if *and* can be placed between them. They describe different qualities of the same noun and may be separated by a comma rather than *and*.

◆ a long, boring movie (a long *and* boring movie)
◆ an expensive, rare gem (an expensive *and* rare gem)

Some adjectives are not coordinate, and therefore no commas are used to separate them.

◆ dirty blue jeans
◆ a retired staff sergeant
◆ an exciting volleyball game

Notice that you would not write:

◆ dirty and blue jeans
◆ a retired and staff sergeant
◆ an exciting and volleyball game

Adjectives usually precede the word they describe; when they follow the word they describe, they are set off with commas.

◆ **(Usual order)**   The loud and unruly crowd stormed the soccer field.
◆ **(Inverted order)**   The crowd, loud and unruly, stormed the soccer field.

Exercise 11–5

Add commas to the following sentences wherever needed. If a sentence does not need a comma, write "C" in front of it.

1. The Picasso painting which was donated last week was stolen yesterday.
2. Jogging my favorite form of exercise is now impossible for me because of a recent back injury.
3. Drew Carey the star of Jack's favorite television show will perform a standup comedy act at the Improv Club next week.
4. The lab monkeys have escaped.
5. Liam loves to tell hilarious stories of his childhood in New York.
6. The popular city councilman was easily reelected.
7. Lisa squirmed in her seat during the unexpectedly awkward moment in her job interview.
8. Alexis' brother who owns a fashionable restaurant brings meals to the homeless people of his neighborhood every Saturday.
9. The rain unexpected and drenching forced us to cancel the soccer game.
10. Anyone who arrives after the start of the opera will not be seated until the intermission.

More Uses of the Comma

Use a comma to set off contrasted elements.

◆ Her birthday is in July, not August.
◆ Jeff always gets a hotel room downtown, never in the suburbs.

Use a comma to set off quoted material.

◆ Georgia announced proudly, "I've been promoted to president of the company."
◆ "My wife just gave birth to twins," Dennis said.

Use commas to set off the year in complete dates.

◆ November 22, 1963, is a day that everyone living at the time will always remember.
◆ On August 6, 1945, the first atomic bomb was dropped.

When only the month and year are given, the comma is optional.

◆ **(Correct)**   The first commercial telecast took place in April 1939.
◆ **(Correct)**   The first commercial telecast took place in April, 1939.

Use a comma to separate the elements in an address.

◆ United Nations Plaza, Riverside Drive, New York, New York

© 2001 Addison-Wesley Educational Publishers Inc.

Within a sentence, place a comma after the final element in an address.

◆ Her office at the United Nations Plaza on Riverside Drive, New York, is her headquarters.

Abbreviations standing for academic degrees are set off by commas on both sides.

◆ James F. Dwyer, Ph.D., will address the graduating class.
◆ A plaque recognizing her contributions to the community was given to Judith Walsh, M.D. (*Notice that only one period is necessary at the end of a sentence.*)

Use a comma to prevent misreading. In some sentences it is necessary to use a comma even though no rule requires one.

◆ **(Confusing)**   As you know nothing happened at the meeting.
◆ **(Clear)**   As you know, nothing happened at the meeting.
◆ **(Confusing)**   Shortly after he quit his job and moved to Wisconsin.
◆ **(Clear)**   Shortly after, he quit his job and moved to Wisconsin.
◆ **(Confusing)**   While we ate the dog continued to bark.
◆ **(Clear)**   While we ate, the dog continued to bark.

Exercise 11-6

Add commas where necessary in the following sentences. If a sentence does not need a comma, write "C" in front of it.

1. Our tour guide is from Bolivia not Guatemala.
2. Actor Leonardo DiCaprio was born in Los Angeles on November 11 1978.
3. Doctor Linda Costa joined our staff in May 1999.
4. "For Christmas I would like a diamond necklace and a chocolate cake" Sarah announced to her husband "but I would like the cake first."
5. We have nicknamed Professor Sanders our English instructor "Fabio" because of his good looks.
6. Most of the time she can be found lounging by the pool at her West Hollywood California apartment.
7. To Marv his nephew Terry was someone special.
8. Frank Sinatra Jr. was kidnapped in Lake Tahoe California in December 1963.
9. After you've washed the dishes give the dog a bath not just a good brushing.
10. "Uncle Mike broke my Playstation video game" the child whined.

Missing Commas

When in doubt, many writers are tempted to add commas to their sentences. Too many commas, however, can slow down the thought or confuse the meaning. Here are some of the frequent situations that might tempt you to use the comma.

1. Do not use a comma after the last item in a series of adjectives preceding the noun.

   ◆ **(Incorrect)**   She was a dedicated, imaginative, creative, painter.
   ◆ **(Correct)**   She was a dedicated, imaginative, creative painter.

2. Do not use a comma to separate the subject from its verb.

   ◆ **(Incorrect)**   A good night's rest, is the best preparation for a test.
   ◆ **(Correct)**   A good night's rest is the best preparation for a test.

3. Do not use a comma between two words joined by a coordinating conjunction.

   ◆ **(Incorrect)**   Bill plays piano, and tuba in the band.
   ◆ **(Correct)**   Bill plays piano and tuba in the band.

4. Do not separate a verb from a *that* clause.

   ◆ **(Incorrect)**   The Surgeon General has determined, that cigarette smoking is dangerous to your health.
   ◆ **(Correct)**   The Surgeon General has determined that cigarette smoking is dangerous to your health.

5. Do not use a comma to separate independent clauses unless the comma is followed by a coordinate conjunction (see Chapter 9 for comma-splices).

   ◆ **(Incorrect)**   The blaze began at Barksdale Air Force Base, it threatened nearby Bossier City for hours.
   ◆ **(Correct)**   The blaze began at Barksdale Air Force Base, and it threatened nearby Bossier City for hours.

Exercise 11-7

Delete or add commas in the following sentences. If a sentence is punctuated correctly, write "C" in front of it.

1. The human body has 206 bones, that come in four general shapes: long, short, flat and irregular.
2. There are thirty-three, separate, spinal, vertebrae in the embryo, but only twenty-six in an adult.
3. This is because some vertebrae fuse together just before birth.

© 2001 Addison-Wesley Educational Publishers Inc.

4. Gwyneth Paltrow is much admired for her high zygomatic bones, more commonly called cheekbones.
5. The mandible, or jawbone, is the only facial bone that moves.
6. Scottie Pippin is able to slam dunk partly because of his extremely long femurs, tibias, and fibulas, called leg bones by most of us.
7. Each finger consists of, three bones, and the thumb consists of two.
8. Incredibly, the average human bone can tolerate a pressure of 27,000 pounds per square inch, before breaking.
9. Bones are, however, usually broken when they are twisted or when, they receive a blow from the side.
10. It is amusing that, the softer material inside human bones is called, "spongy bone."

The Semicolon

Use a semicolon to separate two related independent clauses when there is no coordinating conjunction to join them.

◆ The law is clear; the question is whether it is fair.

◆ Competition for admittance to medical school is intense; only about one applicant in twenty is admitted.

If you use a comma instead of a semicolon for an omitted conjunction, you will create a comma-splice (see Chapter 9 and page 236 in this chapter). There is an exception to this rule in the case of compound sentences in which the clauses are very short:

◆ I came, I saw, I conquered.

Use a semicolon to separate independent clauses joined by a **conjunctive adverb.** Conjunctive adverbs are words like the following: *however, moreover, therefore, furthermore, nevertheless, nonetheless, consequently, otherwise, besides,* and *hence* (see Chapter 9).

Conjunctive adverbs are not conjunctions, and therefore they require more than a comma before them. When they come at the beginning of an independent clause, a semicolon or period should precede them. If they are not preceded by a semicolon or period, the result is a comma-splice.

◆ **(Comma-splice)**   Puerto Rico is not a state, however, its residents are American citizens.

◆ **(Correct)**   Puerto Rico is not a state; however, its residents are American citizens.

◆ **(Comma-splice)**   The Rolls-Royce is an expensive automobile, moreover, its maintenance costs are also higher than for most other cars.

- ◆ (Correct)   The Rolls-Royce is an expensive automobile; moreover, its maintenance costs are also higher than for most other cars.

Use a semicolon to separate items in a series if the items contain commas.

- ◆ Attending the sales meeting were Marino Garcia, the sales manager; Jim Gleeson, vice president; Lisa Crow, advertising manager; and John Jacobs, secretary-treasurer.
- ◆ Candidates for the Most Inspiring Player of the Year Award were Bruce Stoecker, full-back; Don Cohn, tight end; Dick Farley, quarterback; and Joe Rico, fullback.

Exercise 11–8

Add a semicolon or comma where needed in the following sentences and delete any unnecessary punctuation. If a sentence is punctuated correctly, write "C" in front of it.

1. Tran speaks English at school, at home, however, he speaks Vietnamese.
2. The advertising agency selected seven cities as trial markets for the new product: Huntsville, Mobile, and Tuscaloosa, in Alabama, Yakima and Olympia, in Washington, and Carbondale and East St. Louis, in Illinois.
3. The disc jockey didn't play any of my favorite songs, I danced once.
4. Monaco has no famous colleges or universities, however, it has a ninety-nine percent literacy rate.
5. The annual number of marriages in America has increased since the 1980s, so has the death rate.
6. Jessie closed his Manhattan law practice last week, he plans to move to Cedar Rapids to take over his father's farm.
7. Charlene decided to leave before dinner because the roads were becoming icy.
8. I will have to find a job this semester or I will have to get a loan for tuition.
9. Cows will not eat hay that has a musty odor, therefore, farmers must make sure that it is dry before they bale it.
10. During our African honeymoon we visited Zanzibar, Tabora, and Linga in Tanzania, Nairobi, Nakum and Mombasa in Kenya, and Juba, Waw, and Khartoum in Sudan.

The Colon

The colon can be thought of as an equal sign; it tells the reader that what follows it is equivalent to what precedes it. The most common use of the colon is to introduce a list of items after an independent clause:

- ◆ The trade minister stated that his nation offered potential investors several advantages: a good climate, a sound economy, and a reasonable wage structure.

© 2001 Addison-Wesley Educational Publishers Inc.

◆ Yiddish is made up chiefly of words from four languages: Russian, German, Polish, and Hebrew.

The colon is also used to introduce a word or phrase that renames or explains an earlier idea in the sentence:

◆ The Hubble telescope soared into space despite a serious flaw: a distortion in one of its light-gathering mirrors.

The colon can be used between two complete thoughts when the second explains the first:

◆ It was becoming painfully obvious to him: he was being ignored.

A less frequent use of the colon is after a list of items preceding an independent clause:

◆ Cuba, Brazil, and Australia: these are the largest producers of cane sugar.

Do *not* place a colon between a verb and its objects or complements, or between a preposition and its objects.

◆ **(Incorrect)**   Her favorite science-fiction writers are: Ursula LeGuin, Isaac Asimov, and Harlan Ellison.

◆ **(Incorrect)**   For a good day at the beach you must bring: sunscreen, cold drinks, and a radio.

◆ **(Incorrect)**   Charlie Chaplin was easily recognized by: his black mustache, his walk, and his black hat.

A colon can be used to introduce a quotation that does not form part of a clause or phrase in the rest of the sentence:

◆ As Neil Armstrong put his foot on the surface of the moon, he made a statement that has become famous: "That's one small step for man, one giant leap for mankind."

Other uses of the colon are after salutations in business letters and between hours and minutes when referring to time:

◆ Dear Professor Nishimura:
◆ 4:05 p.m.

Exercise 11-9

Insert a colon where needed in the following sentences, and delete any colons that are unnecessary or incorrect. If a sentence is correct, write "C" in front of it.

1. Though Assan and I were in Boston for just one day, we were able to achieve our goal a tour of the city's historical sites.
2. Boston is home to more than fifty colleges and universities, including Harvard University, Boston College, and the Massachusetts Institute of Technology.
3. The North End and Beacon Hill possess quaint features of a bygone era cobbled streets, gaslights, and treacherous brick sidewalks.
4. At the Congress Street Bridge we saw a full-scale working replica of the Boston Tea Party ship and a colorful reenactment of the dumping of tea into the harbor.
5. Assan and I stopped for coffee at the Bull & Finch pub, whose facade and interior were featured in the hit television show "Cheers."
6. I was amazed by the New England Aquarium's four-story, circular glass tank which houses the center's main attractions sharks, turtles, eels, and hundreds of tropical fish.
7. The Old North church, though simple in appearance, was important to visit. Paul Revere spied in its steeple: the two lanterns which sparked his famous midnight ride.
8. Next we toured the 1713 Old State House to see: tea from the Boston Tea Party, one of John Hancock's coats, and the east front where the Boston Massacre occurred.
9. Handwritten documents, tape recordings, and the actual Oval Office desk these mementos at the John F. Kennedy Library touched us deeply.
10. As dusk descended on Boston, Assan and I strolled to the Public Garden for our final treat a ride in one of the famous swan-shaped boats.

Parentheses

Use parentheses to enclose unimportant information or comments that are not an essential part of the passage. In this respect parentheses are like commas; the difference is that they evoke the reader's attention more than commas.

- Mapmakers use a system of medians of longitude (from the Latin longus, "long") and parallels of latitude (from latus, "wide").
- Zora Neale Hurston (who started out as an anthropologist) is one of the finest novelists in American literature.
- Walt Whitman's *Leaves of Grass* (published in 1855) was greeted with hostility.

Dates that accompany an event or a person's name are enclosed in parentheses.

- The Iran-Contra scandal (1988) involved several members of President Reagan's administration.
- Louis Armstrong (1900–1971) invented the popular "scat" style of singing.

Note: Never insert a comma, semicolon, colon, or dash before an opening parenthesis.

- **(Incorrect)**   Eileen Corliss, (my anatomy instructor) was one of the country's best college volleyball players.

© 2001 Addison-Wesley Educational Publishers Inc.

Dashes

The dash is a forceful punctuation mark, but it must be used carefully. It often takes the place of the comma, the semicolon, the colon, or parentheses in a sentence in order to separate emphatically words or groups of words. The difference between the dash and these other marks is that it focuses attention on the items being separated.

Use a dash to mark an abrupt change in the thought or structure of a sentence:

◆ I wonder if we should—oh, let's take care of it later.

Use a dash to make parenthetical or explanatory matter more prominent:

◆ George Halas—one of the founders of the National Football League—was known as "Papa Bear."
◆ The family's belongings—their clothing, furniture, computer, and other possessions—were stolen during their weekend absence.

Use a dash to set off single words that require emphasis:

◆ Sandra thinks about only one thing—money.

Use a dash to set off an appositive or an introductory series:

◆ Only one professional wrestler—Jesse Ventura—has been elected governor of a state.

Note: The use of dashes in this sentence emphasizes the appositive *Jesse Ventura*; parentheses would also be correct, but they would not present the same emphasis.

◆ Leonardo da Vinci, William the Conqueror, Alexander Hamilton, and Richard Wagner—they were all illegitimate children.

Note: A colon could also be correct in this sentence after *Richard Wagner*.

Exercise 11-10

Depending on the desired emphasis, insert parentheses or dashes in the following sentences.

1. My oldest brother the computer programmer who lives in Menlo Park is unable to attend our cousin's wedding.
2. Only one obstacle kept Sue from a career in music talent.
3. The most common American slang terms according to an authority on slang deal with money, sex, and drinking.
4. Mark claimed that it was her intelligence not her wealth that attracted him.

5. Kent's father an acupuncturist lives in San Antonio.
6. Our dinner salad, steak and dessert cost only $6 each with a special coupon.
7. That was my husband not my dentist whom you saw me kissing yesterday.
8. Law, navigation, politics, medicine, war Shakespeare wrote about all of these topics.
9. Charley my pet dog that I told you about is prohibited from entering the house.
10. I read an article in the *Times* or maybe it was the *Post-Dispatch* describing the tornado in Kansas last week.

Quotation Marks

Quotation marks have three main functions: to indicate the exact words of a speaker, to call attention to words used in an unusual sense or in definitions, and to enclose the title of certain kinds of literary and artistic works. In every case, be sure that you use them in pairs; a common mistake is to omit the last set of quotation marks.

For Direct Quotations   Use quotation marks around the exact words of a speaker.

◆ Grandpa announced, "It's time to take my nap."
◆ "I guess I do," the nervous bride whispered.

Notice that a comma precedes quotation marks in a direct quotation and that the first word of the quotation is capitalized. Do not use quotation marks for indirect quotations.

◆ Grandpa announced that it was time to take his nap.

Always place commas and periods *inside* the end quotation marks.

◆ "If you wait a few minutes," she said, "we will walk to the corner with you."

When the quotation is a question or exclamation, place the question mark or exclamation point *inside* the quotation marks.

◆ Ben asked with a smile, "Who left this on my desk?"
◆ "That music is too loud!" my father shouted.

When the question mark or exclamation point applies to the entire sentence and not just to the quotation, it should be placed *outside* the end quotation marks.

◆ Did she say, "I have to go to a sales meeting next Tuesday"?
◆ I'm tired of being told that my writing is "adequate"!

Always place semicolons *outside* the end quotation mark.

© 2001 Addison-Wesley Educational Publishers Inc.

◆ O. Henry's most famous short story is "The Gift of the Magi"; like his others, it has a surprise ending.

◆ The Russian delegate's vote was a loud "Nyet!"; as a result, the resolution was vetoed.

Use single quotation marks around quoted material within a direct quotation.

◆ "We object to 'In God We Trust' on our currency," the lawyer stated.

◆ "My favorite poem is 'Chicago,'" said Imelda.

For Words and Definitions   Use quotation marks to call attention to words used in an unusual sense and in definitions.

◆ I like the symphonies of Charles Ives; my brother's term for them is "cacophony."

◆ The origin of the word "bedlam" is interesting.

◆ The Spanish expression "Adios" comes from another expression meaning "Go with God."

Note: Many writers prefer to italicize (underline) words when used in this sense.

For Titles of Literary and Artistic Works   Use quotation marks to enclose titles of short poems, paintings, magazine articles, television programs, short stories, songs, and any selections from longer works.

◆ **Poems:**   "The Road Not Taken"
                     "Lady Lazarus"

◆ **Paintings:**   "The Last Supper"
                     "Whistler's Mother"

◆ **Articles:**   "The Dangers of Sport Utility Vehicles"
                     "Beginner's Guide to the Stock Market"

◆ **T.V. Programs:** "Ally McBeal"
                     "NBC Evening News"

◆ **Short Stories:** "The Dead"
                     "Raymond's Run"

◆ **Songs:**   "It's My Party and I'll Cry If I Want To"
                     "Every Breath You Take"

Italics

When words that would be italicized when printed are typed or handwritten, they should be underlined.

Underline (italicize) the titles of books, plays, magazines, newspapers, movies, long poems, and the names of ships, airplanes, and trains.

- **Books:**   *Writing for College: A Practical Approach*
                   Beloved
- **Plays:**   *Romeo and Juliet*
                   Sunset Boulevard
- **Magazines:**   *Newsweek*
                   Rolling Stone
- **Newspapers:** *Los Angeles Times*
                   St. Louis Post-Dispatch
- **Movies:**   *Dances With Wolves*
                   Gone With the Wind
- **Long Poems:** *The Iliad*
                   Song of Myself
- **Ships:**   *Old Ironsides*
                   Titanic
- **Airplanes:**   *Spirit of St. Louis*
                   Enola Gay
- **Trains:**   *Silver Bullet*
                   Wabash Cannonball

Underline (italicize) foreign words and phrases that have not yet been adopted as English expressions. If you are not certain about the current status of a particular word or phrase, use a good modern dictionary.

- *caveat emptor*
- *mea culpa*
- *pro bono publico*

Underline (italicize) when referring to letters, numbers, and words.

- Toav received two *B*'s and two *A*'s this semester.
- Several Chinese entrants were awarded *10*'s in the gymnastics competition.

© 2001 Addison-Wesley Educational Publishers Inc.

◆ The word *mischievous* is frequently mispronounced by speakers. (As noted earlier, some writers prefer to enclose words used like this in quotation marks.)

Underline (italicize) words that receive special emphasis.

◆ He lives in Manhattan, *Kansas*, not Manhattan, *New York*.

Exercise 11-11

Supply missing commas and quotation marks, and underline (italicize) where appropriate in the following sentences.

1. Would you please translate the French phrase noblesse oblige for me?
2. Professor Cardenas complained that too many students confuse the words to, too, and two.
3. Who said For people who like this sort of thing this is the sort of thing they would like?
4. Beverly is next in line to be editor-in-chief of the Times-Courier.
5. The Greek letter rho looks like the Roman letter p.
6. My favorite love song said Darnell is Just the Way You Are by Billy Joel.
7. I ordered garlic pizza not garlic pasta.
8. Did you read the Louisville Herald's review of the movie Singin' in the Rain?
9. Although the movie Field of Dreams was not believable the references to baseball history were interesting.
10. The expression to love, honor, and obey has been dropped from some marriage ceremonies.

Exercise 11-12

Correctly punctuate the following sentences, using commas, question marks, quotation marks, or italics (underlining).

1. Isabel Allende the Chilean novelist has written a humorous book about the pleasures of food titled Aphrodite.
2. Faster Than a Speeding Photon an article in Discover Magazine by David H. Freedman asks whether Einstein was wrong in stating that nothing can travel faster than the speed of light.
3. Have you read The Van and The Snapper two novels by Irish writer Roddy Doyle.
4. We rode the Ski Express train to Vermont where we skied several uncrowded slopes which we had read about in Yankee Magazine.
5. Janice was asked to lead a discussion of three poems by Audre Lorde titled Hanging Fire The Woman Thing and Sisters in Arms.
6. Carol named her Cessna airplane The Bashful Boy in honor of her son.

7. The Queen Elizabeth II still seaworthy and anchored in Long Beach is larger than its more famous cousin the Titanic.
8. I read in the Hartford-Courant this morning that one of Uccello's paintings The Rout of San Romano will be auctioned in Rome next week.
9. In the film The Postman the leading character wins a woman's heart by quoting from the poems Walking Around and Leaning Into the Afternoons by the poet Pablo Neruds.
10. Stardust Magazine recently published a poem titled The Moment which was about Perugino's painting Giving of the Keys to Saint Peter.
11. Zora Neale Hurston one of the most famous writers of the Harlem Renaissance is the author of the novel Their Eyes Were Watching God.
12. The television soap operas All My Children and As the World Turns are viewed by millions of people throughout the world.
13. From his jukebox selections we could tell that Joe was suffering from a broken heart: Change the World by Eric Clapton Blue by LeAnn Rimes and Yesterday by the Beatles.
14. When the X-Files or Frasier is on television Oscar refuses to answer the telephone.
15. Did you know that the Newberry medal is awarded annually for outstanding excellence in literature for children.

The Hyphen

The most common use of the hyphen is to break a word at the end of a line when there is not enough room for the entire word. The hyphen has several other important uses, however.

The hyphen is used to set off certain prefixes.

1. After *ex-*, *self-*, and *all-* when they are used as prefixes.

    ◆ ex-husband

    ◆ self-destructive

    ◆ all-purpose

2. After prefixes that precede a proper noun or adjective.

    ◆ anti-Semitic

    ◆ pro-French

    ◆ un-American

    ◆ pre-Christian

    ◆ trans-Atlantic

3. Between compound descriptions serving as a single adjective before a noun.

    ◆ wine-red sea

    ◆ soft-spoken cop

    ◆ slow-moving train

© 2001 Addison-Wesley Educational Publishers Inc.

4. Between fractions and compound numbers from twenty-one through ninety-nine.

    ◆ three-fourths
    ◆ five-eighths
    ◆ fifty-four
    ◆ ninety-eight

The hyphen is used between syllables at the end of a line. Never divide a one-syllable word. When you are uncertain about the use of the hyphen in the syllabication of a word or in compound words, consult a collegiate-level dictionary.

The Apostrophe

The use of the apostrophe can be somewhat tricky at times, but by following the suggestions below, you will avoid the confusion that many writers have with this punctuation mark. The apostrophe is used for the possessive case (except for personal pronouns), to indicate an omitted letter or number, and to form the plural of numbers, specific words, and letters. In the following pages we will examine each of these uses.

1. Use the apostrophe to form the possessive case.

    a. To form the possessive case of a *singular* person, thing, or indefinite pronoun, add 's:

    ◆ the razor's edge
    ◆ the dog's bark
    ◆ everybody's obligation
    ◆ Giorgio's motorcycle

    If a proper name already ends in s in its singular form and the adding of 's would make the pronunciation difficult, it is best to use the apostrophe only:

    ◆ Ulysses' return (Ulysses's would be difficult to pronounce but is acceptable)
    ◆ Moses' teachings
    ◆ Jesus' mother

    b. To form the possessive case of a plural noun ending in s, add an apostrophe only:

    ◆ the cities' population
    ◆ the soldiers' wives and husbands
    ◆ the cats' tails

    c. To form the possessive case of a plural noun not ending in s, add 's:

    ◆ women's rights
    ◆ children's television programs
    ◆ mice's tails
    ◆ alumni's representative

d. To form the possessive of compound words, use the apostrophe according to the meaning of the construction:

- ◆ Laurel and Hardy's movies (the movies that Laurel and Hardy made together)

But: ◆ Chaplin's and Woody Allen's movies (the movies of Chaplin and Allen, respectively)

- ◆ Her mother and father's home (the home of her mother and father)

But: ◆ Her brother's and sister's homes (the separate homes of her brother and sister)

e. Most indefinite pronouns form the possessive case by adding *'s:*

- ◆ someone's hat
- ◆ everybody's choice
- ◆ anyone's guess

The following indefinite pronouns can be made possessive only with *of:*

- ◆ *all, any, both, each, few, many, most, much, several, some, such*

Not: ◆ Although I hadn't seen my two friends since grade school, I could remember each's name.

But: ◆ Although I hadn't seen my two friends since grade school, I could remember the name of each.

f. Do not use an apostrophe with the possessive forms of personal and relative pronouns.

Correct	Incorrect
his	his'
hers	her's, hers'
ours	our's, ours'
yours	your's, yours'
theirs	their's, theirs'
whose	who'se
its	it's

Remember that *its* indicates ownership, and *it's* is a **contraction** for *it is* or *it has.* Similarly, *who's* means *who is* or *who has.*

© 2001 Addison-Wesley Educational Publishers Inc.

TIPS FOR FORMING POSSESSIVES OF NOUNS

1. Make the noun singular or plural, according to your meaning.
2. If the noun is singular, add 's. If adding the 's makes the pronunciation difficult, add an apostrophe only.
3. If the noun is plural and ends in s, just add an apostrophe. If the noun is plural and ends in some other letter, add 's.

Exercise 11-13

Insert apostrophes in the following sentences where appropriate, and delete apostrophes that are incorrect. If a sentence uses apostrophes correctly, place "C" before it. Reword any sentence as needed.

1. The swimming pool schedule has been changed while its being painted.
2. Karls' grandparents came to this country from Sweden.
3. In recent years the mens rights movement has attracted many followers.
4. Over one hundred guests attended the couples wedding.
5. Is this wallet your's?
6. The mayor continued to ignore the veterans demands when they marched on City Hall.
7. The dog seems to have lost its way home.
8. I suppose it was just somebodys attempt at humor.
9. It was obvious from the appearance of both that they had been in the water.
10. Helen and Eddie's grades in Spanish began to improve after the midterm examination.
11. "Who's on First?" is one of Abbott and Costellos funniest routines.
12. The salesmens' bonus was less than they had expected.
13. The poison could be identified by its deadly smell.
14. The policeman wanted to know whose car was parked illegally in front of the firehouse.
15. Mr. and Mrs. Kellys children surprised their parents with an anniversary party.

2. Use an apostrophe to indicate an omitted letter in contracted words or an omitted number:

   ◆ class of '90
   ◆ 'tis a pity
   ◆ won't
   ◆ the '76ers

3. Use an apostrophe to form the plurals of letters, specific words, and numbers.

◆ Watch your p's and q's.
◆ The yes's outnumbered the no's.
◆ Marlene's lowest grade was in the 80's.

Note: An apostrophe is not necessary for the plural of a year.

◆ Our history prof discussed student activism of the 1960s.

Some writers prefer to form the plural of a number by merely adding *-s*, omitting the apostrophe:

◆ The temperature yesterday was in the 90s.

Do not use an apostrophe when writing out a number in the plural:

◆ **(Correct)**   several sevens and eights
◆ **(Incorrect)**   several seven's and eight's

Numbers

1. If a number requires no more than two words, it should be spelled out.

◆ nine months later (not 9 months later)
◆ forty-one dollars (not 41 dollars)
◆ eighteen billion light years (not 18,000,000,000 light years)

2. If a number requires more than two words, use figures.

◆ 694 tons (not six-hundred ninety-four tons)
◆ 4½ pounds (not four and one-half pounds)
◆ 1372 pages (not one-thousand three-hundred seventy-two pages)

3. Write out a number beginning a sentence.

◆ **(Awkward)**   14 patients at Broadway Hospital were treated for food poisoning.
◆ **(Revised)**   Fourteen patients at Broadway Hospital were treated for food poisoning.

Exercise 11-14

Insert any omitted hyphens or apostrophes in the following sentences, and make any necessary corrections in the use of numbers, quotation marks, underlining, hyphens, or apostrophes. If a sentence is correct, write "C" before it.

1. Approximately 50 yeas and 100 nos were recorded at last weeks vote.

© 2001 Addison-Wesley Educational Publishers Inc.

2. Clarissa said that she was thirty nine and holding.
3. Many Europeans call the letter *z* zed or zeta.
4. Dr. Marissa Holdener prescribed an anti inflammatory drug for the foot problem Ive had for the past 3 weeks.
5. Every morning Mr. Cady walks two and a half miles.
6. The President elect was briefed by the C.I.A. prior to her inauguration.
7. Its been difficult to make the dog sleep in it's house.
8. Youre out of your mind if you think Ill babysit your little brother.
9. Margaret offered her husband $150 if he would lose twenty-five pounds, but I doubt he'll accept the offer.
10. I cant meet you any earlier than 12 o'clock, although its probably too late for you.

WRITING SENTENCES

Using Correct Punctuation

Careless punctuation can irritate our readers and often distort the meaning of our writing. In this exercise you are asked to write original sentences illustrating the correct use of punctuation.

1. Write an original sentence in which commas are used to separate interrupting elements.
2. Write a compound sentence in which a comma may be omitted before the conjunction joining the independent clauses.
3. Write a sentence using a comma after a long introductory prepositional phrase.
4. Write a sentence using a comma to set off an introductory participial phrase.
5. Write a sentence in which you correctly use the dash.
6. Write a brief dialogue (five or six sentences) between two speakers, using quotation marks correctly.

Editing Exercise

Punctuate this passage from the novel Great Expectations by Charles Dickens. The first speaker is an escaped convict. The second speaker is seven-year-old Pip, who is lingering at the gravestone of his deceased parents.

Hold your noise cried a terrible voice as a man started up from among the graves at the side of the church keep still you little devil or Ill cut out your throat

He was a fearful man all in grey with a great iron on his leg his shoes were falling apart he had no hat and an old rag was tied around his head he had been soaked in water smothered in mud cut by stones and torn by briars he limped and shivered and glared and growled his teeth chattered as he seized me by the chin

Oh dont cut my throat sir I pleaded in terror pray dont do it sir

Tell me your name said the man be quick about it

Pip sir

Show me where you live said the man point out the place

I pointed to where our village lay a mile or more from the church

The man after looking at me for a moment turned me upside down and emptied my pockets there was nothing in them but a piece of bread he ate the bread ravenously

Now look here said the man who do you live with assuming I'm going to let you live which I havent made up my mind about

My sister sir mrs joe gargery wife of joe gargery the blacksmith sir

© 2001 Addison-Wesley Educational Publishers Inc.

▶Review Test 11-A

Punctuation

On the line preceding each number, write the letter of the sentence that is correctly punctuated.

_____ 1. a. "Is the coffee ready?" Rita asked Bill.
         b. "Is the coffee ready"? Rita asked Bill.

_____ 2. a. I just toured New England and I want to visit the South next year.
         b. I just toured New England, and I want to visit the South next year.

_____ 3. a. Having received a BS from Princeton University Julie is now
            studying for a PhD at the University of Southern California.
         b. Having received a B.S. from Princeton University, Julie is now
            studying for a Ph.D. at the University of Southern California.

_____ 4. a. She asked me whether I wanted to borrow her copy of Adrienne
            Rich's new collection of poetry.
         b. She asked me "whether I wanted to borrow her copy of Adrienne
            Rich's new collection of poetry."

_____ 5. a. Stop. You're choking me.
         b. Stop! You're choking me!

_____ 6. a. Shall we watch the U.C.L.A. game on N.B.C. or the M.I.T. game
            on C.B.S.?
         b. Shall we watch the UCLA game on NBC or the MIT game on CBS?

_____ 7. a. It must be inspiring, to have a P.E. teacher who excels in triathlons.
         b. It must be inspiring to have a P.E. teacher who excels in triathlons.

_____ 8. a. Jamal is a gentle, intelligent, witty, community, leader.
         b. Jamal is a gentle, intelligent, witty community leader.

_____ 9. a. I enjoy the heat and openness of the desert; however, I also like lush,
            cool forests.
         b. I enjoy the heat and openness of the desert, however, I also like lush,
            cool forests.

_____ 10. a. Send the package to 602 Pico Boulevard, Santa Monica, California.
         b. Send the package to 602 Pico Boulevard, Santa Monica California.

_____ 11. a. That's my eighth grade algebra teacher.
         b. That's my eighth grade, algebra teacher.

_____ 12. a. Sylvia Rousseau, Ph.D., is our new dean.
         b. Sylvia Rousseau Ph.D. is our new dean.

_____ 10. a. The Earl of Sandwich, an English nobleman, gave his name to a well-known food item.

b. The Earl of Sandwich, an English nobleman gave his name, to a well-known food item.

_____ 11. a. Although the dog's collar was found on the beach the dog was never located by its owner.

b. Although the dog's collar was found on the beach, the dog was never located by its owner.

_____ 12. a. Richard Wright's novel *Black Boy* is about the racism that a young Afro-American must overcome on the way to adulthood.

b. Richard Wright's novel "Black Boy" is about the racism, that a young Afro-American must overcome on the way to adulthood.

_____ 13. a. My neighbor last year would often wake me up early in the morning by singing *Home on the Range*.

b. My neighbor last year would often wake me up early in the morning by singing "Home on the Range."

_____ 14. a. Shakespeare's birthday, (April 23, 1564), was also the date on which he died, (April 23, 1616).

b. Shakespeare's birthday (April 23, 1564) was also the date on which he died (April 23, 1616).

_____ 15. a. Many people who are avoiding alcohol now socialize at coffeehouses instead of bars.

b. Many people, who are avoiding alcohol, now socialize at coffeehouses instead of bars.

_____ 16. a. Uncle Don said, "Sylvia's favorite short story, 'The Catbird Seat,' was written by my favorite author: James Thurber."

b. Uncle Don said "Sylvia's favorite short story *The Catbird Seat* was written by my favorite author; James Thurber."

_____ 17. a. Buck burst into the room and shouted "Help. I've been bitten by a snake."

b. Buck burst into the room and shouted, "Help! I've been bitten by a snake!"

_____ 18. a. The examining physician noticed a three-quarter inch scar on Rosa's arm.

b. The examining physician noticed a three quarter inch scar on Rosa's arm.

_____ 19. a. Mrs. Jago warned her students "Expect a quiz on tonight's reading when you come to class tomorrow."

b. Mrs. Jago warned her students, "Expect a quiz on tonight's reading when you come to class tomorrow."

© 2001 Addison-Wesley Educational Publishers Inc.

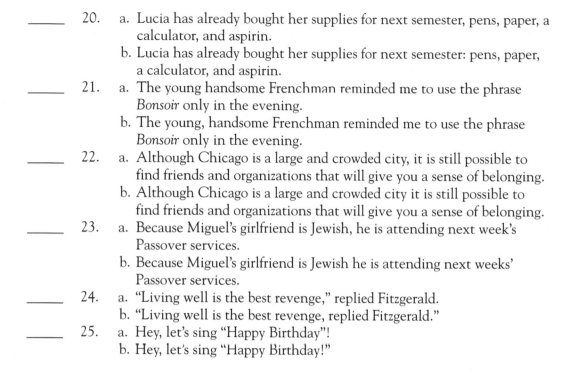

_____ 20. a. Lucia has already bought her supplies for next semester, pens, paper, a calculator, and aspirin.

          b. Lucia has already bought her supplies for next semester: pens, paper, a calculator, and aspirin.

_____ 21. a. The young handsome Frenchman reminded me to use the phrase _Bonsoir_ only in the evening.

          b. The young, handsome Frenchman reminded me to use the phrase _Bonsoir_ only in the evening.

_____ 22. a. Although Chicago is a large and crowded city, it is still possible to find friends and organizations that will give you a sense of belonging.

          b. Although Chicago is a large and crowded city it is still possible to find friends and organizations that will give you a sense of belonging.

_____ 23. a. Because Miguel's girlfriend is Jewish, he is attending next week's Passover services.

          b. Because Miguel's girlfriend is Jewish he is attending next weeks' Passover services.

_____ 24. a. "Living well is the best revenge," replied Fitzgerald.

          b. "Living well is the best revenge, replied Fitzgerald."

_____ 25. a. Hey, let's sing "Happy Birthday"!

          b. Hey, let's sing "Happy Birthday!"

© 2001 Addison-Wesley Educational Publishers Inc.

Writing Paragraphs

Developing Paragraphs by Cause and Effect

"Why did this happen?" "What will happen because of this?" When we ask questions like these, we are thinking in terms of *cause and effect*. The driver who wants to know why his engine keeps dying in traffic, the scientists who ponder the effects of cloning, and the cook who wonders why the soufflé has collapsed are all following a familiar way of thinking: leaping back and forth from effect to cause and from cause to effect.

To demonstrate a cause-and-effect relationship, two patterns can be used: the effects may be stated in the topic sentence, with the causes listed in the body of the paragraph; or the paragraph may move from causes to their effects. In either case, cause-and-effect paragraphs explore why something happened or explain what happened as a result of something else.

In the following paragraph, *the cause*—the 55-mile speed limit—is stated in the topic sentence, followed by its *effects*.

♦ When the 55-mile speed limit was first passed, even its most enthusiastic supporters did not envision its consequences. Automobile owners began to notice that their cars were getting better gasoline mileage because of the reduced speed. Many drivers reported that their cars ran better and needed fewer tune-ups. In many cities, smog levels decreased because of more efficient driving habits. Perhaps the most significant consequence, however, was the decline in the number of automobile-related accidents and fatalities throughout the country.

The next paragraph works from *effects* to their *cause*, which is stated in the concluding sentence.

♦ Jennifer has difficulty sleeping and she is often depressed. She has reduced her diet to two salads a day and has lost over thirty pounds. She weighs only eighty-two pounds and thinks she should lose even more weight. She has few friends and worries constantly about her appearance. Although emaciated, she continues to restrict her intake of food. Jennifer's condition is diagnosed as anorexia nervosa, an eating disorder in which a person loses one-fourth or more of her normal weight, but feels fat and worries about becoming obese. Some researchers believe that this disorder stems from our culture, which emphasizes weight and which encourages young women to be always dieting.

Writing Tips

May the Force Be With You!

Passive verbs are not as forceful or strong as active verbs. For this reason, effective writers tend to avoid them when possible.

To change a passive form to active, find the word that performs the action in the sentence and make it the subject:

subject

Passive: *Senator Marshall* was asked by the dean to speak at commencement.

subject

Revised Active: The *dean* asked Senator Marshall to speak at commencement.

Notice that the revised form is tightened up and more forceful.

When *who* did an action is less important than *to whom it was done*, or when you don't know who or what performed the action, passive verbs are useful constructions:

The suspect *had been seen* in nearby towns.

Helen *was honored* by her coworkers.

Counterfeit money *was substituted* for genuine bills.

Exercise A   ## Using Cause and Effect

Select one of the following topics below and list as many causes and effects as you can think of. Here is an example:

topic: Hunger in the United States

Causes
- low income
- lack of information concerning nutrition and balanced meals
- large families
- inadequate distribution of food surpluses
- emphasis on fatty and starchy foods

Effects
- birth defects
- high incidence of childhood diseases
- high mortality rate among poor
- poor academic performance in school
- undesirable social behavior
- vulnerability to disease

Topics
- cheating in college
- working mothers
- minimum-wage laws
- the Great Depression

© 2001 Addison-Wesley Educational Publishers Inc.

- child abuse
- alcoholism
- the interest in astrology
- the turbulence of the Sixties
- prejudice
- the exodus to the suburbs

Exercise B   Developing a Paragraph with Cause and Effect

Select one of the following topics and develop it into a paragraph, moving from causes to effects or from effects to causes.

- religious conversions
- capital punishment
- the decline in voter registration
- the decline in reading scores
- the growth of conservatism
- the warming trend throughout the world
- the increase in date rape
- the decline of Detroit in the auto world

WRITING PARAGRAPHS

Below are two paragraphs that illustrate cause-and-effect relationships. The first paragraph moves from an effect—headaches in children—to their causes. The second moves from a series of causes to their effect: the creation of a school solely for Indians. Read both paragraphs carefully and then respond to the directions that follow them.

a. Headaches in children are quite rare. They are more frequent in children whose parents complain often about headaches. This is not so much because of inherited physical tendencies, but because children are mimics. Therefore, it is wise for parents to mention headaches as infrequently as possible. Children are susceptible to tension headaches and it is up to a parent to try to discover the cause. Often, just talking about a problem may help a child. Some children try to do too much, or are pushed by family or school to do too much. Even fun activities can be overdone and the child may be exhausted.

—Health Net, *Healthwise Handbook*, p. 97

b. The idea for a school for Montreal's Mohawk children began after a snowball fight between two boys in 1971. Both were guilty, but only one was suspended. The punished boy was Indian and the other was white. As a protest, indigenous children at the school occupied the main auditorium for three days. They felt unwelcome in the school, they said. They had no Mohawk history or language lessons, and they faced daily discrimination. In a school of 2700 students only 400 or so were indigenous. The only Mohawk staff-member in the school was the janitor. A change was necessary. The parents won some concessions from the Quebec government; an Indian counselor was appointed, some native teachers were recruited, and classes in Mohawk history and language were opened. But the people still felt unhappy. In 1978 they called a referendum to decide whether to create an Indian high school. On September 9, 1978 . . . the Mohawk community had set up its own Indian-run school in Canada: the Kahnawake Survival School.

—Julian Burger, *The Gaia Atlas of First Peoples*, in Susan Lobo and Steve Talbot,
Native American Voices, pp. 252–53

Exercise C   Developing a Paragraph with Cause and Effect

Select one of the following topics and write a paragraph moving from causes to effects or from effects to causes.

- the popularity of talk shows
- single-parent families
- heart disease
- voter apathy
- labor strikes
- the growth of on-line shopping
- divorce

Writing Tips

Dashing Through the Snow. . .

Students sometimes confuse the use of the dash with that of the hyphen. These points may help:

Use dashes to set off explanatory matter that you want to make more prominent.

Use a dash to indicate a sudden change in the thought or structure of a sentence. This use occurs chiefly in writing dialogue in a story, or in letter writing.

Use a hyphen—not a dash—to set off certain prefixes, to separate certain compound words, and to show that a word is to be carried over to the next line.

To produce a dash with a typewriter or word processor, type two hyphens, with no space before, between, or after them.

© 2001 Addison-Wesley Educational Publishers Inc.

Computer Activity

With your writing partner, select one of the topics from the "Topics" section on pages 268–70.

Each of you will be writing a paragraph on the same topic, but approaching it from two different points of view. Decide who will write on *cause* and who will write on *effect*.

When you have finished your paragraph, make a copy and exchange computer files.

In tandem, you and your writing partner should have both aspects of the topic, i.e. the causes and effects relating to your topic. Discuss the relationships between these particular causes and effect.

12

Capitalization

The capitalization of words helps the reader and serves as a guide to their meaning. The rules for capitalization are based, in general, on the following principle: the names of *specific* persons, places, and things (in other words, *proper* nouns) are capitalized; the names of *general* persons, places, and things (*common* nouns) are not capitalized.

1. Capitalize the first word in every sentence, including direct quotations that are complete sentences.

    ◆ It has snowed for six days and five nights.
    ◆ Have you washed the dishes?
    ◆ I can't believe it!
    ◆ Mr. Thais said, "My challah has too many raisins in it."

2. Capitalize the first and last words in a title and all other words except *a, an, the,* and unimportant words with fewer than five letters.

    ◆ Phantom of the Opera
    ◆ Catcher in the Rye
    ◆ Last Tango in Paris

3. Capitalize the titles of relatives and professions when they precede the person's name, or when they are used to address the person.

    ◆ Happy anniversary, Mother and Dad.
    ◆ My Uncle Patrick was a mail carrier for thirty years.
    ◆ My advisor is Professor Valdez.
    ◆ I have an appointment with Doctor Shelby tomorrow.

Do not capitalize titles of relatives and professions when they are preceded by possessives (such as *my*, *his*, *our*, and *their*) and when they are used alone in place of the full name.

- ◆ My mother and father have been married forty years.
- ◆ My uncle is a retired mail carrier.
- ◆ My advisor is a professor of Asian studies.
- ◆ My doctor has an office in her farmhouse.

4. Capitalize official titles of honor and respect when they precede personal names.

- ◆ General Colin Powell
- ◆ President George Washington
- ◆ Mayor Giuliani
- ◆ Justice Sandra Day O'Connor
- ◆ Ambassador Rodgers
- ◆ Senator Kennedy
- ◆ Mayor Williams

Do *not* capitalize titles of honor and respect when they follow personal names.

- ◆ a general in the United States Army
- ◆ the governor of the state
- ◆ an ambassador from Canada
- ◆ the mayor of San Antonio

An exception to this rule is made for certain *national officials* (the President, Vice President, and Chief Justice) and *international figures* (the Pope, the Secretary General of the United Nations).

- ◆ The President and the Vice President, with their wives, arrived in Rome last night and were greeted by the Pope and the Secretary General of the United Nations.

5. Capitalize the names of people, political, religious, and ethnic groups, languages, nationalities, and adjectives derived from them.

Czechs
Irish
Japanese
Protestantism

© 2001 Addison-Wesley Educational Publishers Inc.

Latino

Democrats

Communists

African-American

Victorian

Elizabethan

Cubans

Puritans

6. Capitalize the names of particular streets, buildings, bridges, rivers, cities, states, nations, specific geographical features, schools, and other institutions.

Broadway

Wall Street

Empire State Building

Santa Monica Pier

Housatonic River

Passaic, New Jersey

Wheeling, West Virginia

Miami-Dade College

Sing Sing Prison

Somalia

Switzerland

Coney Island

Tellico Plains

Blue Ridge Mountains

University of North Carolina

Howard University

the United States House of Representatives

the United Nations

7. Capitalize directions only when they refer to specific regions or are part of a proper name.

down South

South Carolina

the Middle West

the West Coast

back East
the Near East
in the North
North Dakota

Do *not* capitalize these words when they merely indicate a direction or general location.

the western slope of the mountain

the south of Italy

facing north

northern Montana

on the east side of town

8. Capitalize the days of the week, months of the year, and names of holidays and religious seasons.

Friday

Good Friday

September

the Fourth of July

Father's Day

Ramadan

Passover

Veterans Day

9. Capitalize the names of particular historical events, eras, and special events.

the Civil War

World War I

the Great Depression

the Middle Ages

the Roaring Twenties

World Series

Cannes International Film Festival

Super Bowl

the Trail of Tears

Kristalnacht

© 2001 Addison-Wesley Educational Publishers Inc.

Rodeo Week

the Harlem Renaissance

10. Capitalize the names of school subjects only if they are proper nouns or if they are followed by a course number.

anthropology

Anthropology 101

Portuguese

political science

Political Science 240a

Asian studies

Asian Studies 152

psychology

Psychology 190

11. Capitalize all references to a supreme being.

God

Goddess

the Almighty

the Holy Spirit

the Buddha

the Holy Ghost

the Lord

the Savior

Allah

12. Capitalize personal pronouns referring to a supreme being.

Ask God for His blessing.

Pray for His forgiveness.

Exercise 12-1

Circle every letter or word that should be capitalized.

1. My favorite course at san diego mesa community college was archeology 105, taught by professor diane barbolla, ph.d.

2. I especially enjoyed learning about the works of art and architecture called the seven wonders of the world, which were admired by the ancient greeks and romans.

3. Khufu, khafra, and menkaura make up the group of pyramids of egypt; built between 3000 and 1800 b.c., they are the only surviving wonder which can still be seen.

4. The hanging gardens of babylon, built by king nebuchadnezzar in 600 b.c., lie on a terrace seventy-five feet in the air and are irrigated by the euphrates river.

5. My friend diana, who lives in southeastern greece, told me about the fourth wonder, which was a gold and ivory statue of the god zeus at olympia.

6. The sculptor chares spent twelve years building a statue of the sun god helios that was 120 feet high and overlooked the harbor near rhodes.

7. The largest temple of ancient times was the temple of artemis, near ephesus, greece.

8. The mausoleum at halicarnassus was a giant marble tomb built for mausolus, a statesman of the persian empire—hence the word "mausoleum."

9. When sailing on labor day, I always think of the seventh wonder: the pharos lighthouse of alexandria, which was sculpted by the greek architect sostratos, and stood an amazing two hundred to six hundred feet high.

10. More than 100,000 laborers worked for twenty years to build the great pyramid of khufu, which contains almost three million slabs of limestone.

Exercise 12-2

Circle every letter or word that should be capitalized.

1. In 1533, britain's king henry viii—though already married to catherine of aragon—married anne boleyn and was excommunicated from the roman catholic church by the pope.

2. If I can't save enough money for tuition next semester, I'll not be able to join my family when they take their vacation to western canada.

3. One of the most important religious holidays in the mideast is ramadan.

4. Every fourth of july at our company's party, Mr. Dickerson sings "you give love a bad name" by the hard rock band bon jovi.

5. Thanks to their coach's tough training methods, the water polo team from ukraine won the gold medal at last year's olympics.

6. The former governor said that her memoir, *memories of the mansion*, was factually accurate.

7. We flew pogo airlines from west virginia to western ireland, and then to southern norway.

8. Jennifer and her husband caught several trout in the gulf stream last spring.

© 2001 Addison-Wesley Educational Publishers Inc.

9. A politician from the state of Mississippi revealed that he had been a member of the klan.

10. The oldest university in the united states is harvard, which was founded in 1636.

11. The prince of wales has a country estate at balmoral castle.

12. Floods in the northern part of minnesota damaged the fall crops.

13. Letters written by the explorers of the south pole were read to our geography class by professor brink.

14. Mexico adjusts the value of its peso in accordance with the rise or fall of the American dollar.

15. Applicants for the sales position were required to pass written examinations in english, spanish, and japanese.

WRITING SENTENCES

Using Correct Capitalization

As you saw in this chapter, a word can often be capitalized in one situation but not capitalized in another. In this exercise you will be asked to illustrate such situations.

1. Write a sentence in which "president" is capitalized. Next, write a sentence in which "president" is not capitalized.

2. Following the example above, use the following words in original sentences. For each word, write two sentences: one which requires the word to be capitalized, and one which requires that it not be capitalized.
   uncle (or aunt)
   professor
   university
   street
   college
   west (or another direction)
   day
   biology (or another subject)

Editing Exercise

Supply all missing capital letters in the following paragraph.

When I was a junior at mckinley high school, mister chavez, our teacher, led our american history 101 class on a tour of washington, d.c., our nation's capital. The city was originally carved from the state of maryland. It is located at the head of the potomac river, which separates it from virginia to the southwest. The idea of a national capital city originated at a meeting of congress in 1783 in philadelphia shortly after the war for independence had been concluded. The cornerstone of the capitol was laid by george washington in september, 1793, and in 1800 the offices of the government were moved to the new capitol from philadelphia. The two most famous buildings are the capitol and the executive mansion, which came to be known as the white house. The senate and the house of representatives meet in the capitol, and the president and his family live in the white house. Both buildings are linked to the lincoln memorial by a mall which was originally intended to be a broad, tree-lined avenue like the champs elysees in paris. The streets in Washington are lettered to the north and south, numbered to the east and west, and the avenues are named for the states. Among notable monuments are the lincoln memorial, the jefferson memorial, and the john f. kennedy center for the performing arts. Other impressive buildings include the supreme court, the library of congress, and the treasury. Two famous institutions of learning in the city are howard university and georgetown university. The oldest residential neighborhood is georgetown, where most of the foreign embassies are located. Washington hosts hundreds of national conventions of organizations such as the national association of manufacturers and the national education association. Tourism is also a major source of income, which benefits such nearby communities as chevy chase, bethesda, and silver spring in the state of maryland, and alexandria, falls church, and arlington in virginia. Most tourists visit the city in the spring and summer months. While in the capital we saw several members of congress and we met senator wilson from our state. We also attended the musical play "phantom of the opera."

© 2001 Addison-Wesley Educational Publishers Inc.

Review Test 12-A

Capitalization

Put an "X" next to the number of any word that should be capitalized.

1. Before serving as a (1) general in the United States (2) army, Colin Powell had been assigned to the (3) pentagon.

   (1)_____ (2)_____ (3)_____

2. While driving through the (4) southern part of Illinois, we stopped at Carbondale to visit my (5) brother Elvis, who is majoring in (6) chemistry at Southern Illinois (7) university.

   (4)_____ (5)_____ (6)_____ (7)_____

3. He told us that (8) chemistry 201 is the most difficult course in the curriculum, except for his course in (9) composition.

   (8)_____ (9)_____

4. A (10) preacher from the (11) state of Washington gave the invocation at the dinner for (12) mayor Golding.

   (10)_____ (11)_____ (12)_____

5. Letters by a (13) canadian (14) explorer were read to our class by (15) professor Bennett and a (16) professor from a (17) history class.

   (13)_____ (14)_____ (15)_____ (16)_____ (17)_____

6. My (18) doctor received his degree from the University of Michigan, which is in the (19) city of Ann Arbor.

   (18)_____ (19)_____

7. Innsbruck is in the (20) western part of Austria and is the home of a (21) medieval castle as well as the site of the 1976 (22) olympic ski competition.

(20)_____ (21)_____ (22)_____

© 2001 Addison-Wesley Educational Publishers Inc.

Name_____ Date _____

▶Review Test 12-B

Capitalization

Put an "X" next to the number of any word that should be capitalized.

1. In the opening lines of John Milton's poem (1) *paradise* (2) *lost*, the poet prays to the muses and to the (3) holy (4) spirit for inspiration.

   (1)_____ (2)_____ (3)_____ (4)_____

2. Candidates for a position with the oil company must speak the French (5) language as well as (6) arabic.

   (5)_____ (6)_____

3. Students enrolled in (7) psychology classes are often surprised at the amount of knowledge they are expected to have in such areas as (8) physiology and (9) sociology.

   (7)_____ (8)_____ (9)_____

4. One of the most important (10) moslem (11) religious holidays is (12) ramadan, which is the ninth month of the (13) muhammadan (14) year and celebrated throughout the (15) middle (16) east.

   (10)_____ (11)_____ (12)_____ (13)_____ (14)_____

   (15)_____ (16)_____

5. My subscription to (17) *reader's* (18) *digest* expired while I was vacationing in the (19) mountains of Kentucky last (20) summer.

   (17)_____ (18)_____ (19)_____ (20)_____

6. Walt did a term paper in (21) political (22) science 201; his subject was the (23) supreme (24) court.

    (21)_____ (22)_____ (23)_____ (24)_____

7. The pastor of the (25) church is (26) father Murphy.

    (25)_____ (26)_____

8. We invited Jorge and his family to celebrate the (27) fourth of July with us at a picnic in a (28) park in (29) downtown Indianapolis.

    (27)_____ (28)_____ (29)_____

© 2001 Addison-Wesley Educational Publishers Inc.

WRITING PARAGRAPHS

DEVELOPING PARAGRAPHS BY DEFINITION

When you want to clarify a term that might have several meanings, or when you are asked by an instructor to explain a complex concept or word, you will use *definition* as the organizing principle of your paragraph. Words can be defined in three ways: by a *synonym* (substituting a familiar word for the word to be defined), by a *formal definition* (the kind often used in the dictionary), and by an *extended definition*, which develops the meaning of the word in a paragraph or essay.

Definition by Synonym

Definition by *synonym* is the most concise way to define: a *melee* is defined as "a fight," a *maxillary* as "a jawbone," and *jejune* as "immature." The advantage of a definition by synonym is that it is brief. The danger occurs when the synonym is as confusing as the word being defined. To define *redundancy* as "a tautology," for example, is not very helpful.

The Formal Definition

The *formal definition* can often be expressed in one sentence. It consists of three parts: the term to be defined, the general class it belongs to, and the way it differs from all other members of that class. Here, in chart form, are some formal definitions:

Term	General Class	Differentiation
The *human eye*	is *a bodily organ*	of *sight*.
A *capella*	is *a type of choir*	which *does not use instrumental accompaniment.*
A *binomial*	is *an algebraic expression*	with *two variables in it.*

The formal definition can be very helpful because of its exactness, and therefore is often used by dictionary makers.

Exercise A   Formal Definitions

Using the examples above, select five of the following terms and write a formal definition for each.

apple	anger
soprano	wheelbarrow
misdemeanor	diskette
ski boots	pencil
rock and roll	motorcycle

The Extended Definition

The *extended definition* includes further explanation, examples, or characteristics, and it is the type usually asked for by your instructors. The following paragraph is an extended definition. It names the term to be defined ("sex roles"), the general class it belongs to (a set of social standards), the way it differs from all other members of that class (they prescribe appropriate behavior for males and females), and it gives examples to make the definition clear.

Writing Tips

Writing tips

Paragraphs developed by definition follow no customary pattern. Their organization depends, in great part, on what is being defined and what the writer intends to say about it. Here are some of the questions you might ask before writing your definition paragraph:

- What are some examples of it?
- How many kinds are there?
- What are its parts?
- What is it similar to or different from?
- How is it done?
- What causes it? What are its results or effects?
- A final bit of advice: When writing a definition, avoid using the old cliché, "According to Webster . . . "

© 2001 Addison-Wesley Educational Publishers Inc.

◆ Sex roles are the set of social standards that prescribe appropriate behavior for males and females. Sex-role definitions provide the basis for stereotypes. In Western societies, for example, men are supposed to be dominant, competitive, logical, and unemotional. Women are supposed to be warm, caring, emotionally responsive, and socially adept. The learning of sex roles begins in the preschool years, and by the end of that period, the behavior of boys and girls has become different in many ways. Some of the differences may be due to biological factors. But most of the sex-linked differences in children's behavior can be explained by the ways that parents' expectations and behavior with their children differ according to the child's sex. In addition, other adults who interact with children probably have the same expectations.

Exercise B   Using Extended Definitions

Using extended definition, define one of the following terms or ideas in a paragraph. Underline your topic sentence.

- romance
- a good movie
- sin
- beauty
- macho
- generosity
- happiness
- patriotism
- honesty
- fear

Writing Paragraphs

Both of the following paragraphs are developed by definition. Read them carefully and then respond to the directions that follow them.

a. Granite is the igneous rock most commonly quarried for construction in North America. It is a mosaic of mineral crystals, principally feldspar and quartz, and can be obtained in a range of colors that includes gray, black, pink, red, brown, buff, and green. Granite is nonporous, hard, strong, and durable, the most nearly permanent of building stones, suitable for use in contact with the ground or exposed to severe weathering. Its surface can be finished in any of a number of textures including a mirrorlike polish. In North America it is quarried chiefly in the East and the upper Midwest.

—Edward Allen and Joseph Iano, *Fundamentals of Building Construction*, p. 290

b.   They were master farmers. They settled near the rich alluvial soil of riverbeds in the Southeast to grown corn, the staff of New World life, as well as beans, squash, pumpkins, and tobacco. They had an elaborate trade network among themselves and with other Indians, and crafted beautifully refined objects. They had a complex social structure and a rigid caste system. They were obsessed with death. They built mounds, not only burial mounds like the Adenas and Hopewells before them, but also huge temple mounds. These were the people of the so-called Mississippian or Temple Mound Builder culture.

—Carl Waldman, from *Atlas of the North American Indian*, reprinted in Susa Lobo and Steve Talbot, *Native American Voices*, p. 70

Exercise C   Using Extended Definition

Select one of the following terms and define it in an extended definition of at least 150 words.

- an abstract term such as *loyalty*, *poverty*, or *justice*
- a scientific term
- a slang term that you often use in conversation
- a specialized term unique to a particular sport or hobby
- a term from the visual or performing arts

Writing Tips

Have Pen, Will Query

Have you written an essay, a poem, or a story that you think would appeal to a broader audience? *Poets & Writers,* a magazine which lists names of book and magazine publishers in search of good writing, is available at most libraries and booksellers. The magazine will tell you how and where to submit your work. Many of the editors listed in *Poets & Writers* specifically look for writers who have never been published.

© 2001 Addison-Wesley Educational Publishers Inc.

Computer Activity

Choose a subject from Exercise A on page 286 or B on page 287. Using an extended definition, write a paragraph and underline your topic sentence. Make a copy of only your topic sentence and exchange it with your writing partner, who has performed the same task.

Ask your partner to anticipate what follows your topic sentence by completing the development of the paragraph.

Do the same for your partner's topic sentence.

When your paragraph is returned, decide whether or not you need to clarify your extended definition for your reader. If changes are needed, rewrite your paragraph.

13

Spelling

Some people seem to be born good spellers just as some people are apparently born with perfect musical pitch. Others—and perhaps they are the majority—continue to be plagued by mistakes in spelling all of their lives, to their own embarrassment and the irritation of others. To be sure, mistakes in spelling are not as serious as errors in grammar, word choice, organization, or punctuation, but they are usually more noticeable, and therefore more annoying. Like errors in punctuation, they distract the readers and make them wonder about the writer's credibility and the accuracy of his or her ideas. Whether right or wrong, most people in our society—particularly employers, instructors, and others in positions of authority—regard misspelled words as symbols of carelessness and irresponsibility.

Poor spellers are not necessarily lacking in intelligence or linguistic skill. The poets William Butler Yeats and John Keats were both notoriously bad spellers. But that is no excuse for careless or indifferent attempts to spell a word correctly. Granted, the English language is full of irregularities and inconsistencies; many of the letters in our alphabet have more than one sound, many words have letters that are silent, and others have sounds for which there seem to be no letters. From all of this, one might think that the English spelling system is all chaos and that it is impossible to determine and apply any rules with consistency. The fact is, however, that there *are* some rules and study techniques that will help to improve the spelling skills of even the least confident speller.

SOME SUGGESTIONS

If you are a weak speller, the first and probably most important suggestion for reducing the number of misspellings in your writing is to proofread your papers at least once, looking closely and carefully for words whose spelling you are uncertain of. Too often, students will guess at the spelling of a word or settle for an approximate version, hoping that the instructor will appreciate their creativity and imagination. But a series of misspelled words in an otherwise excellent paper is like spinach in your sweetheart's teeth: it does not enhance the subject. By looking over your papers carefully, you will detect some misspelled words. You may even find it helpful to have a friend read over your work, since writers are often blind to their own mistakes.

Keeping a list of troublesome words is another way of pinpointing and reducing the number of misspelled words that can occur in writing. Such a list would have not only the correctly spelled form of the word, but also its meaning. By training your eye and exercising your curiosity, you will notice the individual quirks and characteristics of words, including their spelling. Of course, having a good college-level dictionary at hand when writing is important, and using it is even more helpful. If your instructor permits, bring your dictionary to class when writing your themes and compositions.

FOUR SPELLING RULES THAT USUALLY WORK

1. *ie* and *ei*

   When *ie* and *ei* have the long *e* sound (as in *meet*), use *i* before *e* except after *c*. The old jingle will help:

   > Put *i* before *e*
   >
   > Except after *c*
   >
   > or when sounded like *a*
   >
   > As in *neighbor* and *weigh*

ie	ei (after c)	ei (the sound of ay)
believe	ceiling	freight
cashier	conceit	neighbor
grief	perceive	sleigh
niece	receive	veil
shriek		vein
thief		weigh

Some exceptions: ancient, conscience, either, fiery, foreign, leisure, neither, seize, species, weird

Exercise 13-1   Writing Words with ie and ei

On the line in each word below, write the letters ie or ei to spell each word correctly. Use a dictionary as needed.

1. sh____ld
2. b____ge
3. ach____ve

© 2001 Addison-Wesley Educational Publishers Inc.

4. dec____ve
5. rel____ve
6. f____ld
7. misch____f
8. y____ld
9. h____r
10. for____gn

2. the silent final *e*

   If a word ends in a silent *e* (as in *hope*), drop the *e* before adding any ending that begins with a vowel. Keep the final *e* before endings that begin with a consonant.

Before a Vowel	Before a Consonant
value + able = valuable	hope + ful = hopeful
hope + ed = hoped	sincere + ly = sincerely
give + ing = giving	nine + teen = nineteen
assure + ance = assurance	state + ment = statement
extreme + ity = extremity	love + ly = lovely
fate + al = fatal	

   Some exceptions: dyeing, hoeing, duly (due + ly), truly (true + ly), noticeable, peaceable, courageous

3. doubling the final consonant

   If a word of one syllable ends with a single consonant preceded by a single vowel (as in *hit*), double the final consonant before adding a suffix beginning with a vowel. If the word has more than one syllable, the emphasis should be on the final syllable.

Single Syllable	Multisyllable
hit + ing = hitting	admit + ed = admitted
slam + ed = slammed	permit + ing = permitting
shop + ed = shopped	repel + ing = repelling
fat + est = fattest	begin + er = beginner
fun + y = funny	prefer + ed = preferred

   Some exceptions: preference, conference, benefited, signaled (also spelled signalled)

4. final *y*

When a word ends with *-y* preceded by a consonant, change the *y* to an *i* when adding a suffix, except those suffixes beginning with an *i*:

> baby + es = babies
>
> twenty + eth = twentieth
>
> likely + hood = likelihood
>
> marry + age = marriage (*but* marry + ing = marrying)
>
> weary + ness = weariness

When a word ends with *-y* preceded by a vowel, do not change the *y*:

> toy + s = toys
>
> monkey + s = monkeys
>
> attorney + s = attorneys
>
> displayed + ed = displayed

Some exceptions: paid, daily, said, laid

Exercise 13-2

Proofread the following sentences, correcting any misspelled words.

1. Carlos spoke with much assureance and confidence to the group.
2. The attornies for the tobacco company conferred before speaking to the reporters.
3. What is the likelihood that you will transfer to State next fall?
4. My grandmother gave me valueable advice before I was married.
5. The firemen were hopefull that they could reach the trapped children.
6. Mona claims that monkies can be taught to read.
7. The men prefered to wear suits and ties to the dinner.
8. The President issued a statment expressing his sorrow at the tragedy.
9. Harold's daily run on the beach was interrupted by the storm last week.
10. A new law passed permiting skateboarding on Warren Avenue.

FORMING THE PLURALS OF WORDS

Most words form their plurals by adding *s* to the singular:

chocolates

dogs

movies

© 2001 Addison-Wesley Educational Publishers Inc.

Words ending in *s*, *ch*, *sh*, or *x* form their plurals by adding *es* to the singular:

classes

crutches

wishes

taxes

The plural of hyphenated nouns is formed by adding *s* to the main noun:

mother-in-law = mothers-in-law

father-in-law = fathers-in-law

court-martial = courts-martial

Nouns ending with *ful* form their plural by adding *s* to the end of the word:

spoonful = spoonfuls

cupful = cupfuls

mouthful = mouthfuls

Some words ending in *f* change to *v* in the plural:

elf = elves

wife = wives

leaf = leaves

half = halves

life = lives

self = selves

Some exceptions: roofs, chiefs

The plural of many nouns that end with *o* is formed by adding *s* if the *o* is preceded by another vowel:

radio = radios

studio = studios

ratio = ratios

zoo = zoos

The plural of many nouns that end with *o* is formed by adding *es* if the *o* is preceded by a consonant:

cargo = cargoes
echo = echoes
hero = heroes
motto = mottoes
potato = potatoes
zero = zeroes

The singular and the plural of some nouns are the same:

fish
deer
sheep
series
means

The plural of some nouns is formed by a change in spelling:

woman = women
child = children
foot = feet
tooth = teeth

Plurals of nouns borrowed from other languages are usually formed according to the rules of those languages. You must memorize their plural forms or use a modern dictionary to check their current status. Here are some examples:

alumna = alumnae
alumnus = alumni
analysis = analyses
basis = bases
crisis = crises
criterion = criteria
datum = data

© 2001 Addison-Wesley Educational Publishers Inc.

dictum = dicta

medium = media

memorandum = memoranda

parenthesis = parentheses

Exercise 13-3

Proofread the following sentences, correcting any plural forms of words.

1. The amount in American dollars was placed in parenthesis in the guidebook for the convenience of the tourists.
2. "Do you have that memoranda from the broker?" asked Mister Bailey.
3. The geologists from the oil company completed their three analysis of the soil.
4. "We can overcome this crises," assured the President.
5. Be sure to add two spoonsful of flour before adding the egg yolks.
6. Some of the characters in the Old Testament had several wifes.
7. The Great Famine in Ireland was caused in part by a parasite that attacked potatos.
8. Echos of the outside traffic reverberated throughout the concert hall.
9. Not wanting to be seen, Jack stuffed his mouth with handsful of jelly beans.
10. I counted over four hundred sheeps before falling asleep.

TWENTY-FIVE SETS OF HOMONYMS: WORDS OFTEN CONFUSED

Many words in the English language are often confused because they sound the same (or almost the same) as other words. Such words are *homonyms*, and the list that follows contains some of those that are most frequently misused by writers.

Look the list over carefully, noting the differences in meaning. For additional words that are often confused, see "A Glossary of Usage" on page 341.

All ready and already	*All ready* is an adjective meaning "entirely ready."
	We are packed and *all ready* to go.
	Already is an adverb meaning "previously."
	Jack pretended to be surprised, but he had *already* heard about the party.
All together and altogether	*All together* means "in a group."
	The families of the bride and groom were *all together* in the reception area.

Altogether means "completely" or entirely."

> We were *altogether* exhausted after the trek through the desert.

Bare and bear

Bare is an adjective meaning "naked" or "undisguised."

> The baby wiggled out of its diaper and was completely *bare*.

Bear as a verb means "to carry or support." As a noun it refers to "a large omnivorous animal."

> The bridge was too weak to *bear* the weight of the trucks.

> While we were in Yosemite, we saw several large *bears* foraging for food in a nearby campground.

Buy and by

Buy is a verb meaning "to purchase."

> When you *buy* a home, you are probably making the largest purchase of your life.

By is a preposition meaning "close to or next to."

> I saw his Hyundai parked *by* the barn.

Capital and capitol

Capital is the leading city of a state, or wealth, or chief in importance.

> The *capital* of Nicaragua is Managua.

> Lorena lives on the interest from her accumulated *capital*.

> The low interest rate was of *capital* importance in holding down inflation.

Capitol is the building in which lawmakers sit.

> The flag of surrender flew over the *capitol*.

Coarse and course

Coarse is an adjective meaning "rough" or "inferior."

> The sandpaper was too *coarse* to use on the table.

Course is a noun meaning "direction" or "academic studies."

> By using a compass, we were able to follow the right *course*.

> The *course* in statistics was helpful in my job later.

Complement and compliment

To complement is "to balance or complete."
> Kareem's new tie *complemented* his suit.

© 2001 Addison-Wesley Educational Publishers Inc.

To compliment is "to flatter." As a noun it means "an expression of praise."

> When anyone *complimented* Bernice, she blushed, because she was unaccustomed to *compliments*.

Consul, council, and counsel	A *consul* is a government official stationed in another country.

> The American *consul* in Paris helped the stranded New Yorkers locate their family.

A *council* is a body of people acting in an official capacity.

> The city *council* passed a zoning regulation.

Counsel as a noun means "an advisor" or "advice"; as a verb it means "to advise."

> The defendant's *counsel* objected to the question.

> The *counsel* that he gave her was based on his many years of experience.

> Saul *counseled* me on my decision.

Forth and fourth	*Forth* is an adverb meaning "forward in time or place."

> When the doors opened, the mob rushed *forth*.

Fourth is an adjective form of "four," the number.

> On my *fourth* attempt, the car finally started.

Hear and here	*Hear* is a verb meaning "to listen to."

> From our room we could *hear* the roar of the crowd.

Here is an adverb meaning "in this place."

> A new restaurant will be opened *here* next week.

Hole and whole	*Hole* is a noun meaning "a cavity."

> The acid etched a *hole* in the coin.

Whole as an adjective means "complete or healthy"; as a noun it means "all of the components or parts of a thing."

> I ate the *whole* cake.

> Her performance as a *whole* was rated superior.

It's and its	*It's* is a contraction for "it is" or "it has."

> *It's* quite an accomplishment, but I received a "C" in math.

It's been a hectic semester.

Its is the possessive form of It.

Every tool was in *its* proper place.

Knew and new

Knew is the past tense of *know.*

Hamid thought he *knew* the combination, but he had forgotten it.

New means "recent."

New evidence was discovered linking smoking with cancer.

No and know

No as an adverb means "not so"; as an adjective, it means "not any, not one."

No, I did not receive my mail yet.

We had *no* opportunity to tell Greg goodbye.

Know is a verb that means "to be aware of."

I *know* that the "No Smoking" sign is on.

Peace and piece

Peace is a noun meaning "tranquillity" or "the absence of war."

The Prime Minister promised *peace* in our time.

Piece as a noun means "a part or portion of something."

Virginia preferred to get paid by the hour rather than by the *piece.*

Principal and principle

Principal as an adjective means "main," "chief"; as a noun it means "a sum of money" or "the head of a school."

The *principal* reason she stayed was loyalty to her family.

Scott repaid the *principal* of the loan and the interest within a month.

The *principal* of my high school encouraged me to go to college.

Principle is a noun meaning "a truth, rule, or code of conduct."

I could never learn the *principles* of the slide rule.

Gambling is based on the *principle* of greed.

Right and write

Right as a noun means "a just claim or title" or "the right-hand side."

© 2001 Addison-Wesley Educational Publishers Inc.

The *right* to speak freely is every American's legacy.

In Ireland we could not drive on the *right*.

Write means "to draw or communicate."

Ben was able to *write* at the age of four.

Role and roll	*Role* is a noun meaning "a part or function."

Role is a noun meaning "a part or function."

The navy's *role* in the revolution was unclear.

Roll as a verb means "to move forward, as on wheels"; as a noun, it means "bread" or "a list of names."

The tanks *rolled* down the main street of the town.

Professor Samuels often forgets to take *roll*.

Scene and seen

Scene is a noun meaning "a view or setting."

The *scene* from my hotel room was unforgettable.

Seen is the past participle of *see*.

Have you ever *seen* a falling star?

Stationary and stationery

Stationary is an adjective meaning "permanent" or "not moving."

The wheels of the car were locked in a *stationary* position.

Stationery is a noun meaning "writing paper and envelopes."

Louis gave me a box of monogrammed *stationery*.

There, their, and they're

There is an adverb meaning "in that place."

Place the packages *there* on the table.

Their is the possessive form of *they*.

They were shocked to find *their* house on fire.

They're is a contraction of *they are*.

They're usually late for every party.

To, too, and two

To is a preposition; *too* is an adverb; *two* is an adjective.

He ran *to* the door.

I'm *too* excited to eat.

It snowed heavily *two* days ago.

Weather and whether

Weather is a noun referring to climatic conditions.

If we have warm *weather* tomorrow, let's eat outdoors.

Whether is a conjunction that introduces alternatives.

It may rain tomorrow *whether* we like it or not.

Whose and who's

Whose is the possessive form of *who*.

Whose car is in my parking space?

Who's is a contraction for *who is* or *who has*.

Who's he dating now?

Who's been eating my porridge?

Your and you're

Your is the possessive form of *you*.

Are these *your* books?

You're is a contraction for *you are*.

You're in big trouble.

Exercise 13-4

Circle the correct word in the following sentences.

1. Toya's reactions were (all together, altogether) different from Maureen's.
2. Did you know that the (capital, capitol) of North Dakota is Bismarck?
3. Doctor Keonig's (coarse, course) in statistics is one of the most difficult that I have ever taken.
4. Huang's tie (complemented, complimented) his shirt.
5. The (council, counsel) met in the conference room of the city hall.
6. The dog licked (its, it's) paw.
7. The (principal, principle) of freedom of speech is preserved in the First Amendment.
8. The Wilsons sold (their, there) home to buy a larger one.
9. Abrupt changes in the (weather, whether) often affect airline schedules.
10. (Who's, Whose) going to help me clean up this mess?

SPELLING LIST

Here is a list of words commonly misspelled in college students' writing. Study these words carefully and memorize the spelling of any you are not sure of.

ably	academic	accommodate
absence	accept	accommodation
abundance	accidentally	accompanied

© 2001 Addison-Wesley Educational Publishers Inc.

accuracy

achieve

achievement

acknowledge

acquaintance

acquired

across

address

adequate

admittance

advice

affect

aggravate

aging

all right

allowed

almost

altar

alter

altogether

amateur

analysis

analyze

anonymous

anxiety

apparatus

apparent

appearance

arguing

argument

athletic

audience

awkward

bachelor

basically

beautiful

becoming

beginning

believed

benefited

boundary

breath

breathe

bureau

business

cafeteria

calendar

campaign

candidate

capital

capitol

career

carrying

ceiling

cemetery

certain

chief

chosen

column

coming

committee

competent

competition

condemn

conscientious

conscious

continuous

criticism

criticize

deceive

decision

definitely

definition

dependent

desirable

desperate

devastating

development

difference

dining

disappear

disappoint

disastrous

disease

dissatisfied

divide

doesn't

effect

efficient

eighth

eligible

eliminate

embarrass

emphasize

enthusiastic

environment

equipped

exaggerate

excellent

exercise

exhaust

existence

explanation

familiar

fantasy

fascinate

February

fictitious

fiery

finally

financially

forehead

foreign

foremost

forth

forty

fourth

fulfill

gases

gauge

glamorous

government

grammar

grievance

grievous

guarantee

guard

guidance

happily

happiness

harass

height

heroes

humorous

hurriedly

hygiene

hypocrisy

imitation

immense

incidentally

incredible

indefinite

independence

innocence

inquiry

insistence

intelligence

intercede

interfere

irrelevant

irresistible

its

it's

jealous

judgment

(*also* judgement)

knowledge

laboratory

legitimate

leisure

lessen

lesson

library

license

lightning

likely

literature

loneliness

loose

lose

losing

maintenance

maneuver

marriage

mathematics

medicine

mileage

mischievous

moral

morale

mountain

muscle

musician

mysterious

naturally

necessary

ninety

noticeable

obstacle

occasion

occasionally

occurred

occurrence

omission

omitted

opposed

optimistic

parallel

pastime

permissible

personnel

physician

pneumonia

possess

preceding

prejudice

presence

© 2001 Addison-Wesley Educational Publishers Inc.

prevalent

privilege

probably

procedure

prominent

pronunciation

psychology

pursue

quantity

questionnaire

realize

recede

recommend

rehearsal

religious

reminiscence

repetition

restaurant

rhythm

ridiculous

sacrifice

safety

salary

Saturday

scarcely

schedule

science

secretary

seize

separate

sergeant

severely

similar

skeptical

sophomore

specimen

studying

succeed

surprise

susceptible

technique

temperament

tendency

theory

therefore

thorough

throughout

truly

Tuesday

twelfth

unanimous

unnecessary

unusual

unusually

usage

using

vacuum

valuable

village

villain

visible

warring

weather

Wednesday

whether

whisper

whole

wholly

who's

whose

women

writing

written

yield

your

you're

Writing Tips

Verbal Vertigo

When you look for spelling errors, your mind can play tricks on you. You think you see letters that are not there, and you ignore those that are there. Reading each line of your paragraph backwards will help you because it forces you to read each word singly, in isolation, instead of in a phrase.

Editing Exercise

Correct any misspelled words in the following paragraph.

Thomas Alva Edison was one of the most imagenative geniuses in the history of technology in the United States. His list of achievments and inventions includes more than one-thousand patents, including those on the phonograph, motion-picture projecter, and the incandescant electric lamp. Born in Ohio in 1847, he moved to Michigan with his family when he was seven years old. He was expeled from school after atending only three months when he was labeled as "retarded" by his schoolmaster. His mother, a former schoolteacher, tutered him at home for the next three years. Despite the lack of an acedemic background, he developed an early interest in science, setting up a small chemical laboretory in the celler of his home when he was ten. Obtaining a positon as night operater with Western Union Telegraph Company, he made several improvments in the operation of the stock ticker and printer. With the money he recieved from the sale of one of his stock printer inventions, he set himself up as a manafacturer of stock tickers and printing telegraphs. In 1876 he built an industrial reserch laboratory in New Jersey and was soon produceing inventions at an unparaleled rate. He rarely left the lab, prefering sceintific experimentation to liesure activities. In 1877 he invented the phonograph. He began work on the light bulb in 1878 and in 1879 demanstrated his carbon filament lamp. In 1883 he accidantally discovered the "Edison affect," which later became the bases of the electron tube. He also perfected motion-picture equipment. He died in 1931 after a liftime of intelectual curiosity and discovry.

© 2001 Addison-Wesley Educational Publishers Inc.

WRITING SENTENCES

Using the Right Word

For each of the following words write an original sentence, using the word correctly in your sentence:

- already
- altogether
- complement
- counsel
- forth
- its
- principle
- role
- stationary
- whether
- whose
- your

© 2001 Addison-Wesley Educational Publishers Inc.

Name_____ Date _____

Review Test 13-A

Spelling

A. *On the line preceding each sentence, write the letter corresponding to the correct word.*

_____ 1. Player representatives and owners of the ball clubs were (a. all together b. altogether) for the last meeting before the strike deadline.

_____ 2. Because her views on abortion contradicted the (a. principals b. principles) of the majority of her constituents, she was defeated in her bid for reelection.

_____ 3. By getting up at five in the morning and arriving at the box office promptly, I managed to be (a. forth b. fourth) in line.

_____ 4. Martin claims that he rides a (a. stationary b. stationery) bicycle one hour a day.

_____ 5. Opponents of gun control claim that the Constitution grants citizens the right to (a. bare b. bear) arms.

B. *On the line preceding each number, write the letter of the correctly spelled word.*

		a.	b.	c.
_____	6.	absense	absence	absance
_____	7.	accidentally	accidentaly	acidentally
_____	8.	begining	beginning	begginning
_____	9.	candidate	canidate	cannidate
_____	10.	cemetary	cematery	cemetery
_____	11.	desireable	desirible	desirable
_____	12.	eligible	elligible	eligable
_____	13.	embarass	embarress	embarrass
_____	14.	garauntee	guarantee	gaurentee
_____	15.	incidentally	incidintally	incidentaly
_____	16.	maintainance	maintanance	maintenance
_____	17.	mathematics	mathamatics	mathemetics
_____	18.	ocasionally	occasionally	occassionally
_____	19.	preceding	preceeding	preceading

_____	20.	recomend	recommend	reccomend
_____	21.	religious	relegious	religous
_____	22.	shedule	schedual	schedule
_____	23.	seperate	separate	separat
_____	24.	unneccessary	uneccessary	unnecessary
_____	25.	Wenesday	Wednesday	Wensday

© 2001 Addison-Wesley Educational Publishers Inc.

Review Test 13-B

Spelling

A. *On the line preceding each sentence, write the letter corresponding to the correct word.*

_____ 1. A man (a. who's b. whose) voice was vaguely familiar answered the telephone.

_____ 2. Because I had been away several years, I did not recognize (a. their b. there) home as we pulled into the driveway.

_____ 3. The (a. peace b. piece) treaty was ratified by all seven nations.

_____ 4. The clerk refused to believe that the (a. hole b. whole) was already in the bicycle tire when we bought it.

_____ 5. On the advice of her (a. council b. counsel), Mrs. Rand refused to testify.

B. *On the line preceding each number, write the letter of the correctly spelled word.*

		a.	b.	c.
_____	6.	acurracy	accuracy	accurracy
_____	7.	aggravate	aggrravate	aggrevate
_____	8.	athaletic	athletic	atheletic
_____	9.	becoming	becomming	becomeing
_____	10.	ceiling	cieling	cieleing
_____	11.	comeing	coming	comming
_____	12.	defenition	definetion	definition
_____	13.	dissapoint	dissappoint	disappoint
_____	14.	environment	enviroment	envirenment
_____	15.	foremost	formost	forrmost
_____	16.	guideance	guidance	guidence
_____	17.	indefenite	indifenite	indefinite
_____	18.	iressistible	irresistible	iressistable
_____	19.	acheivment	achievment	achievement
_____	20.	mileage	milage	milaege
_____	21.	occured	occurred	ocurred

_____   22.   pastime   pasttime   pasetime
_____   23.   pernunciation   pranunciation   pronunciation
_____   24.   restraunt   restaurant   restaurent
_____   25.   wholely   wholly   wholy

© 2001 Addison-Wesley Educational Publishers Inc.

WRITING PARAGRAPHS

A REVIEW

Writing a paragraph forces you to make a number of decisions. You must formulate a topic sentence that can be adequately developed within the confines of a paragraph. You must select the details, facts, and reasons to support that topic sentence. And as you prepare your first draft, you must select the most suitable pattern for developing your paragraph.

Selecting the Best Pattern of Paragraph Development

The pattern that you use will depend on your purpose and your topic sentence. As you have seen in the preceding chapters, several patterns are available. If your purpose is to show your reader how something works or how it came about, you would trace a process. If you want your reader to see the similarities or differences between two things or ideas, you would use comparison and contrast. If you are trying to show your reader what something is by giving illustrations, you would develop your paragraph by giving examples.

The wording of your topic statement will also nudge you toward your choice of development pattern. For instance, "There are three kinds of people who drive sports cars" suggests a paragraph developed by classification. "Most hunting accidents are caused by carelessness" will probably be developed by cause and effect. A term like "feminism," a concept that has several meanings, depending on the person or group that uses it, will probably require an extended definition. By carefully considering your topic statement, you will usually have little trouble selecting the right pattern.

To select the best pattern, ask yourself the questions your reader might ask. The kinds of questions you ask will suggest the method best suited for developing your topic sentence, as the examples below demonstrate.

Topic Sentence:	The behavior of some sports figures is a poor example for our youth.
Questions:	Why do you say that? Whom do you have in mind? Name some examples to prove your point.
Method:	Example
Topic Sentence:	My city is actually comprised of a group of distinct communities or groups.
Questions:	What are the various groups or distinct communities?
Method:	Division and classification

Topic Sentence:	The music that my friends and I dance to is different from that of my parents.
Questions:	What was their music like? What is your music like? How are they different?
Method:	Comparison and contrast
Topic Sentence:	Radiocarbon dating is a very exact way to date organic objects up to 75,000 years old.
Questions:	How is it done? What are the steps?
Method:	Process and analysis
Topic Sentence:	Many college athletes graduate as functional illiterates.
Questions:	Why are they allowed to graduate? Who is to blame? What will happen to them after their athletic careers are over?
Method:	Cause and effect
Topic Sentence:	*Machismo* is an ancient concept that still affects male-female relationships in many cultures.
Questions:	What is *machismo*? What is it not? What are its characteristics? What are some examples of *machismo*?
Method:	Definition

Exercise A   Methods of Development

For each of the following topic sentences, list the questions likely to be asked by the reader. Then select the method of development most appropriate for answering the questions.

1. You don't have to be a genius to set up your personal computer.
2. The Library of Congress System is superior to the Dewey Decimal System for classifying books.
3. The withholding tax on tips has caused many hardships for waiters.
4. My daughter has many more opportunities available to her that were denied my mother.
5. Scientists claim that most men are either Type A or Type B in terms of personality traits.
6. Puppy love can be very painful to those who experience it.
7. Study habits and attitudes toward school are often determined by one's cultural background.
8. The kinds of cars that faculty members drive reveal much about them.
9. American education has come under criticism from the public in recent years.
10. Within the last two years the ranks of the homeless in our cities have increased dramatically.

© 2001 Addison-Wesley Educational Publishers Inc.

WRITING PARAGRAPHS

"Ain't I A Woman?"   Sojourner Truth

Sojourner Truth was born into slavery as Isabella Bomefree, in about 1787. In the first thirty years of her life, Isabella was sold four times—once with a flock of sheep for one hundred dollars. Isabella changed her name to Sojourner Truth in 1843 because she planned to travel the nation telling the truth about the lives of slaves and women. Though Truth never learned to read or write, she was a popular lecturer at meetings of anti-slavery and women's rights organizations. Recently, NASA named one of its Mars rovers "Sojourner" in tribute to Truth's lasting message of fairness and freedom for all people. Truth is best known for the address that follows, commonly dubbed her "Ain't I A Woman?" speech, which she delivered on the topic of women's voting rights at the Women's Convention in Ohio, 1851. Sojourner Truth died in 1853.

"Ain't I A Woman?"
Sojourner Truth

Well, children, where there is so much racket there must be something out of kilter. I think that 'twixt the negroes of the South and the women at the North, all talking about rights, the white men will be in a fix pretty soon. But what's all this here talking about?

That man over there says that women need to be helped into carriages, and lifted over ditches, and to have the best place everywhere. Nobody ever helps me into carriages, or over mud-puddles, or gives me any best place! And ain't I a woman? Look at me! Look at my arm! I have ploughed and planted, and gathered into barns, and no man could head me! And ain't I a woman? I could work as much and eat as much as a man—when I could get it—and bear the lash as well! And ain't I a woman? I have borne thirteen children, and seen most all sold off to slavery, and when I cried out with my mother's grief, none but Jesus heard me! And ain't I a woman?

Then they talk about this thing in the head; what's this they call it? [member of audience whispers, "intellect"] That's it, honey. What's that got to do with women's rights or negroes' rights? If my cup won't hold a pint, and your holds a quart, wouldn't you be mean not to let me have my little half measure full?

Then that little man in black there, he says women can't have as much rights as men, 'cause Christ wasn't a woman! Where did your Christ come from? Where did your Christ come from? From God and a woman! Man had nothing to do with Him.

If the first woman God ever made was strong enough to turn the world upside down all alone, these women together ought to be able to turn it back, and get it right side up again! And now they is asking to do it, the men better let them.

Obliged to you for hearing me, and now old Sojourner ain't got nothing more to say.

| Exercise B | ## Methods of Development |

Write a paragraph of at least 150 words on one of the following topics:

- a time when you encountered discrimination or prejudice
- your ideas for confronting and solving a national problem such as racism, poverty, gender equality, the environment, or education
- racial or gender stereotypes on television or in the movies
- the importance of the right to vote
- possible reasons for nationwide voter apathy in recent years

Writing Tips

Is It Really a Paragraph?

Your mound of words is indeed a paragraph if it

- is a string of sentences that explore one main topic;
- contains a topic sentence that states the main idea;
- explores a topic narrow enough to be developed fully within the paragraph; and
- begins with an indentation of five spaces.

 ## Computer Activity

Don't ever consider your paragraph exercises finished until you have used your computer command to check your spelling. Be aware, however, that the spellcheck will check only spelling. If you are confused about the use of words such as "imply" and "infer," "principle" and "principal," or "effect" and "affect," your spellcheck may not help you.

Use your DICTIONARY and THESAURUS functions to determine correct usage, parts of speech, level of usage, synonyms and antonyms, and variations in spelling.

© 2001 Addison-Wesley Educational Publishers Inc.

APPENDIX

A Checklist for the ESL Writer

Students whose second language is English often have questions about grammar and usage that are not discussed in the other sections of this book. This checklist is for such students. It emphasizes the areas in which ESL writers and speakers have frequent problems.

We realize that merely memorizing these pages would not solve all of your problems with English. Even native speakers of English encounter questions of grammar and usage that can be very confusing. Ask your instructor if he or she can provide *Longman ESL Worksheets* which are available to students who use this textbook. The worksheets have been designed for individual use or independent study, and they can help you identify areas requiring additional attention. An equally important way to improve your mastery of English and become a confident, effective user of the language is by reading and listening to native English speakers and writers.

ARTICLES AND QUANTIFIERS

The use of articles (*a, an, the*) and quantifiers (words like *a few, some, many, a lot of*) can be confusing for anyone who speaks English as a second language. These guidelines will help you use articles and quantifiers in your speaking and writing.

Articles (a/an, the)

A and *an* are called *indefinite* articles. Use *a* when the word following it begins with a consonant sound. Use *an* when the word following it begins with a vowel sound:

a *bear*, a *car*, a *unit*; an *apple*, an *argument*, an *hour*

The is called the *definite* article.

How do you know whether to use an indefinite (*a* or *an*) article or a definite (*the*) article before a noun? For example, when should you write or say "*a* bear" or "*the* bear"? "*A* fire" or "*the* fire"? "*An* orange" or "*the* orange"? Before you can decide which article to use before a noun—or whether none should be used—you have to know whether the noun is *countable* or *uncountable*.

Countable and Uncountable Nouns

Countable nouns are the names of things, people, and ideas which we can count or make plural; they have a singular and a plural form:

- a dog   six dogs
- the salesman   the salesmen
- a phobia   several phobias
- the saucer   three saucers

Uncountable nouns are the names of things we usually cannot count; they have no plural form:

- earth (we don't say "earths")
- weather (not "weathers")
- health (not "healths")
- information (not "informations")

Uncountable nouns have only one form: the singular.

By deciding whether a noun is countable or uncountable, you are ready to decide the kind of article to use with it.

Using Articles with Countable Nouns

When the countable noun is singular, you should use either *a/an* or *the* in front of it, depending on the listener's (or reader's) familiarity with the thing being referred to. When referring to things in general or to things that are not already known to both the speaker and the listener, use the indefinite article (*a/an*) before the noun:

- *A* good mechanic is difficult to find.
- *An* apple was all I had for breakfast.

In these sentences the writer is not referring to a specific mechanic or apple. But when it is clear which thing we mean and we are referring to things known to our listener, we use the definite article *the*:

- *The* mechanic who worked on my car said it needs new brakes. (The listener knows which mechanic is referred to.)
- *The* apple you gave me yesterday was rotten. (Not just any apple; the one you gave me.)

© 2001 Addison-Wesley Educational Publishers Inc.

◆ I watched *a* program on television last night. *The* program was about incurable diseases. (In the first sentence, *a* is used because the listener does not know which program is referred to; in the second sentence, *the* is used before *program* because it has been identified.)

◆ We will need *a* shovel when we plant the rosebushes. (No specific shovel is meant.)

◆ Please give me *the* shovel in the toolshed. (The listener knows which shovel is meant.)

Other Uses of a/an

As explained above, we use *a/an* in front of a singular countable noun when we are introducing it for the first time, without having referred to it before. Here are some other uses of *a/an*:

1. Before singular countable nouns:

   ◆ This is *a* boring movie. (NOT: "This is boring movie.")
   ◆ Would you like *a* cup of coffee? (NOT: "Would you like cup of coffee?")
   ◆ I have *an* idea. (NOT: "I have idea.")

2. To refer to any one member of a class:

   ◆ A professional musician must study for many years.
   ◆ An *isosceles* triangle has three sides.

3. To refer to a particular person or thing when the listener doesn't know which one is meant or when it doesn't matter which one:

   ◆ My cousin bought *an* expensive German car. (The listener or reader doesn't know which expensive German car it is.)
   ◆ Alberto comes from *a* small town in Texas.
   ◆ Could you give me *a* piece of paper?

4. Before a noun when we say what something is, or what something or someone is like:

   ◆ That is *a* good idea.
   ◆ Tony is *a* thoughtful person.
   ◆ Stan has *a* great sense of humor.
   ◆ This is *an* incredible view!

Do not use a/an before uncountable nouns: "a music," "a weather," "a gold," etc. Exceptions are when we are limiting the meaning of certain uncountable nouns in some ways:

◆ He brings *a* certain excitement to his performances. (NOT: "He brings certain excitement.")

◆ Kim has *an* incredible understanding of Asian politics. (NOT: "Kim has incredible understanding of Asian politics.")

Use *a/an* or *the* to make generalizations with most singular nouns:

◆ *A* gesture can often be misunderstood by visitors in a foreign country. (*A* can mean any gesture.)

◆ *The* telephone is being replaced by the cellular phone in many homes. (*The* is used to mean telephones in general.)

By omitting *a* and *the* and making the nouns plural in these sentences, you can make generalizations:

◆ *Gestures* can often be misunderstood by visitors in a foreign country.

◆ *Telephones* are being replaced by the cellular phone in many homes.

Other Uses of *the*

The definite article *the*, as noted above, is used when it is clear which thing we mean. Here are several other uses of *the*:

1. When there is only one of something:

    ◆ London is *the* capital of England.

    ◆ Bill Gates is *the* richest man in the United States.

    ◆ Superman leaped from *the* top of the building.

2. When we mean something in particular:

    ◆ *The* singers at the concert last night were great. (The singers at the concert, not singers in general.)

    ◆ *The* cookies I made yesterday were full of calories. (Not all cookies; a particular group of cookies.)

3. To refer to things in general by using *the* with a singular countable noun:

    ◆ *The* rose is my favorite flower.

    ◆ *The* hippopotamus, despite its appearance, is a very fast animal.

4. To refer to a noun and identify or limit it:

    ◆ *The* argument that I had with my sister was over trivial matters. (*that I had with my sister* limits the argument to a specific one)

© 2001 Addison-Wesley Educational Publishers Inc.

◆ *The* argument against the tax increase was delivered by the mayor. (*against the tax increase* limits the argument to a specific one)

5. To refer to certain nationality words and adjectives: *the rich, the poor, the Germans, the Irish*, etc.
6. With a number of expressions referring to our physical environment: *the city, the country, the sea, the beach, the mountains, the wind, the weather, the universe, the future, the sunshine*, etc.

Do *not* use *the* in the following situations:

1. Do not use *the* with uncountable or plural nouns to talk about things in general. For example, do not use "The books are expensive" when you mean books in general. Similarly, do not use "The life in starving countries is precarious" when you mean life in general.
2. Do not use *the* with singular proper names: NOT: "Mike lives in *the* Chicago." *Exceptions*: Certain geographical names (*The* Bronx, *the* Atlantic, *the* Pacific, *the* Mississippi River, *the* Matterhorn, etc.)
3. Do not use *the* with the names of meals: We usually eat lunch at noon. (NOT: "We usually eat *the* lunch at noon.")
     Exception: Use *the* if you are referring to a specific meal: "*The* dinner that she prepared was delicious.")
4. Do not use *the* when you are thinking of certain places and what they are used for.

     ◆ Mrs. O'Reilly goes to church every Sunday. (NOT: "goes to *the* church")
     ◆ After graduation from high school, Sean joined the army. (NOT: "from *the* high school")
     ◆ On the other hand: The fire at *the* church last week was caused by arson.
        The new high school enrolled new students last week.

These are not the only situations in which articles are used. As you continue to speak and write English, you will become familiar with other rules. In the meantime, consult one of the books mentioned on page 339 when you have questions about their use.

Quantifiers

Quantifiers are words that come before nouns and tell you *how many* or *how much*. Their use can sometimes be confusing, and when used incorrectly, can change the meaning of a sentence. In this section we will examine some of the most confusing quantifiers.

Some and any

Both *some* and *any* can refer to an indefinite or vague quantity or number. They are used when it is difficult or unimportant to specify exactly how much or how many of something we are thinking of. In general, we use *some* in positive sentences and *any* in negative sentences:

- I have *some* money left from my shopping trip.
- I don't have *any* money left to buy more gifts.
- Helen said *something* to me about the matter.
- I didn't understand *any* of her remarks.

Any is common in questions:

- Do you have *any* ideas for your term paper yet?
- No, I don't have *any* ideas. (NOT: No, I don't have *some* ideas.)
- Has *anybody* heard from Luis?

If we expect the answer "Yes," we often use *some* in questions:

- Would you like *some* help with that package?
- Would you like *some* coffee?

Any is used in affirmative statements after words like *never, hardly, without,* and *little* that have a negative meaning:

- We had *hardly any* problem in finding our way to the beach.
- There are *never any* surprises in Professor Forrest's exams.

Use *any* (or *anyone, anybody, anything, anywhere*) when it means "it doesn't matter *which, who, what,* or *where*":

- You can use *any* of these scissors. They're all sharp.
- Students may register *any* time before September 10.
- I dreamed that I could have *anything* I wanted for my graduation gift.
- Fianna said that *anybody* could request a song.

Both *any* and *some* are used in if-clauses:

- If you hear *any/some* news, give me a call.
- If you meet *any/some* of our neighbors, tell them we'll return home soon.

Use *some* in requests:

- May I have *some* more paper, please?

© 2001 Addison-Wesley Educational Publishers Inc.

Much, many, little, few, a lot, plenty

We use *much* and *little* with uncountable nouns:

- *much* energy   *much* optimism   *little* money   *little* admiration

We use *many* and *few* with plural nouns:

- *many* dreams   *many* voters   *few* friends   *few* parking spaces

We use *a lot of/lots of* and *plenty of* with uncountable and plural nouns:

- *a lot of* energy   *lots of* mail   *plenty of* courage
- *a lot of* visitors   *lots of* tires   *plenty of* reasons

We use *much* and *many* chiefly in negative sentences and in questions:

- Our car doesn't require *much* fuel.
- Do you have *many* relatives here?

Much is not usually used in positive sentences. Most speakers and writers prefer *a lot (of)* in such constructions:

- Politicians spent *a lot of* money in the last election. (NOT: spent *much* money)
- There has been *a lot of* thunder and lightning this week. (NOT: *much* thunder and lightning)

In positive sentences, however, *too much* and *so much* are used:

- There has been *too much* rain this week.
- I ate *so much* pasta that I couldn't finish my dessert.

We can omit a noun after *much* or *many* if the meaning is clear:

- You haven't talked *much* tonight.
- Have you seen any football games this season? Not *many*.

Little and *few* are negative ideas:

- There's *little* interest in going on a trip next week.
- She has *few* memories of growing up in Nebraska.

We can intensify the meaning of *little* and *few* by using *very* before them:

◆ There's *very little* interest in going on a trip next week.

◆ She has *very few* memories of growing up in Nebraska.

"A little" and "a few" are more positive; their meaning is closer to "some."

◆ We have *a little time* before the bus leaves. (some time)

◆ *A few* of her records survived the fire. (some records)

Problems with Verbs

If you are not a native speaker of English, you probably run into confusing situations when deciding which form of a verb or tense to use. *Tense* refers to the form of the verb that indicates time. The tense forms do not always agree with divisions of actual time, however. The simple present tense, for example, is not limited to the present time. Furthermore, helping/auxiliary verbs and many adverbs and expressions are used with verbs to indicate time.

In the first section below we will review the twelve verb tenses and their uses, as well as the ways they are formed. Then you will learn to distinguish among the more confusing tenses and to avoid mistakes that even native speakers of English sometimes make.

The Twelve Verb Tenses

1. Simple present tense

    This is the simple present tense:

    ◆ I/we/you/they study

    ◆ He/she/it studies

    The simple present tense is used to speak of things that happen all the time or repeatedly, or are true in general:

    ◆ The sun *rises* in the East.

    ◆ The Star Spangled Banner *is* our national anthem.

    ◆ Helen's father *works* in a bank.

2. Simple past tense
    This is the simple past tense:

    ◆ I/we/you/he/she/it/they studied

    The simple past tense often ends in *-ed*. But many of our common verbs are irregular.

© 2001 Addison-Wesley Educational Publishers Inc.

This means that their past tense form does not end in *-ed* and must be memorized:

Present	Past
buy	bought	We *bought* a house in the country last summer.
go	went	The police *went* with the doctor to the hospital.
hit	hit	A severe storm *hit* the area last week.

The simple past tense is used to talk about actions or situations completed in the past:

- Clark *worked* until eleven o'clock last night.
- World War Two *ended* in 1945.
- Sherry *spent* her inheritance in Paris last month.

3. Simple future tense
   The simple future tense takes two forms:

   - I/we/you/he/she/it/they will study
   - I am/he/she/it/is/you/we/they/are going to study

   The simple future tense is used to describe an action in the future:

   - I *will study* my biology notes tonight.
   - I *am going to study* my lab notes tonight.

4. Present perfect tense

   This is the present perfect tense:

   - I/we/you/they have studied
   - he/she/it/ has studied

   We form the present perfect tense with *have/has* and the past participle of the verb. The past participle often ends in *-ed* (*waited, hoped*), but many important verbs are irregular (*thought, written, done*, etc.). See pages 137–39 for other examples of irregular past participles.
   We use the present perfect tense to describe an action that occurred at an un-specified time in the past:

   - Marta *has* already *mailed* her application for a passport.

   We also use the present perfect tense to describe an action that started in the past and continues up to the present:

   - Marta *has lived* in North Carolina for three years.

5. Past perfect tense
This is the past perfect tense:

- ◆ I/we/you/he/she/it/they had studied

We form the past perfect tense with *had* and the past participle (see the present perfect tense above about irregular forms of the past participle). We use the past perfect tense to describe something in the past that occurred before another action in the past:

- ◆ Fred was very nervous because he *had* never *been* on a blind date before.
- ◆ Sheila knew who the killer was because she *had seen* the movie last week.
- ◆ When I arrived home I discovered that I *had lost* my door key.

6. Future perfect tense
This is the future perfect tense:

- ◆ I/we/you/he/she/it/they will have studied

We form the future perfect tense by using *will have* and the past participle of the verb. The future perfect tense is used to describe an action in the future that will be completed or achieved by a certain time in the future:

- ◆ By next September we *will have lived* in this apartment three years.
- ◆ Claudia *will have completed* the requirements for her degree by the time she is twenty.
- ◆ By the time her treatment for rabies is completed, Michele *will have received* a dozen vaccination shots.

7. Present progressive tense
This is the present progressive tense:

- ◆ I am studying
- ◆ he/she/it is studying
- ◆ we/you/they are studying

The present progressive tense is formed by using the simple present form of *be* (*am, is, are*) and the present participle form of the verb (the *-ing* form).

We use the present progressive tense to describe something that is happening at or very close to the time of speaking:

- ◆ They *are working* in the garden now.
- ◆ Tony *is watching* the game on television.
- ◆ Lou *is taking* a nap.

© 2001 Addison-Wesley Educational Publishers Inc.

8. Past progressive tense
    This is the past progressive tense:

    ◆ I/he/she/it was studying
    ◆ we/you/they were studying

    The past progressive tense is formed by using the simple past tense form of *be* (*was,* *were*) and the present participle form of the verb.
    The past progressive tense is used to describe a continuous action that was going on around a particular past time:

    ◆ What *were* you *doing* when I called you?
    ◆ George *was painting* the kitchen when the doorbell rang.
    ◆ The sun *was setting* on the horizon as our boat pulled out of the harbor.

9. Future progressive tense
    This is the future progressive tense:

    ◆ I/he/she/it/we/you/they will be studying

    The future progressive tense is formed by using the simple future form of *be* (*will be*) and the present participle form of the verb.
    We use the future progressive tense to describe an action that will be going on at a particular moment in the future:

    ◆ We *will be thinking* of you next week on your anniversary.
    ◆ The *dogs will be barking* soon if I don't feed them.
    ◆ Sharon *will be playing* her new guitar in the recital tonight.

10. Present perfect progressive tense
    This is the present perfect progressive tense:

    ◆ I/you/we/they have been studying
    ◆ he/she/it has been studying

    The present perfect progressive tense is formed by combining the present perfect form of *be* (*have been, has been*) with the present participle form of the verb.
    We use the present perfect progressive tense to describe situations which started in the past and are still going on, or which have just stopped and have present results:

    ◆ It *has been snowing* since last Tuesday evening.
    ◆ Mike *has been complaining* about the noise from the new neighbors, but the landlord refuses to do anything about it.
    ◆ We *have been watching* late-night television while on vacation.

11. Past perfect progressive tense
    This is the past perfect progressive tense:

    ◆ I/he/sh/it/we/you/they had been studying

    The past perfect progressive tense is formed by combining the past perfect form of *be* (*had been*) with the present participle form of the verb.

    We use the past perfect progressive tense to describe a continuous activity in the past that is completed before another action in the past:

    ◆ When I received my raise, I *had been working* at the restaurant two months.

    ◆ When Carla returned home, she told her sister that she *had been shopping*.

    ◆ Paul said that he *had been having* bad dreams, and he blamed them on the huge meals he *had been eating* just before going to bed.

12. Future perfect progressive tense
    This is the future perfect progressive tense:

    ◆ I/he/she/it/we/you/they will have been studying

    The future perfect progressive tense is formed by combining the future perfect form of *be* (*will have been*) with the present participle form of the verb. It is used to describe a continuous action in the future that is completed before another action in the future:

    ◆ Jim *will have been working* at the hardware store for seven years next week.

    ◆ Mr. Baylor, my math prof, *will have been teaching* for thirty years this June.

    ◆ Tara *will have been studying* the harp for six months tomorrow.

Tips for Choosing the Right Tense

1. *Knowing how to describe an action in the present*
   Most English verbs have two "present" tenses. Forms like *I study* and *he works* are called "simple present." Forms like *I am studying* and *he is working* are called "present progressive." These two "present" tenses are used to describe several different kinds of time.
   We usually use the *simple present* to describe permanent situations or things that happen all the time or regularly:

   ◆ Ricardo *plays* goalie on his soccer team.

   ◆ I *drive* downtown to my job five days a week.

   ◆ British Columbia *is* on the west coast of Canada.

© 2001 Addison-Wesley Educational Publishers Inc.

We usually use the *present progressive tense* to talk about temporary continuing actions and events that are going on around now:

- ◆ Richard *is playing* goalie today because the regular goalie was injured last week.
- ◆ I *am driving* to work this week because of the subway strike.
- ◆ Marcella *is looking* for an apartment closer to her job.

a. We use the *simple present tense* in the following situations:

In summaries of plays, stories, and movies:

- ◆ In Act One, Macbeth *encounters* three witches in the forest. They *tell* him . . .
- ◆ In today's program Margaret *learns* that her real father *is* . . .

When asking for and giving instructions:

- ◆ "How *do* I *enroll* in the exercise class?" "You *attend* the first session and *fill out* a registration form and *pay* the fee."

With dependent clauses to refer to the future:

- ◆ I'll be ready when you *call*.

With verbs that cannot normally be used in progressive forms:

- ◆ I like the ice cream very much. (NOT: I *am liking* . . . .)
- ◆ I know his telephone number. (NOT: I *am knowing* . . .)

We do not use the simple present tense in the following situations:

To talk about temporary actions that are going on only around the present:

- ◆ The telephone *is ringing*. Shall I get it? (NOT: The telephone *rings* . . . .)

To say how long a situation has been going on:

- ◆ I *have lived* here since 1990. (NOT: I *live* here since . . . .)
- ◆ I *have been studying* English for two years. (NOT: I *study* English for . . . .)

b. We use the *present progressive tense* in the following situations:
To describe changing situations:

- ◆ Helen *is becoming* more confident in her use of chopsticks.
- ◆ Athletes *are growing* taller because of better diets.

To refer to future events in the following constructions:

- ◆ Where *are* you *going* on your vacation next week?
- ◆ She *is leaving* for Cleveland next month.

Note: When the present progressive tense is used to indicate future action, a word or phrase like *tomorrow, next week,* etc., indicating time is usually used.

To refer to repeated actions if they are happening around the moment of speaking:

◆ Why *are* you *rubbing* your elbow?

◆ Fernando *is speaking* to several campus organizations this afternoon.

To describe future events that are decided, or are starting to happen:

◆ "What *is* Phil *doing* this evening?"   "*He's working* on his car." (NOT: "What *does* Phil *do* this evening?"   "He *works* on his car.")

We do not use the present progressive tense in the following situations:

To talk about repeated actions not closely connected to the moment of speaking:

◆ I *ski* once or twice a year. (NOT: I *am skiing* . . . .)

◆ Muriel *cries* every time she *sees* that movie. (NOT: Muriel *is crying* . . *is seeing* . . . .)

With certain verbs that refer to mental states, the use of the senses, and certain other meanings, rather than to action. Such verbs are usually used only in simple tenses.

◆ I *realize* now that I was wrong. (NOT: I *am realizing* now . . . .)

◆ *Do* you *like* anchovies on your pizza? (NOT: *Are* you *liking* anchovies . . . .)

◆ I *doubt* that I have enough time to take a nap. (NOT: I *am doubting* that . . . .)

Here is a list of some common verbs which are rarely used in progressive tenses:

be	know	recognize
believe	like	remember
belong	love	see
doubt	need	seem
feel	own	suppose
hate	prefer	understand
hear	realize	wish
imagine		

Many of these verbs can be used with progressive tenses, but with a change in their meaning. Notice the difference in meaning in the following pairs of sentences:

© 2001 Addison-Wesley Educational Publishers Inc.

◆ I *feel* we shouldn't try to leave now. (NOT: I *am feeling* . . . .)
   But: *I'm feeling* much better now.

◆ I *see* what you mean by that (NOT: I *am seeing* . . . .)
   But: *I'm seeing* Jo Ann next week.

2. *Learning the difference between the simple past and the present perfect tenses*
   Many situations allow us to use either the simple past tense or the present perfect tense:

   ◆ I *solved* the problem. *Were* you able to solve it?
   ◆ *I've solved* the problem. *Have* you *solved* it?
   ◆ Lisa *saved* one hundred dollars this month. I *saved* fifty.
   ◆ Lisa *has saved* one hundred dollars this month. *I've saved* fifty.

In most situations however, the meaning of the sentence requires that we choose either the simple past or the present perfect tense.

   a. We use the simple past tense in the following situations:
      To say when something happened:

   ◆ Her parents *came* to this country in 1980.
   ◆ I *played* basketball yesterday.

      To describe actions that are not connected with the present:

   ◆ Thomas Edison *invented* the lightbulb. (NOT: *has invented*)
   ◆ The United States *was* the first nation to use the atom bomb in war. (NOT: *has been* . . . .)

   b. We use the simple present perfect in the following situations:
      To give news of recent events:

   ◆ There *has been* a severe earthquake in Japan, according to news accounts.

      With *yet* in questions and negative sentences to show that something is expected to happen:

   ◆ *Has* Gerald *arrived* yet?
   ◆ Doris *hasn't received* her grades yet.

      With *ever* and *never*:

   ◆ I *have* never *been* to Sweden.
   ◆ *Have* you ever *been* to Miami?

We do not use the simple present perfect to talk about an event that happened at a specific time:

◆ There *was* a severe earthquake in Japan yesterday. (NOT: There *has been* . . . .)

The present perfect always has a connection with the present; the simple past tense only tells us about the past. If we say that something has happened, we are thinking about the past and the present at the same time. Notice the difference in these sentences:

◆ My father *worked* as a lifeguard when he was in college.

◆ My father *has worked* for the post office for thirty years.

3. *Learning the difference between the simple present perfect and the present perfect progressive tenses*

In general, both the present perfect and present perfect progressive tenses can be used to describe recent actions that have results in the present. The present perfect tense, however, suggests completion or a result. The present perfect progressive tense is used to describe or talk about more temporary actions. Notice the difference between these sentences:

◆ Present perfect progressive: The artist *has been painting* the portrait all week.

◆ Present perfect: The artist *has painted* over fifty portraits.

To show that an action or event is going on at the time of writing or speaking, you can use the present perfect progressive tense:

◆ Charles *has been pulling* weeds and *spraying* the flowers all day.

◆ I *have been studying* all morning.

◆ I *have been thinking* about my brother all day.

◆ *I've been running* on the beach this month.

As you can see, each of the sentences above suggests an emphasis on continuous activity. The *present perfect,* on the other hand, suggests a result or completed activity:

◆ Charles *has pulled* weeds and *sprayed* flowers all day.

◆ I *have studied* all morning.

◆ I *have thought* about my brother all day.

◆ *I've run* on the beach this month.

© 2001 Addison-Wesley Educational Publishers Inc.

Learning to Use Phrasal Verbs

Most verbs in English consist of only one word. Some verbs, however, consist of two or three words: the main verb and a word like *across, away, down, for, in, off, out, up,* and *with.* Such verbs are called "phrasal verbs." and their meanings are usually very different from the meanings of their parts taken separately. For example, the verb *run* has a different meaning from the verb *run into:*

- Larry *ran* the mile when he was on his high school track team.
- I *ran into* an old friend while I was at the library last night.

The verbs *broke* and *broke down* have different meanings, as illustrated by these sentences:

- Mike *broke* his arm while riding his motorcycle.
- His motorcycle *broke down* while he was in Phoenix.

The English language has hundreds of these verbs. You should make a note of the most confusing ones as you hear them.

Sometimes a phrasal verb is followed by an object. In such cases the object can go in either of two positions:

- The referee *called off* the game.
- The referee *called* the game *off.*

Here are other examples:

- Did you *make up* that story?
- Did you *make* that story *up?*

- We decided to *put off* our vacation until August.
- We decided to *put* our vacation *off* until August.

An exception occurs when the object of a phrasal verb is a pronoun (*me/you/it/him/her/us/them*). In such cases, the pronoun must come before the preposition (words like *up/down/in/out/on/off,* etc.):

- Please *wake me up* by seven o'clock tomorrow morning. (NOT: *wake up me. . . .*)
- You can solve the problem if you *break it down* into its separate parts. (NOT: if you *break down it. . . .*)

Common Two- and Three-Word Verbs and Their Meanings

This is not a complete list. The English language contains many others, and you should learn them as you encounter them.

break down	fail or stop
call off	cancel
check into	investigate
clear up	explain
cut down on	reduce
cut off	shut off, stop
figure out	solve or discover
fill in	inform
find out	learn, discover
get off	exit from a vehicle
give up	stop trying
go over	review
grow up	mature
hand in	submit
look after	take care of
look into	investigate
look out for	take care of, be aware of
make up	invent
pick out	select
put off	delay
put up with	allow or tolerate
run across	meet by chance
run into	meet by chance
run out on	betray
show	appear, arrive
speak up	express freely, loudly
stand up for	defend
straighten out	organize
sum up	conclude, summarize
take back	recover, regain
try on	test
try out	compete, apply for
work out	solve, develop

© 2001 Addison-Wesley Educational Publishers Inc.

Common Expressions

This section presents commonly used words and expressions that can be confusing to students of the English language.

Using "used to"

Used to when followed by a verb describes past situations that no longer exist and describes actions that happened in the past but no longer happen:

◆ Sherry *used to smoke*. She *used to smoke* two packs of cigarettes a day. [This sentence means that Sherry smoked regularly in the past but doesn't smoke now.]

These sentences convey similar meanings:

◆ Juan *used to live* in Santo Domingo, but now he lives in Atlanta.
◆ Connie *used to work* at an electronics store, but now she has her own business.
◆ San Diego *used to be* a small navy town, but now it is a cosmopolitan city.
◆ This record shop *used to be* a grocery store.

Used to has no present form. If we wish to describe situations existing in the present, we usually use the simple present tense:

◆ **Past:** Sherry *used to* smoke.
◆ **Present:** Sherry *smokes*. (NOT: Sherry *uses to* smoke.)
◆ **Past:** Lance *used to* snore when he slept.
◆ **Present:** Lance *snores* when he sleeps. (NOT: Lance *uses to* snore. . . .)

To ask questions, the following form is used: *did . . . use to . . . ?*

◆ *Did* you *use to* have a Volkswagen?
◆ *Did* Marino *use to* coach football?

The negative form is *didn't use to . . . .*

◆ *Didn't* you *use to* have a Volkswagen?
◆ *Didn't* Marino *use to* coach football?

Used to describes things that happened in the past and are now finished. Do not use *used to* to say what happened at a specific past time, or how many times it occurred, or how long it took:

- Charlotte *lost* five pounds last month. (NOT: Charlotte *used to lose. . . .*)
- Pedro *lived* in Newport News for two years. (NOT: Pedro *used to live* in. . . .)
- I *went* to the health club twelve times last month. (NOT: I *used to go* to the. . . .)

Do not confuse *used to* and *to be used to*. If a person is *used to* something, it is familiar or no longer new:

- I *used to be* afraid to drive in heavy traffic. (I was afraid to drive in heavy traffic, but I no longer am.)
- I *am used to* driving in heavy traffic. (I am accustomed to driving in heavy traffic.)

Using "when" and "if"

Be careful not to confuse *when* and *if*.
Use *when* for things that are sure to happen:

- *When* we go to lunch today, I think I'll have just a salad.
- *When* you boil water long enough, it turns to steam.

Use *if* for things that will possibly happen:

- *If* he doesn't call me soon, I'll leave for work.
- *If* I buy a new computer, I'll probably get a new monitor with it.
- Please call my brother *if* you go to Cleveland.

Using "since" and "for"

We use *since* to give the starting points of actions or events, particularly from the point of view of a particular present or past end-point:

- Sheila has been married *since* 1998.
- Raul has been studying flamenco *since* his return from Madrid.

Notice that we use *since* when we mention the beginning of the period (*since 1998, since his return*, etc.).
We use *for* to measure how long something lasts:

- Sheila has been married *for* two years. (NOT: *since* two years)
- Raul has been studying flamenco *for* two months. (NOT: *since* two months)

Notice that we use *for* when we say the period of time (*two years, two hours, a long time*, etc.).

© 2001 Addison-Wesley Educational Publishers Inc.

Using "–s" and "–es"

When forming third person singular nouns and pronouns, don't forget that present tense verbs end in *-s* or *-es*:

- ◆ **Incorrect:**   Every day at five o'clock the factory whistle *blow*.
- ◆ **Correct:**   Every day at five o'clock the factory whistle *blows*.

- ◆ **Incorrect:**   Roberta *watch* the news on television while working on her math.
- ◆ **Correct:**   Roberta *watches* the news on television while working on her math.

If the helping verb *do* or *does* is used, add the *-s* or *-es* to the helping verb, not to the main verb:

- ◆ **Incorrect:**   The whistle *don't* blow at five o'clock.
- ◆ **Correct:**   The whistle *doesn't* blow at five o'clock.

Problems with Word Order and Unnecessary Words

Adjectives

When several adjectives come before a noun, they usually have to be placed in a particular order. For example, we say a *beautiful, small, shiny metal* coin, not a *metal, beautiful, shiny, small* coin. Adjectives like *beautiful* are called opinion adjectives because they tell us what the speaker or writer thinks of the object being described. Adjectives like *small, shiny,* and *metal* are called fact adjectives, and they give objective information about something. Opinion adjectives usually come before fact adjectives when they modify or describe nouns.

opinion	fact
a depressing	rainy day
a glamorous	American actress
a boring	political speech

The rules for adjective order can be very confusing, and there is disagreement among writers and speakers on the rules. Nevertheless, the following list will help you arrange them correctly. In general, adjectives should follow each other in this order:

1. Opinion (words like *silly, ugly, intelligent, fascinating*)
2. Size   (*length, weight, height, width*)
3. Age (*old, modern, new, recent*)
4. Color
5. Origin (*British, Western, Oriental,* etc.)
6. Material (*glass, wood, leather, steel,* etc.)

7. Purpose (*coffee* table, *racing* car, *water* bottle)
8. The noun being modified

Examples (the numbers after each phrase correspond to the list above):

◆ a small, ancient, black Japanese wooden cigar box (2 + 3 + 4 + 5 + 6 + 7 + 8)
◆ the impatient German teacher (1 + 5 + 8)
◆ a nostalgic old Hungarian wedding song (1 + 3 + 5 + 7 + 8)

Adverbs in the Sentence

Adverbs can usually appear in three positions in a sentence:
At the beginning:

◆ *Yesterday* a rainbow appeared in the eastern sky.

In the middle:

◆ A rainbow appeared *yesterday* in the eastern sky.

At the end:

◆ A rainbow appeared in the eastern sky *yesterday*.

There are a few situations, however, in which we cannot place adverbs randomly.
Do not place adverbs between a verb and its object:

◆ Maxine plays the piano *beautifully*. (NOT: Maxine plays beautifully the piano.)
◆ Laine *often* forgets her new telephone number. (NOT: Laine forgets often her new telephone number.)

Do not place adverbs before *am/is/are/was/were* when the adverbs say how often something happens (words like *always, never, ever, usually, often, sometimes,* etc.):

◆ Dorothy is *always* on time for her French class. (NOT: Dorothy always is on time . . . .)
◆ Visitors are *sometimes* unaware of the dangers of riptides. (NOT: Visitors sometimes are unaware. . . .)

Unnecessary repetition of the subject of the sentence:

◆ The President *he* gave the State of the Union address last night. (Because *President* and *he* refer to the same person, *he* is unnecessary repetition.)

© 2001 Addison-Wesley Educational Publishers Inc.

Other Problems with Grammar, Spelling, and Punctuation

If you have other questions about grammar, spelling, or punctuation, the following list will tell you where you can get help in this book.

Abbreviations	See page	234
Capitalization		273–84
Comma-splices		197–98
Comparatives and superlatives		14
Dangling and misplaced modifiers		211–214
Irregular verbs		136–40
Past and present participles		42–43; 136–40
Possessives		255–56
Punctuation		233–60
Run-on sentences		195–96
Sentence fragments		189–95
Spelling		291–307
Subject-verb agreement		65–77

ADDITIONAL REFERENCE BOOKS FOR ESL STUDENTS

Irwin Feignebaum. *The Grammar Handbook*. Oxford: Oxford UP, 1985.

Raymond Murphy. *Grammar in Use*. Cambridge: Cambridge UP, 1989.

Jocelyn Steer and Karen Carlisi. *The Advanced Grammar Book*. New York: Newbury, 1991.

Michael Swan. *Practical English Usage*, 2nd ed. Oxford: Oxford UP, 1995.

A Glossary of Usage

This glossary is an alphabetical guide to words that frequently cause problems for writers. Some entries are labeled "colloquial," and some "nonstandard." A **colloquialism** is a word or phrase more appropriate to informal speech than to writing. Although colloquialisms are not grammatically incorrect, they should be avoided in formal writing, and even in informal writing they should be used sparingly. A nonstandard word or phrase is avoided at all times by careful speakers and writers. It is the kind of error sometimes labeled "incorrect" or "illiterate."

If you want to know more about the words in this glossary, consult *Webster's Third New International Dictionary* or a modern college-level dictionary. Other troublesome words that often cause problems for writers can be found on pages 297–302 ("Twenty-five Sets of Homonyms: Words Often Confused") in Chapter 13.

a, an Indefinite articles because they point to objects in a general way (*a* tree, *an* apple); the definite article *the* refers to specific things (*the* tree, *the* apple). Use *a* when the word following it begins with a consonant sound: *a* boat, *a* union. Use *an* when the word following it begins with a vowel sound: *an* hour, *an* engine.

accept, except *Accept* is a verb meaning "to receive," and *except* is a preposition meaning "but," or a verb meaning "to exclude or leave out." "I will *accept* your invitation." "Everyone *except* Henry went to Chicago." "We voted to *except* the new members from the requirements."

advice, advise *Advice* is an opinion you offer; *advise* means to recommend. "Her *advice* was always helpful." "The counselor will *advise* you concerning the requirements for that course."

affect, effect To *affect* is to change or modify; *to effect* is to bring about something; an *effect* is the result. "The drought will *affect* the crop production." "I hope the treatment will *effect* a change in his condition." "The *effect* should be noticeable."

aggravate, annoy These two are often confused. To *aggravate* is to make a condition worse; "The treatment only *aggravated* his asthmatic attacks." To *annoy* is to irritate: "The ticking clock *annoyed* Dean as he read."

agree to, agree with You agree *to* a thing or plan: "Mexico and the United States *agree to* the border treaty." You agree *with* a person: "Laura *agreed with* Herb about the price of the computer."

ain't Although *ain't* is in the dictionary, it is a nonstandard word never used by educated or careful speakers except to achieve a deliberate humorous effect. The word should be avoided.

all right, alright The correct spelling is *all right; alright* is not standard English.

already See *all ready.*

all ready An adjective phrase meaning "prepared" or "set to go": "The car had been tuned up and was all ready to go." *Already,* an adverb, means "before" or "previously": "The car had *already* been tuned up."

allusion, illusion An *allusion* is an indirect reference to something: "He made an *allusion* to his parents' wealth." An *illusion* is a false image or impression: "It is an *illusion* to think that I will soon be a millionaire."

among, between Use *between* for two objects and *among* for more than two: "The hummingbird darted *among* the flowers." "I sat *between* my parents."

amount, number *Amount* refers to quantity or to things in the aggregate; *number* refers to countable objects: "A large *amount* of work remains to be done." "A *number* of jobs were still unfilled."

an See *a, an.*

anyone, any one *Anyone* means "any person at all": "I will talk to *anyone* who answers the telephone." *Any one* means a single person: "*Any one* of those players can teach you the game in a few minutes."

anyways, anywheres These are nonstandard for *anyway* and *anywhere,* and they should be avoided.

awful Don't use *awful* as a synonym for *very.*

- ◆ Inappropriate: The scores of the two teams were *awful* close.
- ◆ Better: The scores of the two teams were *very* close.

bad, badly *Bad* is an adjective; *badly* is an adverb. Use *bad* before nouns and after linking verbs; use the adverb *badly* to modify verbs or adjectives. "Her pride was hurt *badly* (not *bad*)." "She feels *bad* (not *badly*)."

because of, due to Use *due to* after a linking verb: "His embarrassment was *due to* his inability to speak their language." Use *because of* in other situations.

- ◆ Awkward: "The boat struck the buoy in the harbor *due to* the fog."
- ◆ Better: "The boat struck the buoy in the harbor *because of* the fog."

being as, being that These are nonstandard forms and should be avoided. Use *since* or *because.*

beside, besides *Beside* is a preposition meaning "by the side of": The doctor sat *beside* the bed talking to his patient." *Besides* may be a preposition or adverb meaning "in addition to" or "also": "*Besides* my homework, I have some letters to write."

© 2001 Addison-Wesley Educational Publishers Inc.

between, among See *among, between*.

between you and I A common mistake. Use *between you and me*.

breath, breathe *Breath* is the noun: "He tried to conceal the smell of alcohol on his *breath*." *Breathe* is the verb. "The air we *breathe* is contaminated with pollutants."

burst *Burst* remains the same in the past, present, and past participle forms; *bursted, bust,* and *busted* are incorrect or nonstandard forms.

can, may *Can* refers to ability; *may* refers to permission. "After taking only a few lessons, Tom *can* play the trumpet beautifully. Because of the neighbors, however, he *may* play only in the afternoon."

can't hardly, can't barely, can't scarcely These are double negatives and are to be avoided. Use *can hardly, can barely,* and *can scarcely*.

conscience, conscious A *conscience* is a sense of right or wrong: "His *conscience* wouldn't allow him to cheat on the exam." To be *conscious* is to be aware: "I was not *conscious* of the noise in the background."

continual, continuous *Continual* means "repeated frequently," as in "We heard a series of *continual* beeps in the background." *Continuous* means "without interruption": "I was lulled to sleep by the *continuous* hum of the motor in the deck below."

could of A nonstandard form. Use could *have*: "I could *have* gone with him if I wanted."

criterion, criteria *Criterion* is singular; *criteria* is plural.

different from, than One thing is different *from* another, not different *than*.

discreet, discrete *Discreet* means "tactful" (*discreet* remarks); *discrete* means "separate" or "individual" (*discrete* objects). "Henry was *discreet* about the source of his funds. He said that he had several *discrete* bank accounts."

disinterested, uninterested To be *disinterested* is to be impartial: "The judge was a *disinterested* listener in the case." To be *uninterested* is to lack interest: "It was obvious that Jack was *uninterested* in the lecture because he dozed off several times."

double negatives Unacceptable in formal writing and in most informal situations except for humorous effect. Double negatives range from such obvious errors as "I don't have no paper" to more subtle violations (I can't scarcely" and "It isn't hardly). Avoid them.

due to, because of See *because of, due to*.

effect, affect See *affect, effect*.

eminent, imminent *Eminent* means "distinguished" or "famous"; *imminent* describes something about to happen. "The arrival of the *eminent* preacher is *imminent*."

enormity, enormousness *Enormity* means "atrociousness"; *enormousness* means "of great size." "The *enormity* of the crime shocked the hardened crime reporters." "Because of the *enormousness* of the ship, it could not be docked in the local harbor."

enthused Nonstandard. Use "enthusiastic." ("He was *enthusiastic* about our plans for next summer," *not* "He was *enthused* about our plans for next summer.")

except, accept See *accept, except*.

farther, further Use *farther* for physical distance ("They live *farther* from town than we do") and *further* for degree or quantity ("Their proposal was a *further* attempt to reach an agreement").

fewer, less Use *fewer* for items that can be counted, and *less* for quantity. "*Fewer* jobs are available for young people this summer." "He paid *less* for that car than I paid for mine."

finalize Avoid this term; use *finish*.

flaunt, flout *Flaunt* means "to show off": "To *flaunt* his strength, Carl picked up the coffee table." *Flout* means "to disregard or show contempt for": "*Flouting* the sign posted in front of the store, Mister Burkett parked in the 'No Parking' zone."

good, well *Good* is an adjective, never an adverb: "She performs *well* (not *good*) in that role." *Well* is an adverb and an adjective; in the latter case it means "in a state of good health": "I am *well* now, although last week I didn't feel very *good*."

hanged, hung Criminals are *hanged*; pictures are *hung*.

hisself A nonstandard term. Use *himself*.

if, whether Use *if* to introduce a clause implying a condition: "*If* you go to summer school, you can graduate early." Use *whether* to introduce a clause implying a choice: "I'm not sure *whether* I will go to summer school."

imminent, eminent See *eminent, imminent*.

imply, infer "To *imply*" is to hint strongly; "to *infer*" is to derive the meaning from someone's statement by deduction. You *infer* the meaning of a passage when you read or hear it; the writer or speaker *implies* it.

irregardless Nonstandard. Use *regardless*.

is when, is where Avoid these expressions to introduce definitions.

- ◆ Awkward: "A sonnet *is when* you have fourteen lines of iambic pentameter in a prescribed rhyme scheme."
- ◆ Better: "A sonnet is a poem with fourteen lines of iambic pentameter in a prescribed rhyme scheme."

its, it's *Its* is a possessive pronoun meaning "belonging to it." *It's* is a contraction for *it is*. See Chapter 5.

kind of, sort of These are colloquial expressions acceptable in informal speech but not in writing. Use "somewhat" or "rather" instead.

leave, let *Leave* means "to go away," and *let* means "to allow." Do not use *leave* for *let*. "Please *let* (not *leave*) me go."

liable, likely, apt *Liable* means "legally responsible" or "susceptible to"; *likely* means "probably"; and *apt* refers to a talent or a tendency. "He is *liable* for the damage he caused." "Those rain clouds indicate it's *likely* to rain this afternoon." "She is an *apt* tennis player."

© 2001 Addison-Wesley Educational Publishers Inc.

like *Like* is a noun, verb, adjective, and preposition; do not use it as a conjunction: "He acted as if (not *like*) he wanted to go with us."

loose, lose "To loosen" means to untie or unfasten; "to lose" is to misplace. *Loose* as an adjective means "unfastened" or "unattached." "He *loosened* his necktie." "Did he *lose* his necktie?" "His necktie is *loose*."

may, can See *can, may*.

maybe, may be *Maybe* means "perhaps"; *may be* is a verb phrase. "*Maybe* we'll win tomorrow." "It *may be* that we'll win tomorrow."

must of Nonstandard. Write (and say) "must have," and in similar constructions use "could have" (not "could of") or "would have" (not "would of").

myself *Myself* is correct when used as an intensive or reflexive pronoun (I helped *myself* to the pie," and "I hurt *myself*"), but it is used incorrectly as a substitute for *I* and *me* as in the following: "My brother and *myself* were in the army together in Germany." "They spoke to George and *myself* about the matter."

off of Wordy; use *off*. "Sean jumped off (not *off of*) the diving board."

precede, proceed To *precede* is "to go before or in front of"; to *proceed* is "to continue moving ahead." "Poverty and hunger often *precede* a revolution." "They *proceeded* down the aisle as if nothing had happened."

quiet, quite, quit Read the following sentences to note the differences: "I wanted to get away from the noise and find a *quiet* spot." "They are *quite* upset that their son married without their permission." "When college starts next fall, he will *quit* his summer job."

raise, rise *Raise* is a verb meaning "to lift or help to rise in a standing position." Its principal parts are *raised, raised, and raising*. *Rise* means "to assume an upright position" or "to wake up"; its principal parts are *rose, risen*, and *rising*.

set, sit To *sit* means "to occupy a seat"; the principal parts are *sit, sat*, and *sitting*. *Set* means "to place something somewhere," and its principal parts are *set, set*, and *setting*. See Chapter 7.

shall, will Most authorities, writers, and speakers use these interchangeably. Follow the advice of your instructor.

somewheres Nonstandard. Use *somewhere*; similarly, avoid *nowheres*.

theirselves A nonstandard term. Use *themselves*.

try and Use *try to*: "Some men wear toupees in an effort to *try to* hide their baldness."

who, whom Use *who* when the pronoun is a subject; use *whom* when it is an object. "*Who* bought the flowers?" "To *whom* were the flowers given?"

you, you're *Your* is a possessive form; *you're* is a contraction for *you are*. "*Your* dinner is ready." "*You're* the first person to notice that."

© 2001 Addison-Wesley Educational Publishers Inc.

A Glossary of Grammatical Terms

This glossary is an alphabetical guide to the grammatical terms used in this book, as well as to other helpful words. Some entries contain references to other terms or to sections of the text in which they are discussed in detail. For further references and explanation, you should consult the index.

abstract noun A noun that refers to an idea or quality that cannot be identified by one of the senses. *Examples:* shame; delight; tolerance. See also *concrete noun.*

action verb See *verb*

adjective A word that modifies (limits or describes) a noun or pronoun. "The concert was *long*, but it was *exciting*." (The adjective *long* modifies the noun *concert*, and the adjective *exciting* modifies the pronoun *it*.) See Chapter 2.

adjective clause A dependent clause that modifies a noun or pronoun. "The delegates *who voted for the amendment* changed their minds." (The adjective clause modifies the noun *delegates*.) See Chapter 8.

adverb A word that modifies (limits or describes) an adjective, a verb, or another adverb. "He cried *softly*." (*Softly* modifies the verb *cried*.) "They are *extremely* wealthy." (*Extremely* modifies the adjective *wealthy*.) "He left the room *very* hurriedly." (*Very* modifies the adverb *hurriedly*.) See Chapter 2.

adverb clause A dependent clause that modifies an adjective, verb, or another adverb. "I think of her *when I hear that song*." (The adverb clause modifies the verb *think*.) "He became angry *because he had forgotten his keys*." (The adverb clause modifies the adjective *angry*.) "The band played so loudly *that I got a headache*." (The adverb clause modifies the adverb *so*.) See Chapter 8.

agreement The correspondence of one word with another, particularly subjects with verbs and pronouns with antecedents. If the subject of a sentence is singular, the verb is singular ("My *tire is* flat"); if the subject is singular, pronouns referring to it should also be singular ("The *carpenter* forgot *his* hammer"). Plural subjects require plural verbs, and plural pronouns are used to refer to plural antecedents. ("My *tires are* flat." "The *carpenters* forgot *their* tools.") See Chapters 4 and 6.

347

antecedent A word or group of words a pronoun refers to. "Jimmy, *who* used to play in a rock group, decided *he* would go back to college to complete *his* degree." (*Who, he,* and *his* all refer to the antecedent *Jimmy.*) See Chapters 2 and 6.

appositive A word or phrase following a noun or pronoun which renames or explains it. "London, *the capital,* was bombed heavily." "The author *Mark Twain* lived in Connecticut." In the first example, *the capital* is a nonessential appositive because it is not needed to identify the word it follows. In the second example, *Mark Twain* is an essential appositive because it is needed to identify the general term *author.* Only nonessential appositives are set off by commas. See Chapters 5 and 11.

article *A, an,* and *the* are articles. *A* and *an* are indefinite articles; *the* is a definite article. Articles are usually regarded as adjectives because they precede nouns. See Chapter 2.

auxiliary verb A helping verb used to form verb phrases. The most common auxiliary verbs are forms of *be* ("am," "are," "is," "have been," and so on) and *have* ("had," "has," and so on); others include the various forms of *do, can, shall, will, would, should, may, might,* and *must.* See Chapters 2 and 3.

case The form of a pronoun or noun to show its use in a sentence. Pronouns have three cases: the *nominative* or subject case (*I, he, she, they,* and so on), the *objective* case (*me, him, her, them,* and so on), and the *possessive* (*my, his, her, their,* and so on). Nouns change their spelling only in the possessive case (*Larry's, man's,* and so on). See Chapter 5.

clause A group of words containing a subject and a verb. A clause may be either independent or dependent. Independent clauses may stand alone as simple sentences. The dependent clause must be joined to an independent clause. "The restaurant was closed by the health department [*independent clause*] because the chef had hepatitis [*dependent clause*]." See Chapters 3 and 8.

collective noun A noun that names a group of persons or things, such as *army, committee, flock.* Collective nouns usually take singular verbs ("The troop *was* ready to leave") except when the individual members are thought of ("The class *were* arguing among themselves"). See Chapter 4.

colloquialism An informal word or expression more appropriate to speech than to writing.

comma-splice The misuse of a comma between two independent clauses in a compound sentence: "Herb's sister studied architecture in college, she designed the new office building downtown." Comma-splices can be corrected by substituting a semicolon for the comma or by inserting a coordinating conjunction after the comma. See Chapter 9.

command See *imperative sentence.*

common noun A noun that names a general category or class of persons, places, or things: *city, tool, song.* Common nouns are not capitalized except when they begin a sentence. See also *proper noun* and Chapter 2.

comparative degree The *more, less,* or *-er* form of those adjectives that can be compared.

comparison The change in the spelling of adjectives and adverbs to show degree. The degrees of comparison in English are *positive* (*slowly, loud*), *comparative* (*more slowly, louder*), and *superlative* (*most slowly, loudest*). Some modifiers cannot be compared: *round, dead, unique, full,* and so on.

© 2001 Addison-Wesley Educational Publishers Inc.

complement A word or expression that completes the sense of a verb, a subject, or an object. See *direct object, indirect object, predicate adjective, predicate noun,* and *predicate pronoun.*

complex sentence A sentence containing one independent clause and at least one dependent clause: "The grain embargo *that was announced last year* was criticized by the farmers." The dependent clause is italicized. See Chapters 3 and 8.

compound Two or more words or word groups linked to form a single unit. For instance, two nouns can form a compound subject: "*Merchants and businesspeople* were united in their opposition to the new tax"; and two verbs can function as a compound predicate: "She *danced and sang* in the leading role."

compound-complex sentence A sentence containing at least two independent clauses and one or more dependent clauses: "Although the demand for oil has declined, the price of gasoline continues to climb, and the OPEC nations threaten a new price hike." See Chapter 8.

compound sentence A sentence with two or more independent clauses but no dependent clauses: "She wanted to read the book, but someone had previously borrowed it." See Chapters 3 and 8.

compound subject Two or more subjects governed by the same verb: "*You and I* should meet for coffee tomorrow." See Chapter 3.

concrete noun A noun naming something that can be perceived by one of the senses. *Examples:* butter, elevator, scream, buzz. See also *abstract noun.*

conjunction A word that connects words, phrases, and clauses. See also *coordinate conjunction, subordinate conjunction,* and Chapter 2.

conjunctive adverb An adverb that connects independent clauses after a semicolon: "I had looked forward to seeing the movie; *however,* after reading the reviews I changed my mind." See Chapter 9.

contraction A word formed from the union of two words, with an apostrophe replacing the missing letters: *hasn't* (has not), *I'm* (I am).

coordinate adjectives Two or more adjectives of equal importance that modify the same noun: "The *tall, scowling* doorman finally let us in."

coordinate conjunction A word that connects two or more words, phrases, or clauses of equal rank. The most common coordinate conjunctions are *and, but, for, or, nor, so.* See Chapter 2.

correlative conjunctions Pairs of conjunctions used to join parts of a sentence of equal rank. The most common correlative conjunctions are *either . . . or; neither . . . nor; not only . . . but also; both . . . and.* See Chapters 2 and 10.

dangling modifier A modifier that has no word in the sentence for it to modify. It is left "dangling" and consequently ends up modifying an unintended word, as in the following: "Raising his bow triumphantly, the violin concerto ended in a crescendo." See Chapter 10.

dangling participle A participle serving as a modifier that has no word in the sentence for it to modify: "Looking out the window, a car drove by." See Chapter 10.

declarative sentence: A sentence that states a fact or makes a statement: "The capital of Kentucky is Frankfort."

demonstrative pronoun: A word used as an adjective or a pronoun to point out an item referred to. The demonstrative pronouns are *this, that, these,* and *those.* See Chapters 2 and 5.

dependent clause A group of words containing a subject and verb but unable to stand alone. A dependent clause must be subordinated to an independent clause in the same sentence: "*If you are on the honor roll,* you may be eligible for reduced insurance rates." See Chapters 3 and 8.

direct object A word that receives the action of the verb: "She helped *him* with the math problem." "I pried the *lid* off the can." See Chapter 5.

elliptical construction A construction in which one or more words are omitted but understood: "He is heavier than I (*am*)."

essential modifier A word or group of words necessary for the identification of the object being identified: "The man *with the checkered vest* wants to talk to you." Essential modifiers can be words, phrases, or clauses; they are not separated from the words they modify by commas. See Chapter 11.

exclamatory sentence A sentence expressing emotion, usually followed by an exclamation point: "Stop that yelling!" See Chapter 2.

formal language Language appropriate to formal situations and occasions, as distinguished from informal language and colloquialisms.

fragment See *sentence fragment.*

fused sentences See *run-on sentence.*

gender The grammatical expression of sex, particularly in the choice of pronouns: *he* (masculine), *she* (feminine), and *it* (neuter), and their related forms.

gerund The *-ing* form of a verb when it is used as a noun: "*Jogging* is one of the most popular forms of exercise among Americans."

helping/auxiliary verb See *auxiliary verb.*

imperative sentence A sentence expressing a command: "Please turn off your motor."

indefinite pronoun A pronoun that does not refer to a specific person or thing. Some of the most common indefinite pronouns include *anyone, someone, few, many,* and *none.* See Chapters 5 and 6.

independent clause A group of words containing a subject and a verb and capable of standing alone. See Chapters 3 and 8.

indirect object The person or thing receiving the direct object, and usually placed in a sentence between an action verb and the direct object: "Jay's lawyer gave *him* several documents to sign." See Chapter 5.

© 2001 Addison-Wesley Educational Publishers Inc.

infinitive The form of the verb preceded by *to*: *to hesitate, to think, to start,* and so on. See Chapter 3.

informal language Language appropriate to informal situations and occasions. Informal language often uses contractions and colloquialisms.

intensive pronouns Pronouns that end in *-self* or *-selves* and emphasize their antecedents: *myself, yourself, himself, ourselves,* and so on. See Chapter 5.

interjection A word or phrase expressing emotion but having no grammatical relationship to the other words in the sentence. Interjections include the following: *Yes, no, oh, well,* and so on. See Chapter 2.

interrogative pronoun A pronoun that is used to form a question: *who, whom, what, which, whose.* "*Who* wants to play softball?"

intransitive verb A verb that does not require an object: "They slept." See also *transitive verb.*

inverted order A sentence that is not in the usual word order of *subject-verb-object.* "Angry and dejected was he." See Chapter 3.

irregular verb A verb that forms its past tense or past participle by changing its spelling: *bring* (brought); *think* (thought); *run* (ran). See *regular verb* and Chapter 7.

linking verb A verb that connects a subject in a sentence with another word (usually a noun, pronoun, or adjective) that renames or describes the subject. "The bacon *was* crisp." "You *seem* bored." Common linking verbs are *to be, to seem, to become, to feel,* and *to appear.* See Chapters 2, 3, and 5.

main clause See *independent clause.*

mass noun A noun referring to something usually measured by weight, degree, or volume rather than by count. Mass nouns are words like *assistance* (we don't say *one assistance, two assistances,* and so on), *money,* and *height.*

misplaced modifier A word or group of words misplaced in the sentence and therefore modifying the wrong word: "I watched the parade *standing on the balcony.*" See Chapter 10.

modifier A word or group of words describing or modifying the meaning of another word in the sentence. See Chapter 10.

nonessential modifier A word or group of words modifying a noun or pronoun but not essential to the meaning of the sentence. Nonessential modifiers are set off by commas: "My father, *who was born in Illinois,* was a metallurgical accountant." See Chapter 11.

noun A word that names a person, place, thing, or idea. See Chapter 2.

noun clause A dependent clause functioning as a subject, direct object, predicate nominative, or indirect object in a sentence: "He told me *what I wanted to hear.*" See Chapter 8.

number The form of a word that indicates one (*singular*) or more than one (*plural*). See Chapters 4 and 6.

object A word or group of words receiving the action of or affected by an action verb or a preposition. See *direct object, indirect object,* and *object of preposition.*

object of preposition A word or group of words following a preposition and related to another part of the sentence by the preposition: "Vince drove his motorcycle across *the United States.*" See Chapter 2.

object pronoun A pronoun that is used as an object. It may be used as an object of a preposition: "Sit by *me*"; the object of a verb: "Call *us* for more information"; or as an indirect object: "Fiona gave *me* the flowers." See Chapter 5.

participle The *-ing* form of a verb (the *present participle*) when it is used as an adjective (a *swimming* pool), or the *-d, -ed, -t,* or *-n* form of a verb (the *past participle*) when it is used as an adjective (the *painted* house).

past participle See *participle.*

person The form of a pronoun or verb used to show the speaker (*first person:* I am), the person spoken to (*second person:* you are), or the person spoken about (*third person:* she is). See Chapter 6.

personal pronoun A pronoun that changes its form to show person: *I, you, he, she, they,* and so on. See Chapter 5.

phrase A group of words lacking both a subject and a verb.

plural More than one. See also *number.*

positive degree The form of the adjective or adverb that makes no comparison: *heavy* (positive degree); *heavier* (comparative degree); *heaviest* (superlative degree). See also *comparative degree* and *superlative degree.*

possessive pronouns Pronouns that show ownership: *my, mine, your, yours, his, her, hers, its, our,* and so on. See Chapters 2 and 5.

predicate The verb, its modifiers, and any objects in a sentence. The predicate makes a statement about the subject of the sentence.

predicate adjective An adjective that follows a linking verb and modifies the subject: "We were *happy* to get the news." See Chapter 2.

predicate noun A noun that follows a linking verb and names the subject: "Harry is the *captain* of the lacrosse team."

predicate pronoun A pronoun that follows a linking verb and identifies the subject: "My closest friend is *you.*" See Chapter 5.

preposition A word that shows a relationship between its object and another word in the sentence. Common prepositions include *at, to, behind, below, for, among, with,* and so on. See Chapter 2.

prepositional phrase A preposition and its object: *on the table, above the clouds, for the evening,* and so on. See Chapter 2.

present participle See *participle.*

pronoun A word that takes the place of a noun or another pronoun. See Chapters 2, 5, and 6.

pronoun antecedent See *antecedent* and Chapter 6.

pronoun form The form of a pronoun based on its use. Pronouns change their forms when they are used as subjects or objects, or to show possession. See also *case* and Chapter 5.

© 2001 Addison-Wesley Educational Publishers Inc.

pronoun reference See *antecedent* and Chapter 6.

proper adjective An adjective formed from a proper noun: *Italian* painting, *African* nations, *Irish* whiskey. Proper adjectives are usually capitalized except in phrases like "china cabinet" or "french fries."

proper noun A noun referring to a specific person, place, or thing. Proper nouns are capitalized: *Denver*; *Mr. McAuliffe*; *Taj Mahal*. See Chapter 2.

reflexive pronoun A pronoun ending in *-self* or *-selves* and renaming the subject. Reflexive pronouns are objects of verbs and prepositions; "He perjured *himself*." "They went by *themselves*." See Chapter 5.

regular verb A verb that forms its past tense by adding *-d*, or *-ed*: *start, started; hope, hoped*. See also *irregular verb* and Chapter 7.

relative pronoun A pronoun that introduces an adjective clause. The relative pronouns are *who, whom, whose, which, that*. See Chapters 5 and 8.

restrictive modifier See *essential modifier*.

run-on sentence Two independent clauses run together with no punctuation to separate them: "Her uncle works as a plumber in Des Moines he used to be a professor of philosophy in Boston." The run-on sentence is corrected by placing a semicolon or a comma and coordinate conjunction between the two clauses. See Chapter 9.

sentence A group of words containing a subject and a verb and expressing some sense of completeness. See Chapter 3.

sentence fragment A group of words lacking an independent clause and therefore unable to stand alone. See Chapter 9.

sentence types Sentences classified on the basis of their structure. There are four types of sentences in English: simple, compound, complex, and compound-complex. See also *complex sentence, compound sentence, compound-complex sentence, simple sentence*, and Chapter 8.

simple sentence A sentence containing one independent clause. See Chapter 3.

slang An informal word or expression not accepted in formal writing by careful or educated users of the language. Slang is usually short-lived or temporary, and should be used sparingly.

split infinitive An infinitive with a modifier between the *to* and the verb. Split infinitives are avoided by most careful speakers and writers. Some examples: *to really want; to hardly hear*.

squinting modifier A modifier that makes the meaning of a sentence ambiguous because it modifies two words at the same time: "We stood around *nervously* waiting to be introduced"; "I asked them *politely* to leave." See Chapter 10.

standard English The English of careful and educated speakers and writers. See Chapter 1.

subject The part of the sentence about which the predicate makes a statement. See also *predicate* and Chapter 3.

subordinate clause See *dependent clause*.

subordinate conjunction A word that joins a dependent clause to an independent clause. See Chapters 2 and 8.

superlative degree The *most, least,* or *-est* form of those adjectives and adverbs that can be compared: *most beautiful; least valid; greatest.* See also *comparative degree, comparison,* and *positive degree.*

tense The form of a verb that shows the action as being in the past, present, or future times. The most common tenses are simple present, present perfect, simple past, past perfect, simple future, and future perfect. See Chapters 2 and 7.

transitive verb A verb that requires an object in order to complete its meaning: "We *saw* the accident." "They *helped* their neighbors." See also *intransitive verb.*

verb A part of speech that describes the action or state of being of a subject. See Chapters 2, 3, and 7.

voice Transitive verbs can be either in the *active voice* or in the *passive voice.* When the subject in the sentence performs the action described by the verb, they are in the *active voice.*

◆ Reverend Jackson performed the ceremony.

When the action described by the verb is done to the subject, transitive verbs are in the *passive voice.*

◆ The ceremony was performed by Reverend Jackson.

verb phrase A verb that consists of helping verbs and a main verb: "Sal *will* not *arrive* on time"; "I *may have lost* your jacket"; "We *have won* the lottery!" See Chapters 2 and 3.

© 2001 Addison-Wesley Educational Publishers Inc.

Answers to Selected Exercises

(**Note:** Answers are provided for odd-numbered exercises in odd-numbered chapters, and for even-numbered exercises in even-numbered chapters.)

CHAPTER 2

Exercise 2-2 1. 2; 2. 1; 3. 2; 4. 1; 5. 3; 6. 3; 7. 2; 8. 3; 9. 2; 10. 2; 11. 1; 12. 1; 13. 1; 14. 2; 15. 3

Exercise 2-4A 1. twenty; 2. crash; 3. Japanese; 4. popular; 5. derives; 6. stems; 7. have; 8. famous; 9. gross; 10. popular

Exercise 2-4B 1. previously; 2. brightly; 3. first; 4. Later; 5. brightly; 6. very; 7. Meanwhile; 8. increasingly; 9. closely; 10. specifically

Exercise 2-6 1. and, but; 2. and, yet; 3. Neither/nor; 4. and, and, either/or; 5. but

CHAPTER 3

Exercise 3-1 1. wails, vibrate; 2. describe; 3. moves, compress, pileup; 4. happens, expand; 5. changes; 6. comes, increases; 7. creates; 8. reaches, passes; 9. declines, stretch, reach; 10. call.

Exercise 3-3 1. have decided; 2. has been inhabited; 3. are reputed; 4. can be heard, surround; 5. are made, can appear; 6. are painted; 7. will abandon, see, are steamed; 8. has been dreaming, are served; 9. could spend, have vowed; 10. has preserved, is, has been named

Exercise 3-5 1. b; 2. a; 3. c; 4. a; 5. b; 6. a; 7. a; 8. a; 9. c; 10. b; 11. a; 12. c; 13. a; 14. b; 15. c

Exercise 3-7 Answers will vary.

Exercise 3-9
1. *Subjects*: Acupuncture, it; *Verbs*: is, is used
2. *Subjects*: word, treatments; *Verbs*: comes, are

3. *Subjects:* Needles, they; *Verbs:* are inserted, are twisted
4. *Subjects:* location, part; *Verbs:* depends, corresponds
5. *Subjects:* Acupuncture, needle; *Verbs:* is used, is placed
6. *Subjects:* acupuncturist, needle; *Verbs:* is used, is placed
7. *Subjects:* explanation, twisting; *Verbs:* is, stimulates
8. *Subjects:* nerve, other; *Verbs:* is, is
9. *Subjects:* impulse, it; *Verbs:* reaches, closes
10. *Subjects:* Acupuncture, numbers; *Verbs:* encounters, are investigating

CHAPTER 4

Exercise 4-2 1. a; 2. a; 3. b; 4. b; 5. b; 6. a; 7. a; 8. b; 9. b; 10. b

Exercise 4-4 1. a; 2. b; 3. a; 4. a; 5. a; 6. a; 7. b; 8. b; 9. a; 10. a; 11. a; 12. a; 13. a; 14. b; 15. a

Exercise 4-6 1. b; 2. b; 3. a; 4. b; 5. b; 6. a; 7. b; 8. b; 9. a; 10. b; 11. b; 12. a; 13. b; 14. b; 15. b

CHAPTER 5

Exercise 5-1 1. "A": we; 2. "A": he, it, who; "B": he; 3. "A": They; 4. "A": I, we; 5. "C": you, I; 6. "A": It, who, he; 7. "A": it, who; "B": you; 8. "A": We, we, they, we; 9. "A": who; 10. "A": I

Exercise 5-3 1. a; 2. b; 3. b; 4. b; 5. a; 6. b; 7. b; 8. b; 9. b; 10. b; 11. b; 12. a; 13. b; 14. b; 15. b

Exercise 5-5 1. a; 2. a; 3. a; 4. a; 5. b; 6. a; 7. a; 8. b; 9. b; 10. a; 11. a; 12. b; 13. b; 14. a; 15. b

CHAPTER 6

Exercise 6-2 1. a; 2. a; 3. a; 4. b; 5. b; 6. b; 7. a; 8. a; 9. a; 10. a; 11. a; 12. a; 13. a; 14. b; 15. b

Exercise 6-4 Answers will vary.

CHAPTER 7

Exercise 7-1 1. arose; 2. struck; 3. dived *or* dove; 4. dug; 5. burst; 6. bore; 7. grew; 8. became; 9. gave; 10. began

Exercise 7-3 1. present perfect; 2. present; 3. future perfect; 4. present perfect; 5. past perfect; 6. past; 7. present; 8. present; 9. past perfect; 10. past; 11. present perfect; 12. past prefect; 13. present; 14. present perfect; 15. future perfect.

Exercise 7-5 Answers will vary.

Exercise 7-7 1. set; 2. sat; 3. sit; 4. set; 5. sit; 6. set; 7. set; 8. sat; 9. set; 10. sat; 11. sat; 12. sat; 13. set; 14. sitting; 15. sat

© 2001 Addison-Wesley Educational Publishers Inc.

CHAPTER 8

Exercise 8-2 1. No commas needed. 2. prevalent, and 3. radio, but 4. performers, yet 5. decade, but 6. annually, and 7. declining, so 8. concerts, for 9. No commas needed. 10. No commas needed. 11. platinum, and 12. multi-platinum CDs, and 13. decade, yet 14. other CDs, and 15. No commas needed.

Exercise 8-4 Answers will vary.

Exercise 8-6
1. (The Great Smoky Mountains) *which are in the Appalachian Highlands of Tennessee and North Carolina*
2. (Joe) *who is a trained naturalist.*
3. (birds) *that live in the Smoky Mountains*
4. (heights) *where majestic ravens and hawks make their nests*
5. (sunrise) *which is the most active time of day for bird activity and viewing*
6. (deer, bats, woodchucks, and skunks) *which are numerous and easy to spot*
7. (coyote and bobcat) *that inhabit the Smokies*
8. (bears) *that are so prevalent in the Smoky Mountains*
9. (tricks) *which usually keep bears from attacking*
10. (noises) *which bears hate*
11. (Joe) *who is familiar with animals and their customs*
12. (trees) *that were behind us*
13. (stream) *that trickled nearby*
14. (Cataloochee Creek) *which runs through lush meadows and softly sloping dales*
15. (violets and azaleas) *which sweeten those gentle Smoky Mountain breezes*

Exercise 8-8
1. when I heard/that Princess Diana had died
2. Where we spend New Year's Eve
3. that *Cats* was Broadway's longest-running show
4. Why Salt Lake City leads the world in the consumption of Jell-O
5. how he injured his knee while watching television
6. what the speaker said
7. that Reno is farther west than San Diego
8. What Lincoln said that afternoon at Gettysburg
9. how others act/what they are told
10. how to make Irish soda bread
11. that Mozart liked to play billiards
12. that the chemistry test had been cancelled
13. that resolving poverty requires the cooperation of all segments of society
14. Whatever he does/by those who work for him
15. about who was responsible for the Great Depression of the 1930s

CHAPTER 9

Exercise 9-1
Corrections of fragments will vary.

1. Throughout much of human history (prepositional phrase)
2. Correct
3. Consisting of silk sails stretched across bamboo frames (participle phrase)
4. To perform a variety of tasks (infinitive phrase)
5. Measuring weather, delivering love notes, and carrying signals (participle phrase)
6. Correct
7. To fly in stunt formations or even hover (infinitive phrase)
8. To make parachutes for American soldiers in World War II (infinitive phrase)
9. Throughout the fabric after the kite is accidentally punctured (prepositional phrase)
10. Coming in a variety of complex styles and costing as much as a hundred dollars or more (participle phrase)

Exercise 9-3 Sentences 1, 4, and 9 are correct. Corrections of run-on sentences will vary.

Exercise 9-5 Sentences 2 and 5 are correct. Corrections of comma-splices will vary.

CHAPTER 10

Exercise 10-2 Sentences 5, 12, and 15 are correct. Corrections of sentences with squinting modifiers will vary.

Exercise 10-4 Sentences 6 and 14 are correct. Corrections of sentences with illogical comparisons will vary.

Exercise 10-6 Sentences 8, 11, and 14 are correct. Corrections of sentences with faulty parallelism will vary.

CHAPTER 11

Exercise 11-1

1. Your application should be mailed to D. A. Coleman, 19 W. Bond Street, Richmond, VA 23219.
2. Dr. Lehane and Ms. Garcia will sing duets today at 2:30 p.m. at the concert hall on Seventh St. in Des Moines.
3. Did you hear someone yell "Fire!"?
4. My little sister asked me whether there is a Santa Claus.
5. "Do you believe in Santa Claus?" I asked her.
6. The newspaper columnist told our class that he types on an IBM Selectric typewriter that he purchased when he worked at the UN.
7. My daughter earned her degree from UCLA but also took classes at USC and the U. of Arizona.

© 2001 Addison-Wesley Educational Publishers Inc.

8. My alarm rings promptly at 7:00 a.m. every day, but this morning I overslept and missed my favorite TV program and my appointment with Dr. McAndrews.
9. Holy cow! I've just won the state lottery!
10. The world's first alphabet was developed by the Sumerians around 3000 B.C.
11. The Rev. Martin Luther King, Jr., gave a rousing speech at the Lincoln Memorial in Washington, D.C.
12. No! I can't believe it!
13. Did you remember to wind the clock and put out the cat?
14. I wonder whether forces from NATO should be sent to enforce the cease-fire.
15. Please take your shoes off when entering the mosque.

Exercise 11-3

1. two million,
2. Correct
3. to the public,
4. admired by all,
5. Correct
6. Anglo culture,
7. costumes, / contests, / pow-wow,
8. rhythm,
9. snuff cans, / Jingle Dance,
10. Correct
11. Native American,
12. seating, / for dancers,
13. is done,
14. Prayer Songs, / Memorial Songs,
15. of California,

Exercise 11-5

1. Correct
2. Jogging, / exercise,
3. Carey, / show,
4. Correct
5. Correct
6. Correct
7. Correct
8. brother, / restaurant,
9. rain, / drenching,
10. Correct

Exercise 11-7

1. 206 bones / flat,
2. thirty-three separate spinal vertebrae
3. Correct

4. Correct
5. Correct
6. Correct
7. consists of
8. square inch
9. or when
10. amusing that / is called

Exercise 11-9

1. our goal:
2. Correct
3. bygone era:
4. Correct
5. Correct
6. main attractions:
7. in its steeple the two lanterns
8. State House to see tea from
9. Oval Office desk:
10. treat:

Exercise 11-11

1. Would you please translate the French phrase *noblesse oblige* for me?
2. Professor Cardenas complained that too many students confuse the words "to," "too," and "two." (*Note:* Italics are also acceptable for words used in this sense.)
3. Who said, "For people who like this sort of thing, this is the sort of thing they would like"?
4. Beverly is next in line to be editor-in-chief of the *Times-Courier*.
5. The Greek letter *rho* looks like the Roman letter *p*.
6. "My favorite love song," said Darnell, "is 'Just the Way You Are,' by Billy Joel."
7. I ordered garlic *pizza*, not garlic *pasta*.
8. Did you read the *Louisville Herald*'s review of the movie *Singin' in the Rain*?
9. Although the movie *Field of Dreams* was not believable, the references to baseball history were interesting.
10. The expression "to love, honor, and obey" has been dropped from some marriage ceremonies.

Exercise 11-13

1. while it's being painted
2. Karl's
3. men's
4. the couple's wedding
5. yours
6. veterans'
7. Correct
8. somebody's

© 2001 Addison-Wesley Educational Publishers Inc.

9. Correct
10. Helen's and Eddie's
11. Abbott and Costello's
12. salesmen's
13. Correct
14. Correct
15. Kelly's

CHAPTER 12

Exercise 12-2

1. Britain's King Henry VIII, Catherine of Aragon, Anne Boleyn, Roman Catholic Church, Pope
2. Canada
3. Mideast, Ramadan
4. Fourth of July, "You Give Love a Bad Name," Bon Jovi
5. Ukraine, Olympics
6. Memories of the Mansion
7. Pogo Airlines, West Virginia, Ireland, Norway
8. Gulf Stream
9. Klan
10. United States, Harvard
11. Prince of Wales, Balmoral Castle
12. Minnesota
13. South Pole, Professor Brink
14. (sentence is correct)
15. English, Spanish, Japanese

CHAPTER 13

Exercise 13-1

1. ie
2. ei
3. ic
4. ei
5. ie
6. ie
7. ie
8. ie
9. ei
10. ei

Exercise 13-3

1. parentheses
2. memorandum
3. analyses
4. crisis
5. spoonfuls
6. wives
7. potatoes
8. echoes
9. handfuls
10. sheep

© 2001 Addison-Wesley Educational Publishers Inc.

Credits

pages 29–30   From "What the Black Man Wants" by Frederick Douglass

page 30   From *Biology: The World of Life*, 6th ed., by Robert A. Wallace. Copyright 1992 by Harper Collins Publishers, Inc., p. 283

page 30   From *Psychology: An Introduction*, 3rd ed., by Josh R. Gerow. Copyright 1992 by Harper Collins Publishers, Inc., p. 700

page 34   *Native American Voices*, Susan Lobo and Steve Talbot, eds. Copyright 1998 by Addison Wesley Longman, Inc., pp. 266–77. Reprinted with permission.

page 35   From *Management: Leadership in Action*, 5th ed., by Donald C. Mosley, Paul H. Pietri, and Leon C. Megginson. Copyright 1996 by HarperCollins Publishers, Inc., p. 555. Based on "Oprah Winfrey," *Current Biography Yearbook 1987*, pp. 610–14; Barbara Harrison, "The Importance of Being Oprah," *New York Times* Biographical Service, June 1989, pp. 558–64; Richard Zoglin, "Lady with a Calling," *Time*, August 8, 1988, pp. 62–64; Lawrence Ingrassia, "A Select Few Poised to Lead Business into the '90s," *Wall Street Journal*, Centennial Edition 1989, p. A5; Matt Roush, "Her Empire Grows with ABC Series," *USA Today*, May 11, 1990, p. 1D; "Cutting Out the Middlemen," *Forbes*, October 1, 1990, p. 166; Peter Newcomb and Lisa Gubernick, "The Top 40," *Forbes*, September 27, 1993, p. 97; Steven Zausner, "All the Money," *Forbes*, October 18, 1993, p. 22; "King World in Agreement to Continue Oprah Show," *Wall Street Journal*, March 18, 1994, p. 3; Paul Noglows, "Oprah: The Year of Living Dangerously," *Working Woman*, May 1994, pp. 52–55; Eben Shapiro, "Publishing: Oprah Makes Huge Bestseller of a Cookbook," *Wall Street Journal*, May 4, 1994, p. 1; Tracey Wong Biggs, "Oprah Takes a Dream and Runs with It,"

USA Today, October 24, 1994, p. 1; and Gretchen Reynolds, "A Year to Remember: Oprah Grows Up," *TV Guide*, January 7, 1995, p. 14.

page 63   *Cold Mountain*, by Charles Frazier. Copyright 1997 by Atlantic Monthly Press, p. 213.

page 63   *Writing for College*, 3rd ed., by Robert E. Yarber and Andrew J. Hoffman. Copyright 1996 by HarperCollins Publishers, p. 42. Reprinted with permission.

page 85   *Cape Cod*, by Henry David Thoreau. New York: Penguin, 1987, p. 39.

page 85   *Cold Mountain*, by Charles Frazier. Copyright 1997 by Atlantic Monthly Press, p. 139.

page 108   *Writing for College*, 3rd ed., by Robert E. Yarber and Andrew J. Hoffman. Copyright 1996 by HarperCollins Publishers, p. 40. Reprinted with permission.

page 132   *New Gardening Book*, by Better Homes and Gardens. Copyright 1990 by Meredith Corporation, Des Moines, Iowa, p. 237.

page 160   *I Know Why the Caged Bird Sings*, by Maya Angelou. Copyright 1969 by Random House. New York: Bantam, 1993, p. 146.

page 162   *Aphrodite*, by Isabel Allende. Copyright 1998 by HarperCollins Publishers, pp. 109–10.

page 162   *The Art of Being Human*, by Thelma C. Altshuler and Richard Paul Janaro. Copyright 1997 by Addison Wesley Longman, p. 462. Reprinted with permission.

page 187   *New Gardening Book*, by Better Homes and Gardens. Copyright 1990 by Meredith Corporation, Des Moines, Iowa, p. 12.

page 209   *Healthwise Handbook*, by Health Net. Copyright 1990 by Healthwise, Inc., Boise, Idaho, p. 167.

page 209   *Modern Human Physiology*, by Frederick D. Cornett and Pauline Gratz. Copyright 1980 by Holt, Rinehart and Winston, pp. 231–32.

© 2001 Addison-Wesley Educational Publishers Inc.

page 231   *Hike Los Angeles*, by Dennis Gagnon. Copyright 1991 by Western Tanager Press, Santa Cruz, California, p. 19.

page 269   *Healthwise Handbook*, by Health Net. Copyright 1990 by Healthwise, Inc., Boise, Idaho, p. 97.

page 270   "Surviving Schools: The Mohawks in Montreal," from *The Gaia Atlas of First Peoples* by Julian Burger. Copyright 1990 by Gaia Books Ltd., London, pp. 252–53. Reprinted with permission.

pages 288–89   *Fundamentals of Building Construction*, by Edward Allen and Joseph Iano. Copyright 1990 by John Wiley and Sons, Inc., p. 290.

page 288   *Atlas of the North American Indian*, by Carl Waldman. Copyright 1985 by Carl Waldman, p. 70.

© 2001 Addison-Wesley Educational Publishers Inc.

Index

© 2001 Addison-Wesley Educational Publishers Inc.

© 2001 Addison-Wesley Educational Publishers Inc.

© 2001 Addison-Wesley Educational Publishers Inc.

© 2001 Addison-Wesley Educational Publishers Inc.